03 ' 07. 13

With best wishes

WHAT'S NEXT?

WHAT'S NEXT?

Nancy Vlasto

UNITED WRITERS
Cornwall

UNITED WRITERS PUBLICATIONS LTD
Ailsa, Castle Gate, Penzance, Cornwall.

British Library Cataloguing in Publication Data:
A catalogue record for this book is
available from the British Library.

ISBN 9781852001490

Printed in Great Britain by
United Writers Publications Ltd
Cornwall.

I dedicate my book to all those people,
especially my late parents, who have encouraged
and befriended me and accepted me
for being the person I am.

Acknowledgements

My thanks to:

John and Margaret Kelly for their immense help with the scanning of numerous photos and advice during the process of writing my book; Ada Ajegbu (neé Nwakanma) for the practical setting up of the book; David Oram and Peter Stokes for editing and printing information in the church newsletter; the late Graham Child, of JaggerPrint, for his encouragement; Patrick Wright, Roger Chown and his daughter Xanna, Joachim Leibschner, Jill Raine, Sharon Wright and Dr Peter Weston for their general support and advice, and last but not least Chun-Eng Frost, my general assistant and typist, to whom I am indebted, for her wonderful support, tolerance and good humour. This book would never have been completed without her encouragement and efficiency.

Introduction

I thought long and hard about writing this autobiography, but the need to 'put my house in order' and the confusion of so many past activities in my mind, have propelled me into sorting out the events of the past years. Because of my diverse interests and activities, I have deliberately chosen to write this in the form of a diary so that the events are in some sort of sequential order and also able to connect together where necessary. Perhaps the reader might understand my difficulties as they read through this book, and I hope that the dates and how one event relates to another will be helpful and of interest.

The war, of course, coming as it did during my school and early working days, had a dominating influence on my life and continues to do so. I also want to demonstrate that if you want to do something enough you will most likely succeed in doing it. I am so grateful that, despite not having married or had children, I have been able to lead a full and hopefully useful life.

In these pages, and with the help of photographs, I have endeavoured to show how fortunate I have been in the many opportunities in life that opened up for me and the use I made of them. Many of these were made possible, in the early years, by the generosity and care of my parents.

Aside from the different professional and voluntary trainings I have undertaken, I have also been involved in many sporting and musical activities. It has been impossible to list them all as I have sung in well over fifty-six choral concerts, performed as a solo singer in twenty-three concerts and competed in about twenty music festivals (where I learnt much from the adjudicators' comments), and all that arose from a life as a church chorister for over 60 years.

Much of my book has been recalled from letters, notes, diary entries and the like. I wish to convey my sincerest apologies for any inadvertent errors of names, events and dates in this book which may have been mistaken in my memory. Eighty-five years is a long time to remember details.

About My Parents

Notice in *The Times* 22.04.1919:

> 'The engagement was announced between Michael Vlasto FRCS, only son of Helen Vlasto 24 Porchester Terrace W2 and Miss Chrissy Croil, younger daughter of Mr and Mrs Croil of 3 Garden Terrace, Aberdeen, Scotland.'

My parents married in St James Church, Aberdeen, Wednesday June 18th 1919 at 1.45pm. Later they were to have a second marriage service in the Greek Orthodox Church, Moscow Road, Bayswater which friends in the south of England and the Greek community were able to attend.

My father, Michael Vlasto's family, originally came from the Greek Island of Chios off the Turkish coast, but when it was invaded by the Turks in 1822 they fled in their boats to Marseille, France. My father had two sisters, Fanny and Netta, who married and settled in Marseille. He was born in Paris and lived with his mother. He also went to school in Paris. His father had died when he was 10 years old. His mother then brought him to London where he was to be naturalised British. He attended Winchester College and then trained as a Doctor at University College Hospital in London. He played for and captained the United Hospitals Football Team which he founded. He also took the team to the USA. He became an eminent Ear, Nose and Throat surgeon and had a private practice at 26 Wimpole Street (later moving next door to No. 27). He attended St Luke's Hostel (later renamed Hospital) for the Clergy, the West London Hospital in Hammersmith, Queen's Hospital for Children in Hackney and the West Herts Hospital, Hemel Hempstead.

My mother Chrissy Croil was of Scottish descent. She was born in Milwaukee, USA where her parents were on holiday. The family lived in Aberdeen where she attended St Margaret's School. She had a sister, Gladys, and two brothers, Thomas and George.

My parents met in the 1914-18 war when my father was a Royal Naval Surgeon and my mother a Red Cross VAD nurse with the Royal Navy. They were both working in Malta in the Bighi Hospital and met on one of the wards.

Chapter One

I was born in my parents' front bedroom at 16 Porchester Terrace, Bayswater, London W2 on February 1st 1926 in the small hours of the morning, weighing in at around 7lbs (my mother couldn't remember precisely).

I was the youngest of four. My elder sisters Helen born 1920, Christian born 1921 and my brother Michael (Pogy) born 1923. My brother, being only three years older than myself, was to be my closest family 'friend' during the early years of my life.

1926 was a year remembered not for my arrival but for its association with the general strike, when people were on the bread line and many were unemployed and very poor. My yells for sustenance must have brought about some diversion and may even have predicted the future use of my voice that was to bring me so much happiness in the years to come.

Our house was to be found half way down Porchester Terrace, a lovely old Victorian building. During the First World War a bomb had unceremoniously landed plumb through the drawing room ceiling and left an enormous cavern into which my parents had gazed whilst they deliberated as to whether to buy it. Thank goodness they did, for it became our much loved family home for many years. It was bordered, like other houses, with a walled garden at the front and a large garden (by London standards) at the back.

It was a three-storey building with steps down to a large basement containing a kitchen, scullery, pantry and maid's bedroom. The ground floor was composed of a large, beautiful drawing room at the front overlooking the road, which was mainly reserved for visitors and where we were not allowed to go unless invited. My father had his little study with a coal fire at the back overlooking the garden. Here he sat every evening, after finishing his day's work as an ear, nose and throat surgeon, to type his own letters and send out bills to his private patients.

In the evenings and at the weekends I remember sitting on my parents' laps in the cosy chairs in the study and being read to; I am sure it was in this way, at quite an early age, that I learned to read myself.

Next to the study was the dining room which had French windows leading on to a balcony with iron steps down into the garden. Here we ate together as a family when we grew out of nursery meals. This was where we performed our Christmas plays. The bow window became our stage and one of us, usually me, played the piano adjacent to the stage.

From an age when we could stand on our own two feet, we used to perform for our doting and tolerant parents, grandmother, aunt and any friends whom they could muster. There were curtains we could pull across whenever we needed to, this was useful on the occasion when my pants fell down! What fun we had and how good for us it was. I remember 'selling' tickets with a ticket collector's outfit, clipping second hand, pink, blue, white and yellow tickets collected from previous journeys on the buses. I don't think we asked for money – I think we were just grateful that anyone had turned up to fill the seats we had hopefully put out!

My bedroom was on the top floor, my two sisters had the room next door and my brother's room was next to theirs. As my sisters were so much older and later on were to go to boarding school, my brother and I were left alone at the top of the house. After being sent to bed we used to get up and dance and giggle on the landing half way down the staircase and were continually being told to 'go to bed'. We used to throw ourselves down the long flight of fourteen stairs, our hands only going on the banisters half way down, and land with a thud at the bottom. Sadly, one day my brother fell forward on to the radiator at the bottom and cut his head. He had to go to hospital for stitches. I can only admire our parents' tolerance of these antics, which continued with renewed energy but probably with a little more care as it never happened again!

The result of this event was that my brother was moved down to a small room next to their's on the middle floor (which was also where the nursery and bathroom were positioned) and I was left alone at the top of the house. I was very frightened of the dark and, finding myself alone, I used to cry myself to sleep when my father refused to leave the landing light on. Later on they used to leave it on for a certain length of time which improved matters. When, in the holidays, my sisters returned home, I remember the feeling of relief that I was no longer alone.

On rare occasions my sisters would take me into their room for about half an hour and I'd get into bed with one of them. They used to show me what they could see out of their two windows, and then the shadows on the walls made by the street lights filtering through the leafy branches of the trees outside making patterns on the ceiling and walls of their room as they waved in the wind. Then with the sudden turning on of the street light directly outside our house by the lamplighter, I used to tip-toe back to my room and get into bed a much happier person. The lamplighter, coming on a bicycle, was someone who fascinated us as children for he seemed to appear from nowhere carrying a long pole, with this he extended his arm and lit the gas holder in the lights spaced along the terrace. In the morning he would return to extinguish them.

First thing in the morning I would wake to hear the sound of the stair carpets being brushed. Every morning the maids cleaned the sinks and the toilets. The rest of the day they cleaned and polished the rooms or cooked the meals and prepared tea in the pantry. They also used to carpet-sweep the carpets, as there were no hoovers in those days, and polished the silver and furniture.

Meals in the nursery were fun and, always wearing our pinafores, we were encouraged to talk and share our experiences of the day. Our parents did their best to enable us to extend our knowledge and interest in many areas of life.

Our nursery had a fireguard with a brightly polished brass edging along the top which fitted right round the open coal fire. Beside this stood our rocking horse; perhaps this was my first important encounter with horses which were to dominate my interest later in life.

When we were a little older, we all six sat around the table for meals together. My father would arrive last and do the 'rounds' of us four children, feeling our neck glands from behind, before wishing us good morning. I really did not enjoy him doing this, but perhaps he hoped to pick up any illness before it developed, although in those days there wasn't much he could do to prevent it happening. His clothes smelt of anaesthetics, the scent of ether stays with me to this day. On the chauffeur's day off, he often took me with him to collect the car, which was a few hundred yards down Porchester Terrace almost opposite where the Underground trains surfaced on their way to the West End. There was a mews with several garages along the side of it and a T-junction at the end. Ours was the one in the middle, which was lucky because my father was a pretty awful driver! In later years he told me that he had never looked in the driving mirror. This did not surprise me! And this is perhaps why I did not learn to drive until I was in my forties! My father regularly smoked a 'smelly pipe' when he exchanged places with my mother, who was a superb driver. The relief would have been complete had it not been for him puffing the smoke under all our noses.

I used to be appallingly car sick and I have often wondered whether it was caused by a combination of a smoky car, fear of his dreadful driving skills or the verbal maths tests he used to throw over his shoulder for my poor brother to answer. We tried to help him, when we were able, but I don't think any of us girls were prodigies in mathematics, and neither was my father, come to that, and I don't think even he knew the correct answers! I have always reacted badly to tension and I found these times difficult to handle even from a young age.

We had a much loved wire-haired terrier called Michael. As my father's and brother's names were Michael, I have no idea why we decided to give him the same name! Perhaps that is why he became 'Mikey' and my brother 'Pogy'. Mikey seemed to have a very calm nature, putting up with being hugged, sat on, and harnessed to our old cart to pull us for rides around the garden. He lived to the ripe age of thirteen. He might have lived longer but he was very independent, taking himself for walks in the park at the end of our terrace, across the main Bayswater Road. We were told he used to wait at the traffic lights until a pram came along and then cross over beside it! Sadly it was this

15

independence that caused him to lose his life. A taxi driver brought his body back to us. He was lying on the front step of the cab beside the driver like a limp doll. We were all heartbroken as he was our much loved friend and playmate. Later my parents attempted to fill his place in our lives by buying a bulldog we named Kim.

We had three tortoises named Hezekiah, Jemeriah and Jeremiah, I have no idea why! We used to 'race' them from one end of the lawn to the other. If you have never seen a tortoise racing, you must have difficulty imagining it. They used to peep out of their shells to see what was going on. Then they appeared to get a whiff of the tantalising lettuce leaf we were holding in front of them. So first one foot, and then, a few minutes later, another foot would move as they rocked and rolled their way up the lawn (as we shouted encouragement) in the hope of a mouthful of their favourite food. I don't remember how long these races took but I guess even a snail would have done better. I know that mine had a repeated 'list to port' and was always veering off to the left, and once even did a complete circle and a half setting off back to the start. I don't think they thought it was particularly funny but we certainly did!

In our youth my brother and I were often in the bath together; we quite enjoyed 'messing about' with boats etc. One night he attached a clothes peg to my nose and pulled it – hard. When I asked him what he was doing, with tears streaming down my face, he said, 'It turns up, so I'm straightening it for you.' I have looked at clothes peg in a different way ever since.

My mother had a gas ring under one end of the bath and we had to be careful not to sit there; on this she used to make us cocoa before we went to bed. At bedtime our parents always came to say goodnight and tucked us in and my mother said prayers with us. I still remember the sounds that came to me from the garden during the summer when the window was wide open, birds singing, my father mowing the lawn, the voices of anyone sitting at the far end of the garden and then the voice of my mother, 'Nancy, go back to bed,' – and *that* even when I was peeping between the curtains. At other times she would call up the stairs, 'Nancy, whatever you are doing stop doing it!' I still think we were sent to bed too early, it was very frustrating and very boring, especially on light summer evenings. We were not allowed to read in bed.

16

From the beginning I was a strong character, determined and difficult to handle. (My two sisters never tired of telling me this!) Nowadays I take some comfort in the knowledge that Winston Churchill had similar attributes.

As I grew older I graduated from a baby's pram to a toddler's pushchair. Far less comfortable, the wheels juddered on the hard pavements, my feet bounced up and down on the foot rest and my bottom on the hard little seat; it was most certainly not built for comfort. Our dear Mikey used to trot stolidly along, his little head pointing forwards, his lead attached to the handle bar. His head bobbed up and down parallel with mine as he tried to keep up.

The pram pusher was usually the nurse who looked after us. We went through a number of them, probably because they couldn't cope with me! My sisters had the benefit of a Belgian Governess, Lydie (whom we called Miél) who spoke French all the time with them; I was three when she left so did not retain as much of the language as they did.

My preferred activity as a child was bowling my hoop with a wooden stick; something I spent hours doing, which I am sure not only gave me excellent exercise but was a great activity encouraging hand-eye control and estimation of angles and distances. I cannot understand how it went out of vogue and is no longer encouraged for younger children today. (When I later worked with young severely handicapped children I introduced this activity which they found difficult but thoroughly enjoyed.) I would really like to see the hoop and stick brought back to life.

As soon as I could walk reasonable distances, my mother took me everywhere with her. First thing in the morning we went down into the kitchen and sat at the freshly scrubbed wooden table. 'Say good morning to cook,' prompted my mother, which I dutifully did. She then discussed, and made notes, of what meals we were going to have that day and for the week ahead and any shopping that was required. Then the house maid, too, was asked if she had enough polish or anything else with which to do the housework.

Armed with shopping bags we visited our local shops in Leinster Terrace. By standing on my toes I could watch the butcher cutting up the meat. Then on to Oakshotts for other items. There we asked the shopkeeper to cut off the rind of our bacon strips. He then cut the rind up into little pieces for us to feed the gulls at the Round Pond in Kensington Gardens. We would hold up a piece and they would swoop down and snatch it from our fingers. Another favourite shop was the greengrocer where we could buy one penny or two penny bananas which we took home with us as, in those days, we children were not allowed to eat in the street!

It was in this street that I was famously to get myself into a lot of trouble. We were only allowed one sweet a day after lunch; this was not enough for me! Spying a six penny piece on my nurse's dressing table, I thought she might not notice and forget it was there. I quickly took it and put it in my pocket and crept around to the sweet shop on Leinster Terrace and bought five packets of chewing gum. I remember my stomach was churned up inside with fright for not only had I stolen the money but I had gone to the shop which I was not allowed to do on my own. On getting home I shut myself in the lavatory and tearing all the paper off the packets, put them in my pocket. I then proceeded to suck all the sweet coating off each piece and suddenly realised that I was going to have to dispose of all the gum. What *was* I to do with them? All the time I was waiting for my mother's calls to find out where I was! I could only swallow three packets of gum and had to decide what to do with the rest. Eventually, I decided the only thing to do was to put them down the lavatory and pull the plug, but to my horror they remained in full view at the bottom of the pan! By the evening, I was in deep trouble! I was vomiting copiously and doubled up with pain. The family doctor was sent for and various treatments were prescribed. I was afraid to tell them about my escapade! My mother suddenly had a bright idea, and going round to the sweet shop asked if by any chance they had seen me recently. The response was, 'Oh yes, madam, she came in this morning and bought some chewing gum.' At last the mystery was solved, the doctor informed and the correct treatment given. But I still had to explain how I came by the money. Although they were relieved to have solved the problem, the stern 'dressing down' they gave me ensured that I would never again steal anything from anybody, a lesson well learnt!

On Wednesdays, through our childhood years, we used to have lunch at our grandmother's beautiful flat (my father's mother, we called her by the Greek word Giagia) at the other end of Porchester Terrace. (It was to be utterly demolished by a high explosive bomb during the 1939-45 war.) We regularly had pilaf rice and chicken for the main course and ice cream inside an orange for pudding. Her maid Annie was a good friend of ours and we always visited Ella the cook in her tiny kitchen to thank her for cooking the meal. Years later I named one of my dogs after the maid. At the end of the meal two events held us spellbound. One was my grandmother putting her head backwards, dropping pills down her throat and following this with a drink from her glass; our eyes were glued to this ritual event. My mother always appeared to look the other way but I thought it was hilarious. The second event was when she would take a cube of sugar and dip it into her black coffee until it was fully absorbed and then she would pop it into OUR mouths! This was called a 'canard' (or duck), though I have never fully understood why. While the adults sat talking we children were sent into the drawing room where *Puck* and *Chicks*, children's papers, awaited us. I loved Wednesdays.

My poor mother was not so lucky as her parents and two brothers, Tom and George, lived in Canada. She was only to see them three times during the years of her married life. She never complained but I know how desperately she missed them and, in those days, there were no planes to take her to their side in a matter of hours. Her sister Gladys lived in Cupar, Fife in Scotland. She was married to Angus, and they had two daughters, Mary and Kirsty. I was rather envious of them because they had a pony which lived in the field alongside the house. My father, having lost his father at the age of ten, and his sisters living in Marseille, also saw little of his family; travel was so much more difficult in those days.

When we were young certain obligations were required of us. A MUST was to have our bowels open before we went to school! Shouts from upstairs of 'I have *been*' and calls from downstairs of 'Have you *been* yet?' were vitally important events of the day! The other was eating porridge. Once I was kept back from school because I wouldn't eat my porridge at breakfast; I hated porridge and eggs, a fact to which my parents took great exception. The first time I ate and enjoyed eggs was when I was at boarding school with chicken pox; I hadn't eaten for days and was sent up a boiled egg with bread and butter. I ate both and have never looked back!

Dressing took a long time. In the winter we wore gaiters which had rows of little buttons the length of them and we used hooks to do them up and undo them. They took ages to do, although with time I managed to speed up a little. We wore liberty bodices over our vests in cold weather. We wore pinafores at meals and horrible rubber pants when playing on the beach. The sand got between our skin and the elastic! Hats were usually worn when going out and *always* in church. We also wore gloves which were bought on the ground floor of Whiteleys.

Memories of these times include 'going to rest' after lunch on my bed. I found this very frustrating as I felt full of life and fretted at being stuck at the top of the house with no one to talk to. I am sure this was good practice when I was two or three years old, but I believe it went on for far too long. I think, now, that it was more for my parents' benefit than for mine!

I used to lie listening to the sounds of London: the clip-clop of the cart-horses as the coal men delivered their load of bags of coal to the houses, including ours; the bell ring and 'stop me and buy one' of the ice cream man on his tricycle contraption with a box full of different ice creams, they were either Walls or Elderado; the cries of the rag and bone man in his cart and the sound of his horse's hooves; the cooing of pigeons outside in the gardens and the birds in the trees. As already mentioned, the maid used to brush the stair carpet every morning but in the afternoon she would get the scrubbing board out and start rubbing the clothes on it. I really wonder how quickly our clothes became threadbare with the rough handling they received but it certainly got them clean!

Things happened right outside the house, such as the knife grinder coming by on his bicycle whose bike was fixed so that, on using the pedals, he held the knives against a kind of belt to sharpen them. There was a 'hurdy-gurdy' man who came round wheeling his musical instrument, an organ on wheels activated by turning the handle, and played its individualistic music. He was accompanied by a little monkey in a red coat who jumped off to collect the money we were offering to give to his master. I didn't want to laugh at his antics and thought there was something wrong about his captivity.

My parents, always wanting to expand our knowledge of the world, hung three very large maps on the walls of our nursery.

One was of the world, one was of Europe and the other was of England. With all the countries and counties clearly named, we soon found a way of having fun with them. When having meals in the nursery in our early years we used to play 'I Spy' saying things like 'I spy a country beginning with. . .' or 'I spy a county beginning with. . .'' I think this was of enormous help in our being able to place counties and countries when we were asked, or when people talked about them, as we grew up. This developed into capitals of countries. I am surprised that these days children seem to know so little of their own or other countries.

As we gravitated from the nursery to the downstairs dining room certain indulgences came our way, such as 'white tea'; this consisted of milk, a tiny *drop* from the tea pot and the cup filled with hot water from the water jug. We felt that we were really growing up when we achieved this development in our drinking habit. We were limited to one or two sweets when, on occasions, we had them in the house. These would be after lunch treats. As you have discovered, I always did and still do have a craving for sweetness and chocolate in particular. Occasionally, my mother made a gorgeous soft kind of fudge which we devoured at great speed! She and I had very similar tastes in food.

Meals, heralded by the beating of the gong in the hall, were wholesome and plentiful and we were 'waited on' at the table by one of the maids (the parlour maid) who wore an attractive plain uniform with an apron and pretty lace decoration round the neck and cuffs. There was also a scullery maid and a cook downstairs. I was fond of them all and I used to go down and talk with them sometimes, sitting at the kitchen table.

I think we were encouraged to eat more than necessary. For example at tea time we had to 'eat two slices of bread before you have cake' (I think psychologists would call this deferred gratification!) and we were offered second helpings of the first and second courses at lunch, which I always accepted! I adored steamed chocolate pudding with chocolate sauce. (Even now I buy little ones from Marks and Spencer!) At the end of the meal we had to ask, 'Please may I get down?' and receive permission from our parents.

Two things I disliked as a child. Our mother used to arrange for a dress maker to come to our house and make our dresses. I hated it when she kept turning me round to take my measurements. The other was hair washing days, when my mother had to handle me firmly as I would not stand still and followed this with pouring *vinegar* over our hair before the final rinse. It certainly made our hair soft and removed the soap but OH! the smell!

Getting around London was very interesting. We used to take a 12 or 88 bus to go along Bayswater Road to get to Oxford Street where my mother did a lot of her shopping. For years she held an account with Selfridges. We had our hair cut at the 'Bobba' shop! I used to scream when Miss Glover, the long suffering hair dresser, came near me. She wore a white wimple over her hair. My mother thought it reminded me of the nuns who nursed me when I had my tonsils and adenoids out in St Luke's Hostel for the Clergy! In Oxford Street and elsewhere, men and women plied their trade selling hot chestnuts. They had a burning red brazier on a cart and filled little white bags with piping hot chestnuts – it was painful to hold them but Mum and I adored them. I loved London; there were always things to do there. As my sisters and brother were all at school, I spent a great deal of time with my mother.

Getting on a bus was rather like climbing Everest! The step up was so big for one so small but I loved our outings on buses. The conductor would call out, 'All aboard! Move along the bus please,' and then he would pull the string which rang a quite noisy bell which goaded the driver into action. As we got on the bus we all called out, 'Bags sit next to mum,' 'Bags two,' 'Bags three,' the last one didn't need to say anything, as it was obvious he or she was the last one to book their place in the row. This caused great amusement amongst the other passengers. My feet dangled helplessly from the seat and I pressed against my mother on one side and some poor passenger on the other. The conductor came round calling out 'fares please' with an accent on the 's' perhaps to make sure we knew he was coming. In a wooden holder there was an assortment of coloured tickets – pink, yellow, blue, green, orange and white all depicting different lengths of journey which were frequently checked by the ticket inspector men who jumped on and off the buses, at will, like crickets. The top of the bus was open as was the stair case leading up to it. We used to love climbing the big stairs up and down and enjoyed the view from the top, especially the front seat. Later, of course, a roof covered the top and steps and the weather (affecting where we sat) was no longer a factor in decision making.

Trams, too, were similarly open on top with canvas which covered each line of seats separately. My brother and I used to have great fun playing hide and seek under these. My poor mother must have dreaded getting on a tram and was continually trying to make us 'behave'. We were mainly responsive to her admonishment as we were thankfully quite strictly brought up to obey our parents and to know right from wrong. I believe that, on occasions, I was given a smack on my legs or bottom which never did me any harm.

When we went out, one of the instructions for our safety was, 'Hold my hand. If we get separated go up to a policeman, take his hand and tell him you are lost.' Policemen were two a penny in those days and I didn't need any encouragement to find one and get his full attention! They used to blow their whistle when there was trouble to get other police to come to their aid. There were police 'boxes' at quite frequent intervals with a blue light on the top which flashed when the phone rang inside. These were kept locked but there was an outside phone for public use.

At the great age of four I was sent to join my two sisters at Norland Place School (NPS), Holland Park. My first memories of it were being told to 'put on your apron' before playing in the sand trays which, I believe, were metal lined and came up to about the height of my stomach. All manner of shapes and sizes of cylinders, cubes and trowels were there with which to explore the sand and to begin to make cognitive sense of the world around us. I believe most of the teachers had been Froebel trained (which I only found out many years later when my own connections with Froebel were made). I was to remain at NPS for the next six years.

I do not have particularly happy memories of the school which was probably *my* fault rather than theirs. I do remember being pretty naughty! One of my tricks was to put up my hand to go to the toilet – rather more often than necessary. I remember the lined writing books to improve our handwriting. I came on a letter I had written to Father Christmas which indicated how much I had needed help in this area. We were somewhat regimented, forming lines to go anywhere, especially 'line up to go to lunch'. My memory of lunches is confined to one particular dish. It was of a thick stew – the gravy almost solid – served with dry boiled potatoes and dry white haricot beans; I hated it. Grace was said at the beginning and end of every meal. The national anthem was played at every opportunity and the Union Jack displayed on the raised platform at times of special events. There were pictures of King George V and Queen Mary on the wall.

In contrast I thoroughly enjoyed singing in the school choir. I was selected for the choir early on and loved every minute of it. I remember being in the second row and trying madly to balance on a very wobbly form. Playtime was spent in the paved playground between the two buildings of which the school was comprised. Our sports ground was at Gunnersbury Avenue, Chiswick. We took a picnic tea for sports lessons. I always had banana sandwiches and orange juice.

I was very proud of my uniform. In the winter we wore a dark blue skirt and light blue blouse with school tie or a serge-type dress and navy blue blazer with our badge on the pocket. Our hats were also dark blue (and felt soft and furry to the touch) with a ribbon of the school colours around it. Grey socks up to our knees and black shoes completed our outfit. In the summer we wore pretty pale blue flower pattern dresses with white socks and straw hats again with the school ribbon round them.

The two school buildings were joined by a passage on the second floor. There was a 'glass room', as it was named, where children being punished were sent. I spent quite a lot of time in there. It was supposed to make us embarrassed as the staff kept passing to and fro through it. I used to try to illicit a smile from them but, as I remember, without much success.

My sisters Helen and Christian were still at the school when I arrived but shortly afterwards moved on to their boarding school. I was to follow later. They, poor things, witnessed the dreadful accident outside the front of the school of a car knocking down and killing the French school mistress, I don't believe they ever forgot it.

There was great excitement when we heard of the birth of Princess Margaret Rose. I bet we sang the national anthem – though I don't remember. Another event of that time was the dreadful 'burning up' of the British R101 airship on the way to India. Events like this were prayed for in school. The school had close charity connections with the Holland Park Mission and we used to knit and pass on clothes for the children.

Quite early on I showed signs of being good at sports. By the time I had left school, at the age of ten, even though there were girls and a few boys who stayed on until they were sixteen or so, I played for the hockey and cricket first teams.

However, one of my most embarrassing moments was when I was about 9 years old playing in a first team match alongside 16 and 17 year olds and partnering the school's captain at the crease. I was receiving the ball and belted it with all my might out towards the boundary. We made two runs and then I heard 'Stop! Stop!' I didn't know who was saying this and, keen to make my mark and as many runs as possible, I set off charging up the pitch. To my horror I realised that my partner was walking back to the club house and there were cries of derision from our supporters. I know now that I hadn't fully understood the rules and didn't realise why it was she (and not myself) who walked disconsolately off the pitch! She had been 'run out'! I then did exactly the same thing to the vice captain! Needless to say I did not get a very warm welcome from the team when I was eventually 'bowled out' with a very high score.

At school the next morning not a soul would talk to me. It took me some time to realise what a heinous crime I had committed and that word had gone round that I had got the captain *and* the vice captain 'run out' and that I had been 'sent to Coventry' (when no one would talk to me) for the rest of the day. When I got home the tears flowed and my father explained to me what I had done. Once I realised that although I could bat, bowl and field ahead of others of my age group, my understanding of the rules of the game were not as far ahead, this was unlikely to happen again!

Sports day was one of the highlights of my years at NPS. I used to win the skipping, egg and spoon, and other races involving an extra activity incorporated with running. However I was never much good at sprinting (then called the running race). I also won the 'throwing the cricket ball' every year, I think this was because my father used to take me into Hyde Park to practise on the grass areas adjoining Bayswater Road. He was very good at helping me in this way and I appreciated him doing so.

I was always a very nervous and highly strung child. I was terrified of the unknown, a problem which has followed me throughout life. When thunder storms arrived I used to sob

b

uncontrollably despite my parents explaining that it was 'just the clouds bumping into each other'. Another sound over which I got very upset was hearing carol singers in the distance and then getting closer; again I was inconsolable until my parents invited them into the house, then for some reason I stopped crying. There was an occasion when my mother took me to Horse Guards Parade to see Trooping the Colour. We had wonderful seats near the front but unfortunately one of the soldiers fainted right in front of us, falling flat on his face. Naturally his face was covered in blood and all I could do for the rest of the performance was to sob into my hands, much to my mother's distress.

Possibly because of my father's connections and through his medical work, we were given invitations to many annual public events which we would never otherwise have had. I remember being in the front row of the Mansion House balcony and watching the procession of the Lord Mayor's show passing by and *how* we enjoyed it!

My brother was at Wagners School in Kensington, and my mother and I used to walk down through Kensington Gardens (near the borders of the Embassy buildings and to the right of the play area) to collect my brother after his school had finished playing their football games. Then we would go home to tea. I remember my mother giving the playground a wide berth and when we asked if we could go on the swings she would say 'no' because there were 'dirty' children playing in there. In those days there were thousands out of work in considerable poverty and hygiene was not the priority of the day – *that* was food and housing.

Most days I went with our nurse for a walk in Kensington Gardens with our beloved Mikey. My favourite place was the Round Pond. There I used to sail my boats. Sometimes it was the wind-up motor boat and at others it was a sailing boat or remote controlled motor boat. We used to tie string on to the end of them so that they wouldn't get away from us. Having thought this large pond (more like a lake) was quite deep, I remember how we laughed when one of the men looking after it, waded out to rescue a boat which had broken down in the middle and the water only came up just around the calves of his legs.

Learning to ride a bike was quite a nightmare for me. My parents used to hold the saddle while I struggled to get my balance. On my sixth birthday, I went into the drawing room and found a beautiful new shiny red bike. After that I had no further problems. In fact, I became quite adept at negotiating my way between the trees in the park. Later, as an adult, I used to cycle around Marble Arch and Hyde Park Corner, so this was good practice for the future!

My mother arranged for me to have ballet lessons with Miss Sheen at Wigmore Hall. I loved going there and it triggered my desire to continue with this later. We also used to go to a gym class at Miss Brettel's, another activity I much enjoyed. We all went there but I don't believe that any of the four of us were ever able to climb up the rope!

Sometimes my mother and I would peer through the railings of 145 Piccadilly, the home of the Duke and Duchess of York, to watch the princesses Elizabeth and Margaret Rose playing with their dolls, prams and bikes in the garden.

At home the milk was delivered in churns (unpasteurised of course) and the coal was delivered by men wearing long black 'hoods' which covered their foreheads and hung down their backs where they carried the heavy sacks of coal. I can still remember the 'oily' smell that came with them mixed in with the 'horsey' smell of their beautiful cart horses. The men had to stagger down five steps to get into our cellar where they unloaded their sacks. Outside most houses there were 'manholes' which covered a circular entrance where coal could be poured down into cellars. Every now and again the chimney sweep would come with his brushes to clean our sitting room chimney. Mum would put down dust sheets all around the floor to protect it from the soot.

At Christmas our grandmother and great aunt (her blind sister) would take us by taxi to a pantomime or theatre. We rarely used taxis – they were considered a luxury – so it was very exciting. I can still remember sitting on the little seats backing on to the taxi driver. In those days he would get out and open the doors for us! To this day I still feel a certain amount of guilt when I use a taxi.

This year, 1934, I was 8 years old. School continued and I went on putting up my hand to go (unnecessarily) to the toilet. Our motto, 'Follow the light uphold the right' was a hard one to deal with! I know I tried to improve my writing but I was no good at sums. I could march beautifully around the school hall and had no difficulty talking politely with visitors to the classroom, but I found sitting still quite difficult to do. In this day and age I might have been thought to have 'attention deficit hyperactivity disorder' (ADHD).

As always, in the Easter holiday we went as a family to Littlestone-on-Sea in Kent. My father used to book a floor at Popes Hotel which included bedrooms and a lovely big sitting room overlooking the greensward and the sea. I believe this was his favourite time of the year. We would get in the car and he would take the wheel and drive us through the beautiful leafy lanes where we found the woods in which primroses and bluebells were growing. We would all tumble out of the car (gratefully, as I have already indicated, he was a terrible driver!) carrying picnic baskets etc., and find a spot to make a base for our picnic. Down went the rugs and baskets and four white handkerchiefs for our game of football. Then we would all go off in different directions to pick flowers (now forbidden!) and look for trees to climb. Later we would have our picnic and finally, after a game of football, return to our hotel, my father smoking his revolting pipe and my mother (thank goodness) doing the driving. I made a visit in 2005 to retrace my steps and found the Popes Hotel demolished and replaced by a block of flats.

In the morning we went riding. We would sit on the hotel steps waiting for the 'clip-clop' sound of the horses and ponies trotting up the long road leading from their stables. As they came into sight I felt butterflies in my stomach, firstly because I loved them but secondly because I felt quite nervous when riding. When the tide was out we rode on the glorious stretches of sand and when it was in we rode through the surrounding countryside. Our horses were called Peter, Billy, Roly and my pony was a grey called Daphne. She was a bad tempered little beast, who ignored all requests to 'trot on' or 'walk' and did exactly what she wanted, pulling hard at the reins which I found difficult to hold. This especially happened as we turned for home and her mind appeared to be one-tracked as she sensed the 'dinner' that awaited her back in the stables! She enjoyed the odd bite on your arm when standing beside her and sometimes gave a surreptitious side kick with her little hooves! My memories of Littlestone were of cold windy days and games of football on the greensward, where anyone, standing, watching our family antics, was invited to join in. To me this was 'family cohesion' at its best; we laughed a lot and took a lot of good exercise in the process. Time came to return to London and pick up the threads of life at our much loved home.

1934 was an important year for me. I was continuing with my education at Norland Place School when, one day, my parents called me into the drawing room. I was going to Canada with my mother to visit her parents in Summerland, British Columbia. I learned later that it was because I was 'too naughty' to be left at home. My poor sisters were most unhappy that I was being rewarded for my bad behaviour and they, who were so good, were being left behind. They, in future years, frequently reminded me of this!

We went by train from London to Liverpool where we boarded the liner *The Duchess of York*. She was a beautiful ship and had everything from shops, swimming pool, a gym where there was an electric 'Bucking Bronco' horse and where I spent many hours, to libraries, entertainment rooms and dance floors. It took us six days to cross the Atlantic. On board was a large contingent of Oxford Group members which upset my mother for some reason. One of the conditions that I was allowed to travel was that I had to learn all my times table up to 12x. I am sure my mother wished they had not done that, because I had always had a shocking memory and found it extremely difficult to learn them by rote, so everyday we were going '2x2=4, 2x3=6' and so on. By the time we docked back in Liverpool a month later, I knew them! Apart from this our days were spent playing shuffle board, lying on deck reading, using the gym or I played in the children's room. Supper was early for children, so it was nice for my mother that once I was tucked up in our cabin, she could meet with other passengers at dinner. I was fascinated to watch the whales and dolphins which swam alongside the liner. We watched them dive down under the ship and rushed over to the other side to see them come up.

One night, at two o'clock in the morning, the emergency bell went and we had to put on our life belts, go up on deck and stand beside our allotted life boat. As we did so we saw that on one side of us we were right beside and leaning against an iceberg and through the thick fog we could see there was a ship right alongside us on the other. They were tense moments as the other ship went into reverse and, although 'juddering' us, gradually pulled away from our side. There must have been great relief among the crew: my mother only stopped shaking as we went back to our cabin.

We sailed up the St Lawrence River, a wonderful experience with beautiful scenery on either side and little islands dotted along the way. We visited Ottawa where we saw my Uncle George and his family, and Montreal before taking the CNR (Canadian National Railway) train to Kamloops, a three-day-four-night journey across Canada, to the west of the Rocky Mountains. There we were met by my Uncle Tom. It was extremely hot and I remember my mother and my uncle shielding me by the side of the car as I stripped off some of my clothes and changed into a cotton dress. We then had a long journey to Summerland in British Columbia where my grandparents welcomed us at their little cottage on Crescent Beach. Their lakeside home was made of wood – a real log cabin – with a little beach bordering the Okanogan Lake. All night I could hear the waves lapping on the beach outside my bedroom window. My grandparents also owned a large and very beautiful house on a hill just above us, where they stayed in the winter to keep warm and where my uncle lived. Uncle Tom, who had been severely wounded in the First World War and his eyesight badly affected, had taken over the orchard allowing my grandfather to have a well-earned rest.

Neighbours by the lake were a doctor and his wife. They had a son John and daughter Mary, around my age. We used to play baseball type games and football on the large area of grass on the inland side of the cottage. We swam in the lake and I went out fishing with my uncle in his rowing boat (with outboard motor). Once I unexpectedly caught a large salmon-trout! We spent about three weeks there before returning the way we came except, this time, by Canadian Pacific Railway (CPR) boarding the *Empress of Australia* to make the return crossing (an equally luxurious ship) and were met in London by my father and Helen, Christian and Pogy. How glad they were to see us again – I don't think it had been much fun without Mum at home.

Other events which I remember well were the Silver Jubilee celebrations for King George V and Queen Mary, but sadly only eight months later, on 20th January 1936, the King died. My mother took me to see his lying-in-state and the funeral procession through London.

My parents used to take us to the Roehampton Club, of which my father was a member, to swim in the two pools in the summer and to watch the polo being played there. This was another occasion when I got very nervous. When the bell went for the chukkas we used to go on to the pitch to stamp down the divots kicked up by the ponies. The next bell meant they were coming out onto the field again. I was always scared that I would not get off the field before they came galloping across. I didn't like the noise that the ball and the stick made on the surrounding wooden boards either.

At home we always kept busy. We had a musical box called a symphonium; it was wound up by a handle on the side and the metal disc had raised, sharp ratchets depicting the notes it played as it rotated. I much enjoyed playing this. Piano practice also had to be done, daily, once I had started piano lessons with Miss Turner. I used to enjoy making up tunes but as soon as I did my mother would come in and tell me to 'practise properly'. We also had a magic lantern from which pictures were shown onto a screen and we sat, as a family, on chairs in the dining room to view them. It was quite an event.

Social activities included meeting and talking with my parents' friends and quite early on, I was invited to school friends' parties. I loved dressing up in party dresses and wearing little bronze dancing 'pumps' with black elastic holding them on round my white ankle socks. Party food consisted mostly of sandwiches, jellies and cakes and I thoroughly enjoyed them. Games were organised and sometimes we danced. That was when I first found that I not only loved dancing but was good at it, and I was never short of partners for that reason if for no other! Games were often 'Blind man's Buff', 'Hunt the thimble', 'Hanging the tail on the donkey' or 'Hide and Seek'. Dancing was such as forming two lines and dancing 'Sir Roger de Coverley', Musical Chairs or Musical Bumps.

The annual Oxford and Cambridge boat race – unlike today – was *the* event of the year. Street sellers walked around with cards of little dark and light blue wool-made 'men' (about one inch long) with a safety pin at the back which was worn on your coat or dress. There was strong friendly competition and, at school, we used to take one side or the other in our games. It was such fun.

Another thing my brother and I did was to climb into the 'dumb' waiter, the small lift, which we pulled up and down from

31

outside the dining room to the kitchen, by means of a strong pull rope. This was brought to an end when our parents found us doing it. I think they were more worried about our breaking the lift than our breaking any bones!

At the end of the quite large garden at the back of the house, my father had an area surrounded by wire netting and a cement base laid to form one half of a tennis court. He painted a black line across a cemented wall at the height of a net and gave us a wonderful place to play a type of tennis. I spent hours with a tennis racket and ball hitting it backwards and forwards, either on my own or with my brother but we usually ended up fighting over something! I am sure it was this level of practice that enabled me to play tennis to quite a high standard when I was still a child. In the adjoining house a grey-haired elderly lady, Lady Abraham, used to sit in her window watching us and nodding her head at our antics even when we climbed onto her wall to collect mulberries from *her* tree.

Walks in the park continued and one of my favourite places to go was to the Peter Pan statue in Kensington Gardens. I used to love stroking all the little animals, so beautifully carved into the statue, and feel the smoothness and curves around them. I wonder how many other little people had stroked them before and since? Sadly, because of the damage to the statue (I feel a little guilty), the public is no longer allowed near enough to touch it.

In the dark, wintry and foggy evenings one would hear the park keepers warning everyone that it was closing time by calling loudly, 'ALL OUT. ALL OUT!' It was quite an eerie sound in the dank, dripping and muffled darkness of the failing light and often thick fog, and this was another time when I felt very frightened – always afraid we might get locked in. Mikey, our dog, who, when he was alive, always came with us, seemed to be oblivious of everything. There always seemed to be thick fog – thick black coal smoke which went up chimneys and joined the smoke from other London chimneys. It was known as 'pea soup' fog, because of its green tint, which smelt revolting and made us cough and splutter. It visibly swirled around us, limiting the distance ahead one could see.

In past years, men wore top hats for weddings and funerals. My father looked very funny in his and he took our teasing him very well. Sometimes telegrams were sent through the phone or a messenger boy would arrive, message in hand, wearing his pill box hat and asking if there was 'any reply'? I just remember my parents saying, 'No thank you.' I don't believe they ever sent a reply by the messenger boy and I'm not sure how this was done, anyway. All I know is that he got a tip and went away saluting very smartly, jumping down the front steps.

My father never liked speaking on the phone and used to lose his temper frequently with the operator to whom you gave the number (there were no automatic phones in those days). When he got really cross he would say 'my name is *Doctor* Vlasto'. Although as a surgeon he was really known as Mr Vlasto, he thought that being a doctor sounded more important. I also remember him saying 'my good man' when trying to get the better of an argument with the operator and I used to curl up inside with embarrassment.

Something else I remember, that was useful to pre-warn us, was that at night time we could always tell when our parents were coming up the stairs to say good night. There was a very squeaky stair by the top landing which was difficult to circumnavigate.

Some events which come to mind of my childhood will never be forgotten and, on occasions, bring a smile to my lips. Christmas was a very exciting time. Great sheets of different coloured tissue were bought, and glue with several brushes put out beside them on the table. Then we sat around making yards and yards of paper chains and then helped to hang them up all over the downstairs rooms and the hall. They really 'dressed' the house up, along with coloured shades around the lights, and we began to feel Christmas had arrived!

My father had experimented speaking in a quiet voice in the downstairs lavatory and found that his voice came out very muffled through the wall in his study next door. In this way he prepared to have a Father Christmas conversation with me on Christmas Eve. My mother was with me when this great piece of oratory was delivered and I believe I swallowed it 'hook, line and sinker'. He was very pleased with his experiment, as he told me years later. We really did have very caring parents who did everything they could to make us happy.

However, one afternoon I was called into the sitting room by my parents. They both looked quite serious. I was told that I was being too disruptive at Norland Place School and they were being asked to take me away! I remember the ominous silence that followed this shattering news and moving my weight from one leg to the other. "Well, what have you got to say?" I don't think I had anything to say – I remember being quite surprised. "So, we are sending you to Crofton Grange where Helen and Christian are, where we hope you will be better behaved." I think they must have been quite as relieved as I was to think I would be away for three terms of the year. It was to be the start of seven happy years boarding in the depth of the Hertfordshire countryside at Braughing, near Buntingford.

Chapter Two

My mother took me to Derry and Toms in Kensington to buy my new school uniform, thick lisle stockings and new shoes. I was very excited and not a little apprehensive. She seemed to enjoy packing my trunk and ticked each item off the school list as she went along. Three vests, four pairs of knickers, two dresses; one of the items on the list requested, which should be sent with us to school, was a 'rug'. This, it turned out, was to be used out in the garden as we lay on the ground under the beautiful old trees, or in the orchard, when in our free time we wanted just to talk with our friends, read a book or revise our work. Such freedom of choice was much appreciated. My mother and I were very close and I had looked on her as my friend once the endless string of nannies and nurses had left. We had a similar sense of humour which became more alike as I grew older, and I was going to miss her.

And so, at the ripe age of ten years, I arrived at beautiful Crofton Grange School, set in a hundred acres of land and in the company of another girl, Ann Block. I believe there was only a month or two between our ages, though I was the youngest there for the next couple of years.

The headmistress was Miss M.G. Beard, OBE, who had been the principal of Girton College and Putney High School and had a quite brilliant mind. I thought she was an excellent headmistress and over the years at Crofton I became very fond of her and, I think, she of me. She liked children who had character, gave her a firm handshake and looked her in the eye! In a letter to my parents, prior to my going to Crofton, Miss Beard said she hoped I wouldn't be spoilt, being so young, and that my sisters would have to make sure this didn't happen.

She needn't have worried! I was very quickly 'put in my place' by the older girls, to such an extent that I was reduced to tears most days and wrote to my parents begging them to take me away! They didn't. As time wore on I think I got the message and began to be accepted. However, I still continued being very naughty and was often sent to Miss Beard's room for punishment. There she tried to get me to memorise poetry and repeat it to her; she soon discovered that I was genuinely unable to do this (as I mentioned before, I have always had a *very* poor short-term memory) and eventually we resorted to doing crossword puzzles or listening to gorgeous classical music.

One of the 'naughty' (or was it pure mischievous?) things that I used to do was to slip into the dining room and change the napkins round so that I sat next to my friends. The delightful housemaid, Susan, once caught me doing this and gave me a knowing wink; sadly she was to die of cancer not long after and was very much missed by everybody. On one occasion I was sent to Miss Beard for some misdemeanour or other and she told me to go and sit down in her sitting room. I wondered what was going to happen next. First she picked up her *Telegraph* crossword puzzle and started giving me clues. After we had worked on this for a while, she then turned on the 3rd programme, which played classical music, and we sat and listened to this for quite a long time, then she looked at her watch and said: "You'd better go and join the others now."

I am sure that it was due to this understanding of hers that I eventually calmed down, and this in turn made me want to do things to please her. But not before I had gone out of bounds, crawling along ditches to buy chocolates in the sweet shops in Little Nasty and Westmill. I seemed to be 'testing' myself all the time. I never did anything to purposely hurt anyone.

I once went into the forbidden cave, parallel to the middle gate on the drive, in the hundred acres of grounds and, creeping deep into the darkness, my heart pounding, I ran my hands along the wall and let out a scream as I felt a soft body which called out, 'Shut up you fool, it's me.' I still remember the relief knowing that there were others who went out of bounds too!

In an article in *The Express*, dated 27th November 1997, Mrs Jacqueline Lang, one time head teacher of Walthamstow Hall School in Sevenoaks, was quoted saying, 'I always have a soft spot for the ones (pupils) who break the rules provided they aren't doing it in malice.' This describes my impression of Miss Beard, who once said to me, 'When you do something, ask yourself if it would be all right for a hundred people to do this. If it would be, go ahead and do it.' This is one of the maxims which has guided me through my life and I frequently refer to it.

Every weekday we had lessons all morning with a break for a drink and biscuits and lunch at 1pm. We were allowed to help ourselves to as many biscuits as we wanted and my friends and I used to hide under the front staircase with handfuls of them! We played games *every* afternoon, lacrosse and netball in the winter term and tennis and swimming in the summer term. Matches were played during the day on Saturdays and in the evening we danced (all girls together!) to gramophone records. Although this doesn't sound much fun I thoroughly enjoyed it and was quite devastated when I, occasionally, got a 'study mark' as a punishment which meant you missed the evening event and sat doing homework in a classroom!

Another of my school memories was the arrival of a large delicious chocolate cake on my birthday, sent by my mother every year, without fail, to be shared with all in my study and the prefects. All the girls' parents did the same. I believe it must have been sent directly from a shop in London.

My two sisters had been given the opportunity to write to two boys from the East End of London and to send them my brother's old clothes and comics which they had read, and letters and photos were exchanged. This was a programme called Sunbeam Friend set up by the *Daily Mail* in the 1930s (a paper which my parents read daily all the years of their married lives). Having attained the great age of ten years on February 1st 1936, I asked if I could now do the same, only I would like it to be a girl, and they agreed.

So it was that I was sent the details of a ten year old girl, Gwendoline, whose family lived in Poplar in the East End of London. I began writing to her. I believe that the first communication was via the newspaper itself but thereafter we wrote directly to each other. I sent her some of my toys and *Puck* and *Chicks* children's papers and was very thrilled when I got letters back from her. I sent her photos and she sent some to me, I still have one of her with her parents (her father was in army uniform). I am still in touch with Gwen to this day (75 years!) exchanging Christmas cards. In fact, she came to visit me with her husband some time ago, but sadly he has since died. I am grateful to the *Daily Mail* for conceiving this excellent scheme and am very glad that I became part of it.

I am not sure when we first went to Frinton-on-Sea for our summer holidays. All I *do* know was that they were some of the happiest days of my life. I have always loved the seaside from the moment we all shouted, 'I see the sea sixpence for me,' straining our eyes as we approached the sea front and desperate to be the first one, though we never got or expected to get a sixpence!

In the 1930s my grandmother used to take a house at Frinton for a month during the summer holidays and all our family and aunts, uncles and cousins from France and elsewhere used to join her. She organised and paid for everything: the renting of the house, enrolling us as temporary members of the tennis club and the hiring of bicycles for us four children, which she did as soon as we arrived. There was a bicycle shop just off the main shopping street and we were all 'kitted out' with the correct sized bikes. We made full use of them, particularly in the early morning before breakfast when the four of us went off together to explore the villages and surrounding countryside. Having found a slot machine, in what I believe is called Little Holland, where we could buy 1d (one penny) bars of Nestlé chocolate, we frequently found ourselves pedalling in that direction.

My sisters, being older and not particularly interested in bathing in the sea or playing tennis, found little to do. Helen helped our Aunt Fanny with cutting and arranging the many bowls of flowers to fill the downstairs rooms. Christian, who was a budding artist, made a garden house out of branches and straw at the bottom of the garden and spent many hours there drawing and painting.

The first house which I remember that we went to in Frinton was 'Kelvin Lodge', now pulled down, which was on the road running along the greensward on the front. This was a lovely house and had a large lawn at the front, steeply raised at one end to form a wonderful hill down which my brother and I used to race on our bikes. I remember the patterns our wheels made on the dew-covered grass. Physical activity was my great need so I got much pleasure from doing this.

After Kelvin Lodge came our final move to 'Marylands', a lovely house right next to the gravelly road leading into the tennis club. The garden was huge, made up of lawns, flower beds and orchards. A child's haven for hide and seek, we made full use of it and I can still smell the scent of the roses that were everywhere in the garden. The grown-ups used to sit on deck chairs on the long, wide, stone terrace surrounding the brick house. Doors opened out from several of the ground floor rooms tempting one to step out to have a wonderful view over the garden and the golf course beyond.

From a very young age I have had a great love of all animals, horses and dogs in particular, and my excitement knew no bounds when I found ponies on the beach! It cost 6d (sixpence) to ride up to three breakwaters and 1/- (one shilling) for six. They all had their names on the front of their foreheads. Later on, I was to be allowed, by the man who owned the ponies, to lead them when they were giving rides. I doubt very much if this would now be allowed within the current Health and Safety Act, but I really enjoyed being given the responsibility and got an occasional free ride in return!

In those days about twelve steps led down from the path by the beach huts onto the beach. I remember the sea coming up onto the steps when it was particularly rough. Now, large curved concrete blocks – the length of the sea front – protect the land from erosion and risk of flooding. Sadly, it has ruined the look of the beach.

I believe I was the most emotionally and physically satisfied of my family by these summer holidays, but I do not believe my mother or brother really enjoyed them. My mother found little to do while my father played golf or sat and talked in his excellent French with family members. My brother played some tennis and golf but must have found little else to do. I, on the other hand, was blissfully happy either on the beach where I made full use of the sand and sea, on my bike, or more particularly at the wonderful tennis club.

Every day I went to play at the tennis club for the duration of our holidays. I often used to play with my brother, but we had endless arguments and were much happier playing with other juniors! However, in 1935 we played together in the mixed doubles Junior American Tournament and won it! I imagine the public around the 'centre court' must have been well entertained by our conversation together as must have been Pathé News which was filming us.

In the club house, up the stairs, there was a small room which had a tennis table in it. But to me the most important thing there was the ceiling which was covered all over with photos of tennis players from past years: a veritable mine of tennis history at the Frinton Lawn Tennis Club. Recently I paid a return visit to the club and was devastated to find that they had taken down and, apparently, thrown away all those wonderful photos. I was bitterly disappointed and can only hope that some of them were distributed to others, like myself, who cared about them. Some of those depicted were boys I knew who were killed in the Second World War and those happy days of their lives should not have been forgotten.

One of my tennis partners, John Clifford-Turner, was to be my first 'boy friend'. We played tennis together several times and we apparently were quite an attraction to the press! A number of years before his death I visited him and his wife Ann (née Tomkinson) in their lovely home near Frinton. I took with me a copy of one of the programmes with names and results of a tournament John and I had played in together and Ann, looking through it, said, 'Here we are; the singles and you beat me!' I had not realised that she was the person I had played against in the girls' singles. Another of my partners was Christopher (Chris) Boggon, whom I was later to invite to my 21st birthday party.

On a visit to Frinton in 2000, I was given a copy of an article written by the owner of 'Maryland', Mahmea Osborne Alton. She had been asked by her niece, Libby Osborne Hall, to 'jot down' her memories of what Frinton was like in the 1930s. It was from her that my grandmother must have rented the house and she reminded me of, and confirmed, many of the happy memories I had of Frinton. Apparently, Edward VIII and Wallis Simpson had stayed there as had also Winston Churchill.

In December 1936 King Edward abdicated causing great eruptions as he gave up the throne to marry Wallis Simpson. My parents muttered angrily about this for many months. They were

40

particularly unhappy about the embarrassing position into which he had placed his brother (King George VI to be) and also his choice of partner, whom they could not stand! But on 12th May the next year there was great excitement with the coronation of King George VI and Queen Elizabeth as crowds gathered up in London. I went with my mother to join them and saw the royal family come out onto the balcony at Buckingham Palace. My mother took us to see anything of importance going on in London. I believe she enjoyed going herself but I know she mainly did it for our sake.

In 1938 my parents took us for a short holiday to France. We stayed in a small hotel in Dinard. We had a lot of fun there and my brother and I played table tennis in the small front garden bordering the road. I think that, once again, they wanted us to do things as a family, with the impending fear of war drawing nearer. On one particular holiday we went to Elie in Scotland where my mother's parents came from Canada to join us. This was the only time my siblings met them.

Over the winter my father said he was taking us to Switzerland as he was sure that war was pending and wanted us all to go on holiday together. We spent two weeks at the Krönenhof hotel in Pontresina. It was a very happy time, with skiing and skating on the hotel skating rink and a night ride in sledges pulled by horses through the cold moonlit night, which was quite wonderful. The stars seemed to twinkle so brightly in the sky.

We also went to watch the ski jumping at St Moritz and my brother spent the whole time taking photos of the crashes! The photos came out like little back dots on a white background. Now they hardly ever fall; I wonder why it is.

On Christmas Eve we went to the local church. On arriving, we found the door locked. As we stood there shivering in the snow an American family joined us. Just as we were wondering what to do, the Vicar, a little man, bent over and with a bandage round his neck, appeared with a key and, apologising, let us in. The poor man had a boil on his neck and had just come from the doctor and was profusely embarrassed at keeping us waiting. We reassured him and the six of us and the four of them trooped in. We were to be the only parishioners. We then saw the Vicar unlocking the organ; he turned round to apologise to us again and said it would just take a few minutes.

He then acted as Vicar and organist, jumping up and down as the service required. Our family had quite a strong sense of humour but that was nothing compared to the Americans. When it came to the time for offerings to be carried up to the altar the Americans picked up a bowl and put some dollar notes in it. They then passed it to my father who only had a large note in his pocket. To my mother's horror, he started taking change from the American's dollar notes! My mother told him off crossly saying, 'Leave it!' and my father, rather sheepishly, just put his own note into the bowl. By then everyone in our two families were in stitches, which was all *most* embarrassing in the silence of this little church. As the Vicar stood holding his poor neck, my father and the American took the plate up and returned to their seats. The service having come to an end, we thanked the Vicar and he turned to lock the door behind us. We returned to our hotel. I remember this incident with great clarity and not a little wonderment. To me it was a most meaningful service.

We saw the New Year in at the hotel. I was chosen to 'bring in the New Year' and had to sit inside a large simulated flower with four petals over the top of me. This was on a type of sleigh and was pulled into the large dining room. Once there, I had to stand up and say 'Ladies and gentlemen, we wish you a Happy New Year and to our French friends *Nous leurs souétons une trés bonne année.*' But in the event, I forgot to put down the fourth petal at the back and cracked my head on it! My father tried to teach this speech to me all afternoon but, because of my memory problems, I had an awful job learning it. When I got half way through I became stuck after 'Nous leurs . . .'; fortunately all the people rescued me from having to remember the rest. I was overcome with embarrassment and I don't think my father was happy!

Hitler's influence in Germany was causing great unrest in Europe and there was a general feeling of impending war. My father, being a highly intellectual man, always interested in what was going on in the world, in the months before 1938, frequently said that he was concerned about Germany's rise in power. In preparation we were issued with gas masks and had to carry them with us everywhere. They dangled from round our necks and were in awkward square-shaped boxes that were quite cumbersome for young children to manage.

Large silver barrage balloons appeared around London and other big cities. I wondered what war would be like if it were to happen. We began to notice women in green uniforms and, on enquiring who they were, I found out that they were members of the newly formed Women's Voluntary Service (WVS). They came into being as the need for such a service was anticipated and were to play a vital part in the years ahead, many of them paying with their lives.

In anticipation of German planes flying overhead, we did what we could to prevent them from aiming at certain targets. We knew this tactic would disorientate the pilots and navigators and was continued throughout the war. We started putting 'blackouts' on our windows, street lights were turned off and cars and buses were only allowed a tiny cross of light to appear from their headlights. It was very hard to drive safely as it was difficult to see the cars coming towards you, or the backlights of cars in front of you until you were almost on top of them.

'Stone pigs' appeared in the shops. These were to take the place of hot water bottles, rubber being utilised for the war effort. Sugar was to become almost non-existent and I took to using saccharin, which I found left a nasty aftertaste in my mouth. Many people tried to do without sweeteners of any kind. I tried but failed! We all kept dried milk on our shelves as milk was not always readily available. There was a shortage of pencils and paper and as a result writing, in general, was discouraged. We were, however, encouraged to form penfriends across the world and write letters to evacuees and troops who needed letters from home.

At home 'Number 16', my mother, ever aware and always planning ahead, made me do one of the most horrendous tasks for which I have never forgiven myself – nor my mother! I had tame mice which had just produced a litter of babies, all pink and quite adorable. She said, 'Nancy, you have got to get rid of those mice. I am not having them running loose in the house when the bombs come down.' She meant it. I said, 'But how can I do that, Mum?' Her reply indicated she didn't mind by what method but that it had to be done. As I couldn't bring myself to kill them by hand, one by one, I knew I had to do something quickly and, taking the cage, tipped them down the lavatory and pulled the plug. I had nightmares imagining them swimming along the sewers under the roads of London. I still have a guilty conscience about what I did and to this day remember them every time I pull the plug!

Anderson shelters were being built in back gardens to give protection from air raid shrapnel, some people spending every night in them; but my parents decided not to do this and neither did we have them at our school in the countryside.

Many people had left London including our immediate neighbours. My mother removed some bricks out of their adjoining garden wall to allow our hens to get through and exercise and find more food to eat. As soon as the sirens went, a shout went up in our house 'The hens! Get the hens in!' So we clambered over the shed roof to jump down into the other garden and with much difficulty and laughter, guided them back through the wall and shut them up into their wooden shed. That, we thought, would help to protect them from any bomb that might fall!

We, the public, were asked to be alert and if we saw anything out of the ordinary tell the police. So one night, as I was about to get into bed, I turned out the light and went to open the window. As I pulled back the curtains and looked out into the darkness I stood mesmerised. From a top window of the houses backing onto our garden I saw a bright light flashing on and off intermittently as a plane flew overhead. I called my sister who in turn called our parents. They saw it happen and immediately called the police who came around within minutes. After satisfying themselves that there was something funny going on, they left us. They never passed any comment but about a quarter of an hour later the light flashing stopped and never happened again. We had, hopefully, caught our first spy!

On a visit to Yately, Surrey to see my mother's cousin, the late Eileen Tracey, I was introduced to neighbours who had a son called John Priestley. We seemed to take to each other and began phoning, writing and meeting regularly. He used to frequently ask me to sing solos to him on the top deck of buses we went on. (Of course, we made sure there was no one else up there with us!) Our friendship continued over the next few years.

London air space was dotted with more and more hideous silver-grey barrage balloons. Doubtless these deterred some attacks by planes, but indiscriminate bombing of targeted places continued by planes flying above the balloons.

44

As I travelled around London, during school holidays, shopping or going to the theatre or cinema (which mainly remained open throughout the war) I deliberately chose to take the Underground as I felt safer down there. But from early evening, families of Londoners descended into the noisy, smelly stations, lying several deep, end to end, either on lilos or camp beds or on the cold, hard platforms to try to get some sleep. Babies, children, bottles, blankets, thermo flasks, night clothes were all there with them. I think portable loos were replaced daily. A white line about two feet from the edge of the platform was painted to allow people to stand waiting for the next train. I never remember hearing of any casualties but I fear there must have been from such a confined space with live electric rails so close by. I will never understand how the parents of the toddlers and young children kept them from running forwards over the edge. The electricity was disconnected after the last train left and overnight.

To increase security all station names were removed making it extremely difficult to know when you had arrived at your destination! If you turned to your neighbour and asked if they knew the name of the next station you were likely to receive a frozen look and no help. Posters were put up everywhere saying things such as 'Walls have Ears' and 'Keep Mum'! Some showed nuns sitting in an Underground train wearing boots and sporting moustaches with a caption 'Don't trust anyone – they may be spies'! Even road names disappeared and sign posts were turned around the wrong way which also created chaos!

All materials went to the war effort and my parents sorted out rubber and metal items from our house and garden shed and handed them in. We were amazed when, one day, on going for a walk in Kensington Gardens we found all the railings, which enclosed the park, had gone. For a short time sheep were grazed in there, but they disappeared almost as soon as they had arrived. Doubtless they had tried to make their escape too often!

At school we had to knit a 'charity garment' every term. But during the war, we also had to knit sea-boot stockings out of thick oily wool for the sailors or balaclava helmets for the troops. I must admit, sedentary activities (apart from playing the piano or singing) were not my favourite and my charity garments changed from being baby jackets with complicated stitches to much simpler straight up and down vests! I can still remember the fishy oil smell of the wool with which we used to knit the sea-boot stockings. My mother even taught my father to knit and together they made several pairs. At school our food was sparse but adequate. My favourite first course was mashed potatoes with one of the headmistress's hen's eggs fried on top.

I was coming to the age of wearing nylon stockings but nowhere could they be found. People stained their legs and drew a pencil seam line down the back! American visitors were sure of a great welcome if they brought a gift of a pair with them. We did not receive letters from our family in France, because of censorship, but we did occasionally get them from our Canadian families. Our letters were censored both coming in and going out, which was not surprising, in case we gave any vital information to the enemy.

I became Company Leader of our school Guide company and was guilty of making them practise marching up and down beside the school building. However, we were rewarded, when, marching in the armed forces parade service at Braughing Church, we were told that we were the smartest of all the forces there!

Going back to Crofton at the start of the summer term, this time, felt very unreal. From the tension and preparation that comes before an impending war one is transported to the peace and quiet of the countryside with a life totally contained within the school building and grounds. Somehow I did not feel it was quite right to be so protected and cut off from the world outside.

It was decided that on Parents' Day there should be a demonstration of putting out an incendiary bomb. Who should be chosen to do this? 'Nancy!' boomed Miss Beard's voice and I had to practise every evening until the great day arrived. A small fire was lit in the garage (no petrol or car was near!) and the parents crowded round to see this 'interesting' display. I had to crawl across the wet floor on my stomach towards a pile of burning wood with my arm overhead holding the nozzle of the hose. I'm not sure whether it was the water running all over the floor or whether I actually did put it out, but by the applause of the parents I could only think the deed had been done. I just hoped I would never be called to do it in real life. In contrast to this a few of us gave a gymnastic display on the tennis courts which we enjoyed doing. There were fewer parents there, presumably they had difficulty in travelling. Petrol was in extremely short supply and rationed and there was a general feeling of insecurity around. Trying to cross London at night was a hazardous affair and Underground stations were taking 'all night visitors' lying along the platforms as I have mentioned.

During this term at Crofton I took the Grade I ballet exam, the first I had taken but my teacher Mrs Freedman, from Madame Vaccani's school, was keen I should do so. I also took Advanced Home Nursing, First Aid, Silver Life Saving and a gas exam which taught us how to cope in the event of a gas attack. I really wasn't interested in academic work, although I was always able to write stories in literacy. I was lucky in having this most wonderful and kindly teacher by the name of Beatrice Crowell who taught all subjects for our first two years. She was particularly interested in scripture lessons and I did my very best to remember the stories from the Bible that she told us so beautifully. But few of those lessons, in which I only got a pass mark in School Certificate, seemed to remain in my brain. I still can't face anything to do with numbers. One year I got nought for maths. I took one look at the exam paper and put my pen down; I just couldn't face it! This mark was read out in front of the whole school, but I don't remember being particularly embarrassed because I really didn't understand maths at all. To this day I can't count up money properly, as friends of mine will confirm! However, I *could* play the piano and in my last year was in charge of organising the hymns for prayers.

Where I could not shine academically I certainly did in all physical activities and in music. Mention the word sport and I'm rearing to go, at least I used to be. On arriving at Crofton I had to learn to play lacrosse, a quite wonderful game, which I took no time at all to master. As I went through the school I became first vice captain and then captain of the lacrosse, netball and tennis teams and was never so happy as when I was playing any one of them. Home and away matches were equally enjoyable, though I never liked the bus journey to other schools very much.

I have always been very fond of animals, particularly horses and there in the field beside the school building, on the other side of the ha-ha, were cart-horses! I couldn't believe my luck and started getting up early in the morning and going out into the field to stroke them. Attached to the school, but I believe privately run, was a lovely farm where they lived along with cows and calves and from where we got our milk.

One day, I took a deep breath, made sure no one could see me and slipped out of the back gate of the school garden and went into the farm next door. There I met the farmer named Gavin. He was a delightful gentleman and, on showing me around the farm, must have realised how genuinely fond of animals I was. He let me climb on a fence surrounding an outside covered enclosure and get on one of the cart-horses. He then showed me how to hold a calf's head with my hand over its nose and in its mouth so that it could take its first drink of milk out of a bucket. From then on I used to go there whenever I had free time, over several weeks, checking that no one was looking and worked quite hard while I was there. One afternoon, just as I was slipping through the gate, apparently I was seen by one of the staff. The next day Miss Beard sent for me. She told me that she was very sorry but she was going to have to stop me from going to the farm. I was aghast! 'How did you know I was going there?' I gasped, and she said she had known all the time because Gavin had told her. But she told me he was so pleased with my work and my handling of the animals that he asked if I might be allowed to continue. She apparently told him that it was all right until a member of staff reported it. Sadly this is what had happened so she would have to forbid me from going there. I was heartbroken but thanked her for letting me do this as she had, and gave her my word I would not go back again. I never did.

I think I must have been restless in the early morning for I still continued going over to talk to the horses in the fields before breakfast during the next few years and in the final two years I used to take the 1st lacrosse team out before breakfast to practise on the games field. I can't think why they agreed to it, but I think we had good fun making up our own rules and games.

Another time I was tempted by some gorgeous ripe peaches in the walled kitchen garden which I'd seen on my way to our small swimming pool. The kitchen garden, lovingly cared for by Mr Aves, was out of bounds, but I just *had* to have one of those peaches. I was grateful to find a friend who felt likewise and together we crept in and took one each. I can still remember the round, hot, fluffy ball in my hands, when: 'Nancy! Have you been picking peaches? What are you doing in the kitchen garden?'

My mother in the foreground. Grantham, 1914-18 war, prior to her marriage.

My mother with her family on her wedding day. L-R: Tom Croil, Chrissy Croil Senior, George Croil, my Mum Chrissy, Thomas Croil Senior, Gladys Croil

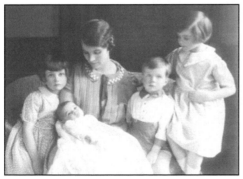

My mother with L-R: Helen, myself, Michael (Pogy) and Christian.

Our beloved Mikey.

My mother and father at 16
Porchester Terrace, London.

My paternal grandmother with
her family around her. I am
the youngest.

Outside Porchester Terrace with
'Monkey Man'.

I am on the right.

Me and Michael (Pogy).

Helen, Christian, Michael
(Pogy) and me.

Pogy and I on Daddy's
tennis court.

Our back garden.

Norland Place School – I am in row two second from left.

Norland Place School.

Me on the right with siblings and
Mikey in Kensington Gardens.

I am holding a hoop and stick.

On Okanagan Lake, Canada, where I caught my first
salmon-trout with Uncle Tom.

Me on Daphne with Pogy and
Mr Noakes, the Popes Hotel
in the background.

The four of us about to set off.

My father got us and anyone
nearby playing football.
(Littlestone-on-Sea.)

Myself diving off the top at
Crofton Grange swimming pool.

My parents would not allow
me to wear a white dress or
socks at this time.

With my partner John Clifford Turner.

Frinton-on-
Sea Junior
American
Lawn Tennis
Tournament –
I am 3rd from
right. Chris
Boggon is 6th
from right.
1938

My Pathé News photograph taken at Frinton-on-Sea.

Myself and Michael – winners of
Frinton-on-Sea Junior American
Tournament doubles, 1935

At Frinton a few years later.

My sister Christian and father helping to fill sandbags on Frinton beach, 1939

I was the youngest in the First Team at Crofton.

The staff at the Downe House summer school of music. My teacher next to me and my sister-in-law to be, Eileen, far left front row.

Crofton School, 1943, my last year.

Kirsty and I, at Farnborough on cycle
trip from Elstead, 1943

Albert McCreary –
Canadian padre.

Christian was captain of the pair
of boats in photo. I once went
with her from the docks to
Paddington train station.

Rognveld Gunn is 5th from left,
his mother to his left.

LIEUTENANT J. R. PRIESTLEY.

LIEUTENANT JOHN RICHARD PRIESTLEY was the
son of the late Lieut.-Colonel H. E. Priestley and of
Mrs. Priestley, Handfords, Yateley, Hants.

He was born 3 February, 1924, educated at Wellington and Oxford, and gazetted to the Regiment 22 May,
1943.

He died of wounds received in action while serving
in N.W. Europe, August, 1944.

A brother officer writes :—

" John Priestley's charming personality at once
impressed itself on all at Ranby, short though his time
was in the Battalion. Possessing an excellent brain,
he was full of enthusiasm and did well in everything
he took up. At the same time he had a very carefree
disposition and a very deep sense of humour. He was
loved by all who came in touch with him, officers and
other ranks, and his death is a very great loss to the
Regiment.

" In his last letter home from his Battalion he
wrote ' I have never been so happy in all my happy
life, as I am here.'
                                        " V. B. T."

Lt. John Priestly with his obituary.

My friend had slipped out of the gate and I was the one to be caught. 'Nothing, Miss Crowell.'

'Nancy, were you picking a peach?'

Tears welled up in my eyes and down my cheek and the peach, which had a large bite taken out of it, was produced from behind my back.

'Come and see me in the classroom after breakfast tomorrow.'

Perhaps it was the several hours that elapsed before we met, perhaps it was the look on my face, or perhaps it was just that Miss Crowell was the most kind, child-centred person I had ever met, that I was not surprised by her reaction. 'I'm disappointed that you did that, you know it was wrong, don't you?'

I said I did and I was sorry, but I *did* love peaches. I can still remember the quiver of a smile at the corners of her lips and I loved her for the gentle reprimand I received. I didn't risk it again though I know others who did!

From before the start of the war and throughout the six years we, the public, were barraged with warnings: 'Put that light out!' 'Wear your gas masks!' 'Pull your curtains shut!' And in the early part of the war, when the fear of a German invasion was everywhere, sirens alerted us that planes were approaching: 'Go to your shelter!' At my boarding school all the girls and staff had routine emergency drills. The fire bell rang (often at about 5 or 6am) and we had to get out of bed, pick up our gas mask box and 'WALK down!' to our respective meeting areas in the garden where our names were read out by a mistress. Once they were sure we were all there we trooped back to our bedrooms, hoping to get another hour's sleep before the 'wake up' bell got us all out of bed again. I was never any good at any of this. I did, and always have, needed at least eight hours' sleep at night, though this was not always possible during the nights of bombing. There in the Hertfordshire countryside we were exceptionally free of some of the worst problems of war.

One day our headmistress told us that Mr Tompset the chauffeur, Mr Aves the head gardener and Mr O'Brien the stoker were forming a small Home Guard to 'protect' the school. They appeared dressed in khaki and, with shovels and pickaxes over their shoulders, marched up and down outside the school building. It was a hilarious sight. None of them, if my memory serves me right, was under 50 years of age and they didn't seem

49

to have the remotest idea what they were supposed to be doing! This was to become even more horrendous when one day they appeared sporting rifles! Apart from the concern of all the girls I remember one of them commenting, 'Let's hope there aren't any bullets in them!' They practised marching up and down with Mr Aves issuing orders and told us that we weren't to worry, they would catch any German daring to come near the school. (*Dad's Army*, on television in later years, was no exaggeration – it really happened!) In 2000, the Queen paid tribute to the more than 1.5 million who served in the Home Guard during the war.

On turning up for a German lesson at school, we discovered that, because of the dire political situation, our German teacher Fraulein Von Kahler had just left to return to Germany. During my German lessons, which I didn't very much enjoy, I used to look out the window and watch the hens our headmistress had bought. She used to go out every morning to collect the eggs to help substitute our food rations. What a wonderful woman!

During the time I was at Crofton I used to spend the holidays at our family home in London and going to ballet classes with Madame Rambert at the Mercury Theatre, at Notting Hill Gate, which was a tiny little theatre with a very small stage and music supplied by gramophone records or a piano. She kindly allowed me to take 'class' with the members of the Rambert Ballet Company, for which my parents must have paid. These were held in a large adjoining hall and here I was fortunate to take class alongside such famous dancers as Maude Lloyd, Sally Gilmour, Elizabeth Schooling and Anthony Tudor to name a few. Madame's daughters Angela and Lulu Dukes were also in the company. I exercised at the bar with members of the company and took part in all the ballet moves they had to do. I was heart-broken though when I realised that, firstly, I was not the right shape *anywhere*! Madame used to pull my stubby fingers saying, 'Nancy, can't you make them any longer?' and secondly, I had led a somewhat sheltered life and nursing was calling me. I shall never forget this wonderful experience and harboured hopes that I might train properly on leaving school. I was very fortunate to be given these opportunities.

Despite some of the changes that have inevitably taken place over the passage of time, I still think of Frinton as a place where I spent some of the happiest days of my life. When now in my 'old' age, I find it difficult to sleep, I think myself back in that beautiful little town with its manicured avenues and wonderful tennis club and very soon get back to sleep. On a return visit I saw the new Frinton Museum; I was so pleased to see the VLASTO arch prominently displayed, straddling the path in the garden charmingly cared-for by the people of Frinton. I feel now that I have never really left there.

Letters from Vaccani regarding ballet lessons at school.

Letter from Marie Rambert.

[I was disgusted when, in 2008, I was to watch a repeat of a so-called 'quirky' (their words) programme shown by the BBC. So incensed and distressed was I by the negative presentation of the town of Frinton and its residents that I was driven to phoning the BBC to complain about its contents. I wrote to the Council of Frinton expressing my disgust at what I had just seen. I found the programme to be hurtful to the people of Frinton and untruthful in its presentation of the town, not to mention how insensitive to the individuals portrayed in a somewhat disparaging manner.]

That summer was our last visit to Frinton as the war was to take over our lives. On September 3rd 1939 war was declared. My father was always sitting hugging his little wireless, but on this occasion we were all sitting round the big wireless in the sitting room together with our French family, only recently over from France, when we heard the news. They had been very anxious and unsettled because of the fear of the imminence of war. It was eerie how they all got up suddenly, saying, 'We have to go.' They rang to book tickets to return to France and those with cars set off for the Channel ferry crossing, scared that they might be unable to return to France before the cancellation of any further crossings. This was the last time we were to see some of them. We all helped making sandbags on the beach ready to be

52

used to protect people's homes and buildings and we were also told these were to be used to prevent bomb damage in strategic places, which was proof that we were definitely now at war. There was none of the usual 'happy-go-lucky' feel in Frinton itself or at the tennis club.

One morning at breakfast, during the holidays, our mother read a cablegram from our grandparents in Canada, offering to have us all to live with them for the duration of the war. Each one of us was asked in turn if we wished to go; none of us wanted to leave. So the generous offer was turned down and we prepared ourselves to face whatever was to come. To make the most of our time, not knowing what the future held for us, we made occasional visits (due to petrol shortage) to members of our extended family.

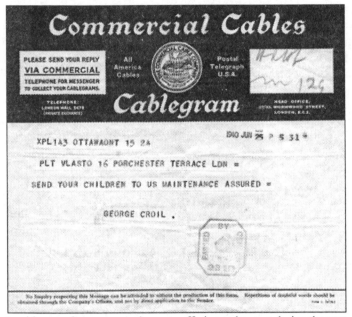

A cablegram from my grandparents offering to have us during the war.

Leading up to the war Britain was in a great state of agitation and uncertainty as we rolled forward, seemingly unable to prevent entry into war. Germany had troops marching into Bohemia, Monrovia and Prague. In April, Italy invaded Albania. The final act which brought us into the war was when Germany invaded Poland. Belgium, Dutch and French refugees were being dive-bombed by German Stukas. Then the Soviet Union invaded Poland from the East.

All these horrors were having their effect on the feelings of the British people although we tried to keep life running as normally as possible. We spent many hours glued to our 'wirelesses'. My parents who had served in World War I were devastated and tears flowed down their cheeks.

Although the Government had been doing its best to assure us that there would be no war, British industry began making guns and ammunition. Air Raid Precaution (ARP) started and we were encouraged to practise wearing gas masks and putting our babies into special respirators as a precaution. At school we had to put on gas masks every Saturday morning at 'prayers' to get used to wearing them. We had fun making 'rude' snorting noises by lifting the side of the rubber face mask, much to the perceived annoyance of Miss Beard. It reminded me of the noise we used to make racing our potties around the nursery floor!

People working in factories had music relayed while they worked. Some tunes became our favourites, such as *Workers Play Time* and *Music While You Work*. It seems amazing now, that King George VI and the Queen went to Canada in June of that year, returning in July – I think we were all quite worried about them going at this time.

Back at school I developed a severe toothache. The school doctor advised that I should go to my dentist in London as it was infected. The matron rang my father and asked him to arrange it. My poor father was in such a state; my mother was in hospital and he was at home alone. He met me at Liverpool Street Station and took me to Harley Street. There I had a nightmare removal of the offending tooth – it was agony. He then took me back to Liverpool Street Station and took me to a café for tea. Unlike me, I couldn't face eating anything (and there were cream cakes!) and it hurt even to drink. With great relief, I am sure, he put me on the train and left. I was in excruciating pain. The train stopped and started all the way back to Braughing and I had to change trains (in the dark) to get onto the Braughing line half way through the journey. Even now, I cannot believe that other people in my carriage did not notice my distress, even though I was doing my best to hide it.

The school car met me at the station and took me back to Crofton. I went straight up to see the Matron. 'What's the matter,' she said. I told her I had had the tooth out, there were stitches in my gum and I was in a lot of pain. She didn't believe I had stitches until she looked in my mouth. Then she took my temperature and sent me to bed.

In the night I felt really ill and by morning couldn't get out of bed without help. She again took my temperature and immediately put her arm around me and walked me to the sick room where the doctor came to see me. The next days were a blur of pain, sleep and being fed liquids. I do not know to this day how ill I was. Perhaps it's just as well!

Once I was well, the headmistress chose me and her niece Dereka, who was also at the school, to weigh the food we ate during 24 hours, so she could approach the government to increase rations to schools. Needless to say we piled our plates up more than ever to prove our point. It worked! Eggs and potatoes were rationed but could be bought in a dried form which then had to be reconstituted. Unless you grew your own green vegetables they were hard to come by. Practically no fruit was available; an orange was a luxury and we didn't see a banana or grapes for years.

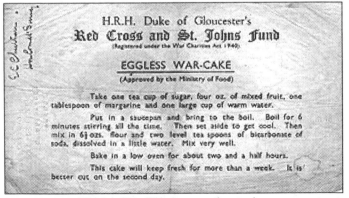

'Eggless War Cake' – a wartime recipe.

We were not allowed radios at school and heard little news. On occasions when we were able to listen, messages were being sent over the radio to France and other European countries keeping them informed of events. This was in code such as 'the sheep are in the pasture, the gates are closed, Jane is with Peter,' etc. We did not understand them and luckily neither did the Germans! It was quite eerie.

Early in 1940, we began to feel the terrible tension that accompanies the fear of what war might bring. Would we be invaded? Girls started leaving Crofton Grange to return to their homes in Scotland, Wales and from across the Channel. Their parents wanted their children near them. My parents, realising the seriousness of the situation, booked our family of six into the Selsdon Park Hotel, Croydon, for a wonderful weekend treat.

At the start of the spring term 1940 the girls returned to Crofton very much aware that we were at war. I had left 16 Porchester Terrace much less happily than in recent years. By now the evacuation of children from London had begun. As my mother and I waited for the train at Liverpool Street Station hundreds of shocked children and parents filled other platforms waiting for trains to evacuate them away from London – where to? No one knew. Mothers were weeping, children were sobbing as they said goodbye. They all had a gas mask in a brown cardboard box hanging around their necks and sported large labels pinned to their coats giving their names and ages. Their parents had no idea where they were going.

At the end of May the great rescue of our troops from the beaches of Dunkirk in France took place. Thousands of soldiers lined the beaches hoping to be rescued. Back here in England, there was a prearranged co-operation of boat owners on the Thames and along the south coast to Sheerness, who phoned their nearest pubs, clubs and friends to take their boats to the nearest point on the coast and await the signal to cross the Channel. This they did with unimagined bravery and rescued approximately 338,000 troops; hungry, exhausted and many wounded. Sadly other soldiers and boatmen were wounded and lost their lives when strafed by German aircraft whilst struggling to return from the beaches. We were devastated when we heard the news, in June, that Paris had fallen. My father was particularly distressed as he had lived and had been schooled there.

From a documentary programme on television, September 2010, I learnt that the first bombs were dropped on Great Britain on 2nd August 1940, on Enfield, Tottenham, among others in the north of England. On September 7th 1940 the *blitzkrieg* began; London was bombed on seventy-six consecutive nights. The Germans sent over 300 bombers escorted by hundreds of fighters. They did not appear to be expecting any resistance but we sent up a large number of fighters led by Douglas Bader. We learnt from the news that fifty-six German planes were shot down on that day. November 2nd was the only exception because of poor weather. I think an apt adjective to describe my experience of these bombing attacks would be horrendous, I was really frightened as bombs came shrieking down. The ground shook and even the movement of the air around me seemed to affect my whole body, pulling me in different directions. The whole atmosphere was very tense. It was quite a relief to return to the comparative peace of the countryside.

At school I began to grow up. I decided I was going to start to work as I was now fifteen years old and would soon have to take responsibilities in the school and be a model for the younger children. I offered to give ballet classes to a few of the girls and to my surprise they accepted! I then wrote a ballet and was given one of the entertainment evenings to perform it, using a mixture of gramophone records and my playing the piano. At that time I had the nerve to write to Marie Rambert to ask if I could borrow some of her dresses for the performance but had a reply to say that they were in use by the company at that time. Following the performance we had lovely compliments from the head teacher and we were all so pleased.

I had been in close contact with one of the girls who contracted chicken pox, so I had to go into quarantine. I was put into a room at the end of a corridor well away from the other girls' bedrooms where, sadly, I remained for the full 3 weeks of the incubation period and there, right in the middle of my back, on the twenty-first day was my first spot! Even the matron sounded quite upset for me! I was put to bed with a high temperature and a sheet, soaked in Dettol disinfectant, hanging down across the door. During those three weeks I really enjoyed getting to know nature: walks in the garden, listening to the birds and going out to my beloved horses in the fields. I believe that the weeks I spent alone in the sanatorium, when in quarantine, helped me to know myself and to find that I was really quite a responsible person!

At the height of my illness my mother came all the way from London to see me. She was not allowed to touch me and I remember being very upset about this, but when no one was

57

looking she gave me a good-bye hug which somewhat made up for it. On my recovery the headmistress sent for me and congratulated me on being so good over this period of time (with reason, as I was rarely good). She said she had cleared it with my parents and I was to go up to London with a group of other girls to see a ballet. I was really grateful. It seems incongruous to be talking about going to the ballet when life was fraught with dangers in this low period of the war. We tried to carry on as normally as possible but air raids at home and abroad were at the front of our thoughts constantly.

From now on I remember changing. Doubtless puberty had 'kicked in' and I started *working* for the School Certificate which I would sit in 1942. I was really due to be made a prefect but, again, Miss Beard saw me in her study. She asked me how I would feel if she didn't make me one because there were several of my year who could be eligible and as I was already captain of games, company leader of The Guides and head of music, she wondered if I would mind? I did! However because, as always, she was honest with me and I saw her dilemma, I agreed. So I ended my days as a Head of Study and was quite happy with this undoubted honour! On Saturdays the whole school met in the library for prayers, to sing hymns and to hear the latest news from the papers. Later we were to have one newspaper delivered to each study.

In the 1942 summer term at Crofton I sat School Certificate. I had already taken Grade 5 in piano playing and now had to take the written music exam. French oral was amazing: as I went into the classroom the examiner beckoned to me to sit down. To my horror, out of the corner of my eye, I could see Mademoiselle's black head bobbing up and down outside the windowsill, on her hands and knees, trying to listen in! I think I did well only because I started naming my uncles', aunts' and cousins' names who lived in Marseille, rolling my r's as best I could! Anyway, I managed to get a merit grade for both those subjects!

Then there was the dreaded domestic science. I had to clean the staffroom, sweeping the floor and polishing the furniture and laying the fire. *Then* came the cooking part. I had to write out a plan for a two-course lunch, pricing the items, and lay and clear away the table, whilst at the same time entertaining our 'guest' examiner. I was absolutely terrified (to this day I am no good at cooking). I made a first course of roast beef and Yorkshire pudding with vegetables followed by apple pie and cream. To my amazement I got a credit for this! I give most of the credit to our delightful teacher, Miss Roberts.

I also took art as a school certificate subject and was faced with painting a little sweet pea in a pot. I really enjoyed this and I managed to get a credit for this too. As nervous as ever, I failed biology and English literature, which did not surprise me, because again, my memory for quotation was hopeless and I only 'passed' in religious knowledge for the same reason. My reward was to receive a leaving present (chosen by myself) of *Black's Medical Dictionary*.

The results were good enough for Miss Beard to send me a postcard at Fulbrook Farm saying, 'The hens ought to lay well after this!' She and my mother used to compare notes on how many eggs their respective hens had laid – I guess she thought that they must have been as surprised and delighted as she was!

Mrs Beard's card – I was equally surprised!

At my last piano lesson at school, my teacher Margaret Channon told me that she had written to ask my parents permission to take me with her to the summer Music School at Downe House School in Newbury Berkshire. It would last a week and she would be there as a chaperone. I got the feeling that she wanted to show me how pleased she was that I had done so well over the seven years I had studied piano and music with her. She could not have given me a better leaving present! Two weeks or so before we went, I received a large parcel containing all the music we were going to sing and study. I had never been so excited and began immediately to sit down at the piano and familiarise myself with it all.

The day to go to Downe House arrived. We went by train and I found myself at this wonderful school surrounded by grassed areas which banked down to a large concert hall where we all congregated in the evening to sing large choral works. During the mornings we attended classes in groups studying motets and madrigals and doing some solo work. In the afternoon we were free to do what we liked and there were tennis courts and a swimming pool. Towards the end of the week there were tennis tournaments for doubles and singles with vouchers as prizes to spend in the music library. I had a very large collection of music to remind me of those days, for I continued going to that Summer School for many years, each year being more fun than the previous. One year, one of the young men on the course stupidly dived into the shallow end of the swimming pool before we could call out to warn him. He cut his forehead badly and had to be helped from the water. He was obviously concussed and I took him straight to the sanatorium. Unfortunately there was no nurse on duty during the holidays so I rang the doctor who was 'on call'. During my week there I nursed him every day until he was allowed up to go home on the last day. I believe that the following year there was a nurse on duty.

If I ever had to fill in a questionnaire about 'what are some your happiest memories of past years' it would be the arrival of the parcel of music, each July, to be used that year at Downe House: so much did I enjoy it. This could also apply to the Surrey County Council courses of music at Gipsy Hill, Kingston upon Thames which I attended for several years, ending up on the staff as librarian. It was to the music department of Kingston College that I later gave much of my music collection.

During my last two terms at Crofton, the matron had allowed me to have some work experience preparatory to my starting my nursing training. I used to go around the different classrooms taking the temperature of all the girls. This was an attempt to catch early signs of illness and infection. I felt quite 'grown up' doing this and it was a good precursor to my moving into the adult nursing world. I was also allowed to look after any sick girls, which I much enjoyed. Armed with these experiences I was ready to apply for admission to University College Hospital to train as a nurse once I had reached my 18th birthday in the following year.

60

Sadly I had to say farewell to Madame Rambert and the Mercury Theatre. The training school, by this time, had moved to the country, from where her daughter Angela wrote me a sweet letter, only the company staying behind; though some of the dancers had joined ENSA and entertained the troops at home and abroad. I wept as I said goodbye and Madame kissed me warmly. Thoughtfully, knowing that I would be upset, my mother came to meet me and we went back home as I fought back my tears.

So back to school, and my last summer term was hectic, to put it mildly: a gymnastic display, a diving display and a solo ballet performance were all on my itinerary for Parents' Day. With the continuation of the bombing in the country, this all made for a somewhat comprehensive ending to my seven years at Crofton Grange.

I was truly sad to be leaving the school I loved. I hugged my friends and the staff as we left in the coach which was to take us to Braughing Station. I was genuinely distressed when it came to the end of my last term at Crofton. I wonder how many could say this? Apart from leaving my friends, I was leaving the sports I loved and which we did every day, the music I enjoyed, and the general environment of my lovely school and, of course, the staff.

I must admit I was not enjoying the thought of rockets crashing down on us and there was a definite sense of fear in the air as we drew into Liverpool Street Station which was covered by a vast glass canopy roof.

As always, my mother was there to meet me and our hug meant more than just 'welcome' – it meant 'Thank God you're still alive and well!' She said, 'I can't believe this is the last time I'll be meeting one of my four children from school.' It must surely have been a very emotional moment for her.

In my suitcase I carried five silver cups, two for tennis (singles and doubles), one for swimming, one for diving and one for reading aloud. As we walked into London they could be heard clanking in my case and we laughed as we realised they would all have to be inscribed with my name, the date and be kept polished. My poor parents had to pay to have them all engraved!

I took a deep breath and faced the fact that I was no longer a schoolgirl and was now a 'Woman of the world!' We linked arms and, disappearing into the Underground, I turned to my mother and said, 'What's next?'

Chapter Three

During the first years of the war, London was not a pleasant place in which to be; the endless wailing of sirens, the queues at almost empty shops, ration books for most things and the endless fear as the drone of planes flew overhead leaving you wondering where the next bomb would land, were all very frightening.

Air raid sirens usually went off at about 4pm in the winter just as darkness was falling. Planes approaching London followed the Thames up to the centre and the Docklands area. Bombs came shrieking down from above and by November the attacks were at their height.

We did a lot of tripping up over pavements as there were no street lights, the only visible lights were the search lights crisscrossing in the black sky. Occasionally they 'picked up' a plane flying in towards us, at which time they all converged to make sure it remained a clear target for the anti-aircraft guns (or ack-ack as they were known) to bring them down on the outskirts of London to avoid the heavily populated areas.

In the cinemas, while films were playing, notices were put on the screen, like sub-titles, saying 'Air raid in progress'. In the theatre the manager would either come on to the stage, leaving the actors static in the background, or the curtain would come down and the manager would tell us there was a raid going on. He would invite us to remain in our seats if we wished as the play would continue; I believe most of us did, it was probably as safe there as anywhere else.

I believe that it was my mother's guidance and faith that, along with prayers and reading of Thomas Akempis at my school. I formed my own religious faith which has been at the base of all my thoughts and activities to this day. During the holidays I used to go to church with my mother at either nearby St Matthew, St Clement Danes Church on the Strand or the Temple Church in the city where they had a superb choir. The latter also had a remarkable choir boy soloist, whom I later found out must have been Ernest Lough, and the organist George Thalban Ball. Sadly this, as well as Coventry Cathedral were badly damaged. Liverpool, Glasgow, Portsmouth, among others, got their share of the bombings too. In December the city of London was set alight and it was called the 'Second Great Fire of London'. We felt helpless.

As already mentioned, on leaving school I decided that I would train as a nurse. My father, wanting to be sure that nursing was really what I wanted to do (I never felt he wanted me to be a nurse), arranged with the Matron of Queen's Hospital for Children, Hackney Road, London E1 where he had been the Ear, Nose and Throat surgeon over many years, that I should work there as a probationer and see how I liked it. My mother came with me to be interviewed by the very delightful Matron Miss Allen at the hospital (sadly neither she nor the hospital still survive). My application was accepted.

In those days nurses were required to sleep in the nurses' home. We were also provided with our uniforms and meals but paid towards them out of our salaries. On the day I started work there my mother, having come with me to the hospital, gave me a brief hug at the nurses' home door and walked off into the distance down Hackney Road. I think both of us were dreading the separation.

My uniform of blue and white stripes with stiff starched collars, cuffs and belt had been laid out on my somewhat spartan bed and I felt a twinge of excitement but a definite squirming in my stomach at the thought of this new world I was about to enter. I found myself changing out of my 'civvies' – as ordinary clothes were known – and struggling into this strange uniform. I couldn't manage to do up the stud at the front of my collar and I had no idea how to turn the flat cap (looking for all the world like a very dead slice of cod) into a proper cap which was to perch uselessly on top of my head.

63

So it was that in October 1942 I found myself in front of the Matron Miss Allen. I knocked on her door and she called out, 'Come in Nurse Vlasto.' This was the first time I was to hear myself given this title! Standing in my starched uniform, as can be seen on the front cover, I felt like the new girl in school. I felt as if I was looking down on myself from above, very uncomfortable and unlike the 'real' me. The scissors in my top pocket and the fob watch pinned to my dress (as we were not allowed to wear watches on our wrists) began to feel like my friends and I frequently fondled them for comfort! *But* as for the revolting thick black stockings. . !

While I was getting dressed earlier, another nurse came into my room asking if I needed any help. So started the beginning of a long friendship with Joy Shepperson – soon to be known to me by the name Sheppie. Sixty-eight years later we are still in touch. Recently she reminded me that when she came into the sitting room on that first day she had found me playing the piano. She said she had never forgotten it. I don't know if she meant that it was well or poorly played! She married and became Mrs John Tuite-Dalton and they had three children.

She helped me to adapt to the weird and wonderful way of the nursing profession. She showed me how to put the wicker laundry basket, once tall and able to contain our dirty clothes but now squashed nearly flat, under the end of the bed, on which to rest our poor aching feet after completing our shifts. In the morning we were called by a sister banging loudly on the door shouting 'Six o'clock, Nurse'. This was our cue to haul ourselves out of bed, put on our uniform and cross to the hospital to have breakfast at 6.30am.

I was sent to work on Connaught Ward where the sister was a very tall, slim and pleasant lady, Sister Smart. The wards were long with cots and small beds lining the walls and there was a constant sound of crying babies to which I was eventually to become accustomed. Most nights sleep was intermittent as the bombs fell around us, but we were so tired and with 'familiarity breeding contempt' we somehow managed to sleep through much of it.

Nursing in those days was very different from now. In each of the wards was a coal fire. One of our duties was to lay and light the fire and keep it fed with coal during the day and night. There was no other heating so it was vital that we did this.

We stood around the Sister's desk, with our hands behind our backs, when we came on duty to get the report of the day or night shift. Then we were given our duties for the shift which included washing or bathing the babies and children (depending how ill they were), cleaning the ward, cleaning the bathroom, giving out medicines and preparing the children for theatre. We also cooked and gave the children their breakfast and prepared and gave the babies their bottles (nurses think they have it tough now!). One of the most stressful duties was 'laying out' any of those who had died in the night.

Considering the terrible times the children were living in they were surprisingly calm. Doubtless their pain and being away from their families and friends was enough for them to deal with. Nurses had to be 'Mum' to many of them and they gave us their love and trust. Visiting times were necessary but unsettling for the children and some of them needed much comforting as their parents left the ward to go home – usually in tears. The parents too, needed comforting.

At that time my boyfriend was John Priestley, a Lieutenant in the Rifle Brigade, and in between receiving letters from him, he used to come and take me out for a meal or just a ride around in a bus and chat. One day he came to see me at the hospital and, after a brief visit, he hurriedly said goodbye as neither of us liked parting. He left behind his leather covered 'stick'. My friend, Johnny, ran after him but she told me, 'I'm sure he heard me but he went on walking. I think he must have wanted you to have it.' Sadly, John was to die in 1944 from injuries received in Normandy. In 2004, having kept it by me for 60 years, I contacted the Rifle Brigade (as it was called then) and arranged, with the retired curator Major K. Gray, to send it to the regiment for their museum. It is with his permission that I have included a photo and the obituary written by his regiment.

The war was at its height: nightly bombings had badly affected the East End of London, particularly in 1941 when the city was heavily attacked and many roads flattened and impassable. By 1943 the attacks were slightly less frequent; however, every evening we had to take all the children down into the cellars with everything needed to nurse them. I still remember covering the top of the teats on rows of bottles with a snow-white cloth and on removing it, finding dozens of cockroaches swimming over

65

them! The poor things must have been bombed out of the ground and as thirsty and in need of sustenance as we all were. They scuttled away! I don't think we wanted to know where they went.

The nursing staff were becoming very weary, getting little rest even when we did get to bed, trying to sleep through the noise of the bombers overhead and the bombs they dropped. As I write this, I cannot believe how we remained sane and able to keep on with our jobs. Eventually it was decided that it was absolutely impossible to continue in this way and we no longer went down into the basement. We just prayed that we did not get a direct hit. Our prayer must have been answered for 'Queen's' remained standing amongst the rubble all around it.

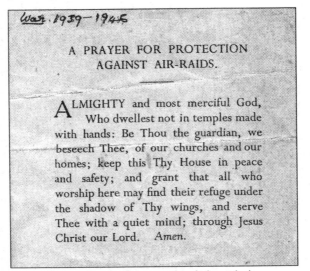

These prayer leaflets were handed out during
the time of the bombings in the 1940s.

We laughed at the smallest incident. There was this famous occasion when early on in my time at Queen's, I carried six tiny metal bed pans, one on top of the other, into the ward to give to the children. Just as the Matron walked in through the swing doors I dropped the lot! Thankfully they were empty but I was extremely embarrassed, especially when all the children burst out laughing!

Despite this, we all managed to find fun in life. One night, when my friend Sheppie and some other nurses had crossed over into the nurses' home, I followed them groping my way in the dark up the stairs to my bedroom. I put out my hand to turn the door handle and let out a piercing scream. There was something cold and wet, like fingers, hanging from it. There were howls of laughter from Sheppie and the others. She had found some raw sausages (goodness knows from where, rationing being as tight as it was) and tied them to my door handle. I have never forgotten this incident and, apparently, neither had she; we still laugh when we recount that night whenever we speak on the phone. She tells me that (sixty-eight years on) she is still recounting it to her grown-up children.

We were given our paltry rations to take home on our days off; rations varied depending on the availability at the time. We were given a minute cube of butter to take home in a piece of greaseproof paper but, by the time I got home, it had liquefied and my mother and I just laughed and threw the *very* greasy paper away! Our ration allowance was ¾ pound of sweets, ½ pound of sugar, ½ pound of butter and ½ pound of tea. To bulk up for the lack of meat we made stews with barley. We had whale meat, rabbit and 'Spam'. Dried eggs were used in place of proper eggs. I recently read that grants were given to farmers to plant and sow their fields.

I still remember the names of some of my patients, even after all this time. Peter Blaby was a little six months old baby whom I loved very much. Another was a black curly headed little boy Michael, very thin and a poor eater, who used to stand in his cot, holding the rails and looking at me with his dark soulful eyes. He used to call me Nurse Elastoplast! He started projectile vomiting and rapidly deteriorated. A post mortem revealed that his brain had literally been 'eaten away' with what must have been cancer.

Some families sheltered down in the Underground every evening before the bombing started. Due to the fetid atmosphere and general lack of hygiene, the babies used to arrive at the hospital with red raw little bottoms and frequently with diarrhoea. The treatment at that time was to paint them with 'gentian violet' a very purple disinfectant. I have memories of rows of cots with little purple bottoms sticking out between sheets tucked in across the bed above and below them.

We had been awaiting some sign of our ability to fire at the planes approaching, which seemed to fly in without interception over the East End of London. On the night of March 3rd 1943, there was a very loud 'crack' sound at the back of our hospital which seemed to shake the building. I turned to one of the nurses and said, 'At last we're firing ack-acks at them.' I can't explain the relief that we felt. Sadly, just down the road at Bethnal Green Station, hearing this terrible noise and mistaking it for a German bomb being dropped, crowds rushed to the Underground station to seek shelter. One hundred and seventy-three were crushed to death and around sixty injured. Such were the terrible tragedies 'at home' in the war.

Mostly we had to make our own entertainment as travel was so difficult and many actors were abroad either with ENSA entertaining the troops or actively in the forces. Despite the gloominess caused by drawn curtains and pulled down blinds, we managed to keep quite cheerful. At dances, as well as foxtrots and Viennese waltzes, we danced the jitterbug and hokey-cokey. We used to go to the Hammersmith Palais and the Theatre Royal, Drury Lane where we danced on and off the stage to various bands. Our partners were mainly men in the forces, in uniform, many from overseas. Stable relationships were rarely formed because of the transience of our lives, as no one knew what their future held or whether we would meet again.

Material for dress making was hard to find but, occasionally, one came across small quantities of parachute silk which was a good substitute. The nurses made little material shades for the ward lights with 'V' sewn on them as a hope for the end of the war. There was so little we could do.

The forces wore uniform in the streets, had free passes, reduced fares on the railways, free cinema tickets and, after the war, medals given to them. However, nurses and doctors had no help whatsoever and really felt like the 'poor country cousins' even though we were quite as much, if not more, in the war as they were at times. How this rankles with me! Sixty-four years on the Land Army had their way and were issued with war medals, some of whom I know lived off the fat of the land and never saw a German plane throughout the war years! What about the hospital staff in Britain? Apparently, because we were not part of the Army, Navy or Air Force, we did not warrant such accolades!

I remember on a holiday visit to a hotel in Burley in the New Forest, I met a young man, Rognveld W. O. Gunn, who at the age of only 20 was in the Coldstream Guards and was to be killed during the war in August 1944. He was a brilliant musician and we used to play duets together for the guests at tea time in the hotel.

My elder sister, Helen, worked for some time in the Free French canteen in London and was to join the Naval Red Cross as a VAD. After nursing at Royal Hospital Haslar in Gosport she was sent to Alexandria to work in the 64th General Hospital until the end of the war. My brother joined the Navy and was sent to America to train in submarines. It was quite amazing and with much gratitude that we all came through the war physically unscathed. Our parents must have had a worrying time.

That year my other sister, Christian, still making Porchester Terrace her base, joined the Grand Union Canal Carrying Company taking coal and other necessities from the London docks to the Midlands. She had remained at our house for some of the war attending the Central Art School and tracing gun parts for the Admiralty in Bath, Somerset. She had also worked at the National Physical Laboratory in Twickenham. She became one of the women who 'manned' the boats (barges) up and down the canal and became captain of a pair of boats. In May 1943 I joined her 'on board' going from the docks just near my hospital to as far as Paddington. At night, in pitch dark, we tied up under a bridge. The bombs rained down around us in the night, but in the morning there were hoots of laughter. Looking into our cabin were four people leaning over the bridge and watching us, almost naked, asleep in our cabin bunks! At that time she was taking coal up north. I didn't realise what had happened but, getting off the boat and walking up Praed Street, I saw people looking at me in a funny way. It wasn't until I got home that I saw in the mirror that my face and clothes were covered in black soot!

One night, when I was on night duty, I was exhausted and asked my ward sister if I could bring my scheduled night-off forward by one evening. Having looked at the state I was in, she realised she had no choice despite having to find a replacement. So I went home to Porchester Terrace and joined Christian sleeping in the bed next to her's in our old nursery. The next night I went back on duty. In the morning, after a night of bombing, my friend Sheppie and I went up on the hospital roof to see what area had been targeted. In the distance, the sky was blood red. I said to her, 'That looks like Bayswater.' I ran downstairs and rang my sister at our house. A plane had flown the length of Porchester Terrace dropping incendiary bombs. My sister had extinguished six bombs with our stirrup pump, one of which had gone straight through my bed into the floor below and there was a large black hole where I should have been sleeping that night! It missed Christian's bed by about one metre. My ward sister said she would never deny a nurse's desperate request to change her night-off duty again. That was the nearest I came to being killed in the war and a very 'near miss' for my sister.

Life in hospital was constrained; we had little time to go out and were mostly too tired to do so anyway. Also there was so much rubble and damage on the roads and pavements it was quite difficult to get about, especially at night. I used to take the number 6 bus to Liverpool Street Station and get on the Central Line to Queen's Road (later called Queensway) to go back to our house.

My father's mother and her sister lived in separate flats further down the road from our house. Unfortunately my great aunt was blind and could be seen walking daily up and down Porchester Terrace, arm-in-arm with her sister. My parents decided that, for

Drawing by Christian of my grandmother and great aunt
Caliope Ionides walking up Porchester Terrace.

the benefit of everyone, they should move out of London to the country while still keeping the Porchester Terrace house for

Christian to use and for any of us to go to as we wished. As the bombings were increasing and needing to get away from it all for the safety of my grandmother and her sister, my parents rented a house called Fulbrook Farm at Elstead in Surrey. My sister Christian gave me an account of the two older ladies sitting in the back of the taxi, with straight backs (they weren't going to be defeated by Hitler) and defiant expressions, furious that they were forced to leave their homes by the events of the war. Their helpers in the house followed behind them in a second taxi. Sadly we didn't anticipate the arrival of the V1 bombs (doodlebugs) which appeared to follow us to the country. Many fell around the Elstead area as Surrey was on the flight path for the V1s.

At Fulbrook Farm there was a cottage in the grounds, a large garden and a pretty grassed central courtyard surrounded by stone walls and enclosed by two large barred gates. Along one end was an enormous empty hay barn. Everyone, including my parents, my father's mother and her blind sister, plus Annie (the maid), Ella (the cook) and Banyard (an elderly retainer who did odd jobs and would never be retired by my grandmother) all lived in the house!

This arrangement became a bit crowded and later, in the early 1940s, my parents decided to move into the charming little two-bedroom cottage by the barn and set about making it *their* home while my grandmother and great aunt stayed at the house. This became a refuge for any of the family needing a break. My mother loved the years they spent there and enjoyed keeping hens, looking after them and feeding them with the parings from the vegetables grown by my father. Every day the pungent smell coming from the 'hen's pot' pervaded the cottage and beyond! But we were more than grateful for the eggs which they laid for us and we much enjoyed picking them out of the nesting boxes in the hen house. My mother then began working, part-time, at a munitions factory in Guildford where she organised the 24-hour fire watch rota. This was the first paid job my father had allowed her to do and *how* she enjoyed it!

My father, having been rejected by the Navy, by virtue of his age and eyesight, grew vegetables in the large kitchen garden and cared for the fruit trees. I believe this was the first experience he had ever had of working on the land and it seemed to help him overcome his disappointment at being rejected by the Navy and

71

having retired from his medical work. For a while he kept on his consulting room but eventually, reluctantly, decided to give up any idea of going back there. The arrival of penicillin during the war was to radically change the work of the ENT surgeon. I was to miss Wednesdays when my mother and I used to go to his consulting room and polish his instruments with Bluebell polish.

During our time in Elstead we did not become much involved with the village but we became aware of a boys' prep school nearby at Littleworth Cross. My parents formed a friendship with the headmaster and his wife, Hal and Nan Milner-Gulland, and their two sons Nick and Robin. They much enjoyed their contact with the school and I used to be invited, with them, to Shakespeare plays which were most professionally performed out in the lovely gardens around the school buildings. It was delightful to meet such polite, well-mannered young boys so obviously enjoying life. Occasionally some of them came to have tea in our barn, which we loved and I believe they did also. (In 2006 I revisited the school with my nephew Peter, who with his brother Richard had been pupils there. It had moved to Danehill, Haywards Heath in Sussex several years before. It was a sad and yet happy occasion to celebrate the life of Nan Milner-Gulland who had recently died; Hal having died before her. I felt it was important for me to be there to represent my late parents.)

I cycled around Elstead quite a lot and on one occasion my cousin Kirsty Brewer (née Macdonald, who recently died) came down from Cupar Fife to stay with us at Fulbrook Farm and she and I (dressed in Guide's uniforms; I don't know why!) went for a long cycle ride through the county of Surrey. I also spent some hours working in the kitchen of a convalescent home for troops off the Hogs Back near Guildford and waiting at tables at a troops' café near Aldershot.

I used to go down to Elstead for a break on my days and nights off and my mother would drive along the Hogs Back in the dark to meet me at Guildford Station and then take me back again when I returned to London. Driving at night, especially in the winter, was a nightmare, as I have described before. Tiny crosses of light only were being allowed on the front and rear car lights and the wind and driving rain or snow battered the car on the exposed road. It was a treat to get away from the noise of war-torn London, but several V1 bombs came down very near our house and Cutmill Ponds.

Two funny events happened at Fulbrook Farm. One day an English army officer opened the gate into the garden leaving a line of soldiers the other side of the gate. He marched up to my father who was digging up vegetables, saluted, then said, 'Excuse me sir, may I have permission to march my men through your grounds?' 'Certainly,' said my father, 'but I want you to be *sure* that you shut the gate behind you.' 'Yes sir. Thank you sir,' and he saluted and marched off back to his men. Once he had returned and with a lot of stamping of feet, got himself into position, he gave the order, 'Forward march, pass down the line, last man shut the gate.' From man to man the order went over their shoulder, 'Last man shut the gate,' and they all walked through, leaving the gate open! The man at the end of the line had obviously forgotten he was the last man. We thought it was hilarious!

The other occasion was when the commanding officer of a Canadian army unit came up to ask my father's permission to use our large barn for his troops. My father said, 'Of course, old chap. There is just one thing I would ask, could you please make sure that they don't pick any apples off that tree near the gate as I have taken a lot of trouble caring for it and it is the only one I have.' 'Certainly sir,' came the reply and he saluted and marched back to tell his men. By the time they left for D-Day a few days later, despite their having put an armed soldier on duty to guard it, there were no apples left and no one knew who took them! What an insignificant event that seems now when many of these men were to die on the beaches as they stormed the coast of France. One of those, whom we heard later had lost his life, was their charming Canadian padre, Albert McCreary, who used to come into our cottage to write letters home to his family. We were all desperately upset.

Soldiers were to be found everywhere: in the cafés, on the streets, manning the 'pill boxes', on the side-roads or lying in the ditches alongside the lanes with their guns at the ready. Our barn was full to overflowing with Canadian troops. One night they disappeared as suddenly as they had come. They went to the coast for the D-Day landings. It was all so eerie, we had no idea what they were doing. Thinking back I don't think we realised what strained times we were living in. Our work, of necessity, was traumatic; nursing sick and injured children was very distressing – quite apart from what was going on outside in the streets around

d

us. We were to keep the cottage until 1945. My mother hated leaving it and so did we.

So, my time at Queen's as a probationer came to an end in March 1944. After a brief break at home, I prepared myself for the years that lay ahead training to be a nurse at University College Hospital (UCH), London.

I took the opportunity during this break at home to visit my cousin in Scotland. I have always been fond of train journeys and found excuses to visit my family in Cupar Fife. Two incidents come to mind particularly. I took a night sleeper on the Flying Scotsman to Edinburgh and at King's Cross I got my hot water bottle out of my case and went up to the engine driver and asked him if he could fill it with hot water for me. This he did laughingly with his mate. My little hot water bottle looked quite minute beside this enormous iron engine but I was profoundly grateful for their kindness and waved a 'thank you' as I disembarked early the next morning in Edinburgh. After this I used to go to the station restaurant where they willingly filled it from the hot water urn.

On the other occasion, when travelling to Edinburgh from King's Cross, as I sat down on my sleeper bunk I noticed, hanging on a special hook above the pillows, two beautiful diamond and other jewelled rings, a pearl necklace and a gold watch. I took them in my hands to ask the sleeping-car attendant what I should do with them. He told me that, if I hurried, I could go to the ticket office to hand them in. I did, but they told me to give them to the Railway Police who were in the station. I found one of them and gave them to him. He asked for my name and address which I gave him. Naïve as I was, it did not occur to me to take his number. It did not occur to me either that he might not be trustworthy. But I fear I never heard another word from anybody and I can only assume that several thousand pounds worth of jewellery was never returned to its rightful owners. I never followed this up – as certainly I should have done – but I was more disappointed that this should have happened and I never heard any more about it. One learns from life's experiences!

Chapter Four

In August 1944, after several weeks of bed rest, I was sent on sick leave to Knowle Park Convalescent Home 'for tired nurses', which was in Cranleigh Surrey, a beautiful private house set in delightful grounds overlooking the countryside.

During the war anyone owning a large private house was required to use it in some form for the war effort and that is how Mrs Berdoe-Wilkinson came to turn her home into a convalescent home and became the Red Cross Commandant-in-Charge. It must have been a major adjustment on her part – turning her sitting room, dining room and every part of the house, with its beautiful furniture, into a virtual hospital with beds and patients everywhere. She could not have imagined, in her wildest dreams, that her home would be used as it was during the war. She was a tall and slim woman, spoke with a lovely Oxford accent and was very much the competent commandant. Nevertheless she treated everyone with courtesy and came to us every day with morning greetings as a host keeping the atmosphere less institutional.

After I had been resting there for a few weeks, she sent for me to go and see her, and asked if I would like to stay on there until I could return to UCH. Until I left, my job would be to do the ordering for all the needs of the Home. I was given a Red Cross uniform and my task was to order all the food and cleaning equipment needed. I did not particularly enjoy doing this but in my free time I used to go into the village to the lovely little parish church or sit in the garden writing letters or poetry. Amazingly one of my poems was published in the September 1944 *Guildford City Outlook*, the first writing I ever had published:

I Wonder Why

I often wondered why the thoughts of battles past and won
Seemed to hover through his mind although his fighting days were done.
I wondered why, instead of peace and quiet, he'd rather have
The whistling of the restless birds as they sang above his head.
I wondered why he raved and shouted out to those that passed,
That he'd live to join and fight again, that those days weren't his last.
He'd been mentioned in despatches and been given the VC;
No word of this he'd mentioned to the patients or to me,
But he died that very evening, and these last words he spoke:
'God bless this good old England, my wife – and give them hope.'

The following two poems printed in the *Surrey Comet*, 19th May 1995, were written in 1944 whilst in Cranleigh.

Invasion of France
Into Battle
Battle! War!
The cries ring out through the stifling night
And the air swallows, catches and holds the echoes,
Swinging through clouds, sunshine, roaring in flight
Till the swaying world stops, and the tideless sea flows once more.

March! March!
Onto the battle front – on and on
Plodding and pulling and praying for sun
A body rolls sideways – a sickening thud don't look back.

Fight! Coward!
The words are throbbing and beating in time
To the rattle of guns and sweat and grime
Are filling my eyes. There they are! Charge men!
Never stopping or resting but on again – till it's done.
Courage! Patience!
The last desperate moments are drawing near to us
Crying and moaning, there lie the best of us.
Thunder and lightning, when is it going to end?
There goes the white flag, there they come round the bend
Men – we have won!

A Tribute to the RAF
(Written in London 1942)
The houses were shaking and quaking
As the bombers flew out overhead
The silvery streaks they were making
Caught my eye as I lay there in bed.
They shone like the crests of the rough sea
Beating against the storm
They hung and they drifted above me
Bright with the light of dawn.
Every morning, all day and at night
They took off, like the busiest bees
In a hive, droning, gaining their height
As they skimmed past the tops of the trees.
Any noise they make we can bear
Those bombers that fly in the sky
For we know that if they were not there
Our pride would not ride so high.
For the boys who with courage and valour
Risk death, for their dear ones at home
They uphold Britain's proud Empire banner
And grind Hitler's Reich to the bone.

I remained in Cranleigh until the doctor signed me off to return
home in early 1945. I was really sad to say goodbye to Mrs
Berdoe-Wilkinson. She had been very kind to me and I had made
several good friends, among them Harold and Jean Warrender (he
was a well known actor), who lived in a flat in the grounds and
had been very kind to me.

Having left Cranleigh, I arrived on 9th April at the University
College Hospital Nurses' Home, Huntley Street, London WC1,
feeling very much like a fish out of water. A few others, of what
was to be Set 86, were sitting uncomfortably at the edge of their
seats in the sitting room waiting to hear what they should do next.
I joined them. We were then taken to our rooms, told to unpack
and put on our uniforms, which were laid out on our beds, and
then to meet again in the sitting room.

Our dresses were made of strong cotton with blue and white
stripes. The hem had to end just below the knee and it had Peter
Pan white collars and similar cuffs to our short sleeves. We also

had black capes lined with soft red material and cross-over red ties to hold them on. They were beautifully warm and we wore them crossing the roads between areas of the hospital. We wore black stockings and shoes with rubber soles for quietness on the wards, something I find sadly lacking in some hospitals today. Perched on our heads were little white caps which were of no use whatsoever!

<table>
<tr><td>Telephone No.
EUSTON
5050 (7 Lines).</td><td>University College Hospital,
Gower Street,
London, W.C.1.</td></tr>
</table>

CARD OF ENTRY

To enter the Preliminary Training School on Monday, 9th April, 1945 at 4 p.m.

Luggage in advance should be addressed to:-

        The Preliminary Training School,
          Nurses' Home,
            University College Hospital,
            Huntley Street,
            London, W.C.1.

Bring your Gas Mask and Ration Book with you.
Please acknowledge this card

My entry card to UCH Nurses' Home.

During the years we were in training, we were moved between wards and departments spending several months in each so that we got wide nursing experiences. We had two hours off during the twelve hour day and two nights off every three weeks on night duty. This 'time off' was like gold dust to us and was essential to maintaining our physical and mental well-being.

Rules were strict in those days: nurses could not be married or widowed, could not receive phone calls except in their free times, hair had to be hidden underneath our caps, no jewellery worn and we were 'not to talk about your private personal problems over your patient's beds'.

'Observation' of the patient was the word repeatedly stressed. Temperatures were taken by mouth and pulse felt at the wrist. The latter was an aid to assess the patients' well being – was it cold, clammy, the pulse thready (thin), strong, irregular and so forth. All these rules were read out to us by the Staff Nurse in charge of us as we sat waiting.

One of my colleagues, Jean Hughes, who was to remain a life-long friend until she died in 2006, told me that the first thing she remembered about me was hearing me play the piano in the sitting room. As she came into the room she heard me asking the other nurses, 'Who wants to come country dancing on the roof?' She and a few others joined me and we had such fun with an old wind up gramophone and an old 'crackly' country dance record. None of us could remember how to do it but, I think, made up our own version and thoroughly enjoyed ourselves.

I doubt if any of us slept well that night. What would the next day bring? In the morning we were woken by our Staff Nurse with a loud knock on the door calling out 'Half past six, Nurse.' The first six weeks were spent in the Preliminary Training School (PTS) and we were taken to the training room for our first lesson in nursing.

The sister-in-charge was Miss Marjorie Houghton. We were shown around the hospital and wards and got a general 'feel' of the place. We spent most of the time attending lectures on basic anatomy, hygiene, treatments and general nursing procedures – such as washing patients, making beds, etc. Then we went for half-day visits to our allotted medical or surgical wards under the watchful eye of the ward sister and staff nurse. Everyone was very helpful remembering that they, too, had been through the initiation of the unknown.

The only sterile equipment was made so by the nursing staff. Every morning, one of the nurse's duties was to 'do the sterilising'. There were steaming sterilisers on the ward, into which went all the instruments, syringes, needles, forceps, catheters, kidney dishes and galley pots. Bandages were washed and hung up to dry before being re-used. We had to fold all the dressings into the correct shape and fill the drums ready for them to be autoclaved elsewhere in the hospital. We wore masks when doing dressings and cleaned the skin before giving injections.

We made beds day after day, over and over again, and we were taught how to clean beds and lockers daily and to make up beds for the return of patients from theatre. The giving of medicines and injections were practised (the latter on oranges), I must admit, with some hilarity.

Then the great day came when we had completed our time in

PTS and started our nursing as probationers on the wards. The work was heavy: physically, mentally and emotionally demanding. I believe I developed problems with back pain quite early on which continued throughout my years of training and beyond.

I started work in a medical ward which I very much enjoyed. The ward sister was a kind and professional person who had high standards and a deeply hidden sense of humour. We stood by her desk, hands behind our backs and were given our 'night report' which had been written by the senior night nurse. Patients were known by their surnames and NOT by bed numbers! 'Nurse, how would you like to be talked of as "bed 17"?' On night duty I dreaded the night sister's 'round' when we were required to go from bed to bed with her, giving her the name of the patient, age, their diagnosis and what treatment they were receiving. There were about 25 beds in a ward and, as I have said already, memory was not my strongest asset! Without my notes this experience was nerve-wracking!

Letter from a grateful patient.

Because it was in the early days of penicillin and antibiotics, patients stayed in hospital for a much longer time than today. They were also kept in bed for longer periods and so we got to know them very well and often knew quite a lot about their families and friends.

Despite the war continuing, we were always looking for ways to relax and have fun. We sometimes went to dances which were held in various venues, where members of British and Allied forces awaited the arrival of nurses or other dance partners. These were recognised centres where you would be sure to find a partner to enjoy the evening to get away from it all. These dances were open to everyone and I don't remember having to pay an admission fee. One of these places was the Hammersmith Palais. Bands such as Victor Sylvester and Joe Loss were much in demand at this time.

Weddings of colleagues were excuses to put on what 'glad rags' we still owned. Occasionally, some of my 'Set' went to the Paddington Turkish Baths which I remember were in the vicinity of Whiteleys. We found walking up and down the very posh marble staircase – stark naked – quite incongruous and laughed helplessly as we did so. I think this helped to relieve a lot of the tension of war we were all feeling. Other times we had parties and made up our own games such as scavenger hunts.

I also joined the Marylebone Church Choir and sang with them on Sundays when my off-duty time coincided with the services. They were a very friendly group of musicians and I was grateful for their tolerance. Eventually it became difficult, with hospital exams, night duty and work, so sadly I had to say goodbye.

Christmas was a wonderful and exciting time in the hospital. As many patients as possible, who were deemed fit enough, were sent home and we all stayed on duty to care for those left behind. Sister told us when we could decorate the ward but said that, sadly, we did not have many paper chains etc., with which to decorate. That morning, when I was cleaning out one of the top cupboards, I found a pair of false teeth (put there some years before, following the death of a patient). I had recently noticed there was a pawn shop in the next street and was suddenly struck by the idea to sell them to get some money with which to buy some more decorations. Timorously I approached Sister with the object on a sheet of surgical lint and told her of my proposition.

She reluctantly agreed to my trying this and so I set off to the pawn shop, full of hope.

I returned with 2/6 (two shillings and six pence) and took it up to the ward and placed it on the Sister's desk. She asked, 'Where did this come from?' When I told her, her shoulders began to shake and she did her best to cover up her amusement. 'Well done!' she said, 'I'll get some decorations tomorrow and then we'll dress the ward ready for Christmas.' As it was war time there was little in the way of attractive decorations but we did our best with what she managed to get. Some of the patients got their visitors to bring in bits and pieces and we became quite festive. Screens were placed in a corner of the ward around a table. There we had mince pies and bottles of anything we could get hold of; mainly wines and soft drinks.

There was a sudden change in the atmosphere as the staff 'let their hair down' and surgeons, registrars, housemen, students and nursing staff all chatted together and had occasional drinks behind the screens. I think the patients enjoyed this camaraderie among us and a good time was had by all. The severely ill and deaths were treated with the same solemnity and care which had always been given by the staff but now brought considerable poignancy to the festive atmosphere.

I remember two male patients especially; one of their names was William. He was terminally ill and in great pain. His wife visited him frequently. I used to call him 'Willie' and he always looked up and smiled when I did this. Years later, I had a letter from his wife saying she would always remember me because of my care for him and the poem I had written for her about him. Another was Albert, who must have been about forty years old but he looked nearer sixty. He had a severe heart condition. He was nursed in an upright position in his bed; his legs were swollen like tree trunks, hanging down over a sterile sheet with fluid draining from them. He never complained up to the time of his death and was much loved by all of us.

The compassion we felt for the patients made our work seem so worthwhile and must have been the means by which we were able to cope with the heavy load of responsibility we bore and the emotional turmoil we inevitably had to face. Letters of thanks received from families of patients we had nursed were always so welcomed and boosted our morale.

Our meals were a problem. It was hard to go over to the dining room smelling the fishy smells of the whale meat after dealing with sputum pots and bed pans! I know of at least two nurses who used to eat the food left on the plates by patients who had poor appetites, some of whom had tuberculosis. The nurses held a special meeting about the food we were getting but were probably not aware at the time of the extreme difficulties facing the country. This was because of the censorship exercised by the press and radio at the time so that the Germans would not be informed of the success of their attacks. Ships crossing the Atlantic were 'running the gauntlet' to evade being bombed as they brought food to us from Canada and America, but sadly, many ended with great loss of life.

War was still everywhere. In February 1945 thousands of British and American bombers set out for Germany, bombing Dresden smashing almost the whole city and reportedly killing over 100,000 people. They flew over our heads in waves and I remember how they blanked out the skies. There were so many of them flying in close formation, bumper to bumper and wing to wing, that one could hardly see the sky. On several occasions I said to myself, "What? *More* planes?"; it seemed incessant.

According to one source, by the end of the war 24,000 had been killed by V1 rockets or 'Doodlebugs'. These were the most terrible and truly frightening war weapons as you heard them coming (sounding like a motorbike) with flames spurting out at the back. They then banked round lower and lower in an arc and you wondered where they would land, leaving your heart in your mouth with apprehension. I believe tens of thousands lost their lives and were injured as a result. Hundreds of guns on the south coast shot down Doodlebugs but it was difficult as they flew so fast. Fighters joined in and brought many down in the Channel.

In March V2 rockets started arriving, fired from the Dutch coast. Figures given in the *Chronicle of the 20th Century* were that they weighed 12-13 tons, flew at more than 3000 mph and were 46 feet long. These rockets managed to get through 'Doodle Bug Alley', which were gaps between the balloon barrages placed in a circle round London. Thankfully these attacks had dwindled by the middle of March.

On April 11th 1945 Buchenwald Concentration camp, where

my paternal uncle, Georges Rodocanachi had been incarcerated and died, was liberated and around the same time the Red Army captured Berlin.

On May 8th Churchill announced the end of the war in Europe and I joined the throng of people dancing and cheering outside Buckingham Palace to celebrate. In London alone at least 39,000 had died and at least 100,000 were left wounded. The relief that peace brought was almost tangible; even the lights returning to the London streets brought back some sense of normality. We joined the crowds surging up the Mall to Buckingham Palace, singing and dancing and hugging the person nearest to us, no matter whom! I believe we cried with relief as I remember choking back tears as we tried to sing *God Save the King* when he, the Queen and Winston Churchill came onto the balcony.

On August 6th 1945 the news came over the BBC that an atomic bomb had been dropped on Hiroshima, to be followed by one on Nagasaki. I don't believe we had the remotest idea at that time, how truly devastating was the effect of these terrible bombs. It was in the belief that we were bringing the war with Japan to an end that we could appreciate the reasons for their use. It seemed that, at that time, little else was talked about and we just prayed for it all to come to an end.

On August 14th it did. The Japanese surrendered and at last a true peace had arrived over our land. Once again we took to the streets to relieve the tension that had built up over six years of terrible war. It brings shivers to my spine as I am writing this. There was a service of victory and thanksgiving held in Westminster Abbey the following month.

I read somewhere that by the end of the war the price of victory was 55 million dead! Half a million houses destroyed and one million damaged, and 55,000 airmen killed in bombing raids. As I read this I held my head in my hands. Had it all been worth it? Who had won? What had they won? In my old age I still cannot answer these questions. I guess that if we had been over-run by Hitler and the Nazis we might not have been around to ask the questions. So we have many people to thank who were injured or gave their lives that we might be free. I found subsequently that I was continually getting 'flashbacks' about the war years.

Although war ended then, it was many years before rationing ended. We would see a queue in the distance and rush to join it not knowing what we were queuing for until word passed down the line, 'They've got some chocolate!' Another queue might be for bananas and so forth. Unknown to us at this time, there were people in France and other parts of Europe literally living on grass in their hunger, so little food was there to eat. So, we were lucky. However, rationing remained due to food shortages. Three years later milk rations went up from one pint to three and a half pints per week. You could imagine our joy when we received the occasional food parcels from relatives in Canada and America.

In February 1947 I 'came of age' (21 years in those days) and my parents, wishing to mark the occasion, discussed with me how we could celebrate it. At this time there were still shortages of venues, money, food, etc. We had to think long and hard about having an 'occasion' due to these constraints. As I was on night duty at the time and therefore free to get up during the day, my parents invited close family members and a couple of my friends to an afternoon tea dance at the Cumberland Hotel at Marble Arch. It was a great success. I was delighted when Chris Boggon, with whom I had played in the doubles at Frinton Tennis Club before the war, was able to join us. This was quite a special few hours of 'living' in a time of adjustment to post-war traumas.

One night, when on duty in the obstetric ward, I developed violent abdominal pain and had quite a large rectal haemorrhage. I was put into a wheelchair and pushed over to the nurses' sick bay in the Private Patient's Wing of the hospital. There I was put to bed and the next day was taken to theatre for a laparotomy (exploration of the abdomen). The surgeon diagnosed TB glands of the stomach, although there seemed to be no association with the haemorrhage. I was returned to my room where I was to remain for some time for bed rest. They used to push me on my bed out onto the balcony, where it was freezing cold. I was supposed to breathe in fresh air but spent most of the time trying to keep warm under the bed clothes! I learned later that it was the coldest winter of recorded temperature since 1814! No nurses or visitors wanted to come out onto the balcony so, eventually, my bed was pushed back into my room and the French doors left open. I was greatly relieved.

Sadly, at this time, three nurses in my set contracted poliomyelitis and one, who was particularly badly affected, was nursed in the room next to mine. Another nurse, in the room opposite, was found to have a tubercular ovary. It seemed that nurses, by virtue of their proximity to infected patients, were particularly vulnerable to any infections they encountered in their work.

At this time my parents had decided that they would like to move permanently to the country and sell our London house, so they started looking in the Westerham area, where my sister Helen lived with her husband. In 1947 they moved to a house, above Pilgrims Way on The Avenue, called 'Betsoms' and were to spend many happy years there.

One night when I went home by train to Westerham, I changed trains as usual at Dunton Green. There didn't seem to be many people around and it was bitterly cold. I went to find a carriage. The train driver called out to me 'Nurse,' as I was in a nurse's outdoor uniform, I walked towards him and he said, 'Do you want to come up? It's warmer up here.' I didn't need to stop to think, in a second I was up beside him with the heat from the boiler warming my frozen hands and feet. 'Can I have a go at driving her?' I asked, never thinking he would say yes. But I can now proudly say that all those years ago I drove the Westerham Flyer train under his guidance and shovelled coal into the boiler to make the steam.

It was to Betsoms I went to complete my sick leave. During the time I went there I did some 'gentle' private nursing in the area. My brother-in-law Aidan was one of the local GPs and was able to find patients for me to look after. He and my sister Helen had taken a cottage in the village after he left the Navy following the end of the war and he had been appointed as GP in the local practice.

One delightful gentleman, who, I was told, needed 'night nursing', had a large bedroom with twin beds in it. After I had settled him for the night with a warm drink he got into bed. 'Now sister,' he said patting the top of the other bed, 'I won't have you sitting up all night. I don't usually need anything, but if I do, I'll call you. You hop into that bed and have a good night's sleep.' I was flabbergasted! I told him that was not something that I should do and he was paying me to sit up and stay awake ready to help him. However, after three days, I was taking off my cap and shoes and lying on the top of my bed, falling fast asleep. In the morning we would both ask each other if we had slept well! To this day I can't imagine why he needed a night nurse or that I descended into such unprofessional behaviour! Luckily, word had not got around that this was my idea of how to behave as I nursed several private patients after that in the locality!

While at home, still on sick leave, I joined the WADS (Westerham Amateur Dramatic Society) and took part in performances of a play called *No Medals* by Esther McCracken which was great fun. The performance took place in the large Women's Institute hall near the station. I used to get there by bus from our house and it felt quite strange to be dressed in WRNS (Women's Royal Naval Service) uniform instead of a nurse's .

One day when thick snow lay on the ground at Westerham and we were walking up the hill past the post office, a hearse came along beside us and started sliding from side to side on the icy road unable to make any progress. It started sliding backwards and the driver beseeched us to help him or he 'would be late for the funeral'. So several of us went to the back of the hearse and started pushing it, with its coffin inside, up the hill. It was hard work and we had a job to stay on our feet, but eventually, with some mirth, we reached the brow of the hill and it went on its way with a thankful wave from the driver.

At another time, when I was attending the funeral of a much-loved cousin who lived in Brasted, we arrived at the churchyard gate and parked the car near the local pub which was right beside the church yard. The publican came out and asked if we minded moving the car because he was expecting the beer to arrive. We replied, 'So are we!' Despite the seriousness of the occasion we all burst into laughter when we realised that our *bier* had a slightly different connotation!

This story reminds me of a little boy of about eight years old whom I was to teach some years later. When my students didn't know what a word meant I wrote it on the back of a piece of paper. That week he had new words to learn. I asked him to write a sentence containing these words so I was happy he knew how to use them. One of the words was 'erect'. He told me he didn't know what it meant. So I wrote on the back 'we put up or erect a tent or a building'. In his homework the next week he had written: 'Today my teacher was on leave so I had to erect with my supply teacher.' Oh dear – how to keep a straight face!

I approached UCH to see if I could return, but the nurses'

Medical Officer said it was too soon and he would see me in three months' time. I decided to make a move back to London and having nowhere to stay I joined Mrs Coward's Trained Nurses Co-operative at 62 St Georges Square, SW1. I was put up at one of their houses where we were given a camp bed with a blanket while we awaited calls to come through from the office allocating nursing jobs as they came in. It was quite a gamble as to who got the next one. It was usually the first person to race to the phone! And so I worked for them for some time, and did private nursing in people's homes or 'specialling' patients who needed one-to-one care in hospital. This was varied and interesting.

One of my patients lived with her husband in a suite of rooms in Grovsenor House, Hyde Park Lane. Following a small gynaecological operation her doctor suggested that she had a private nurse for a few days. Two incidents stand out in my mind. She appeared to think she needed a nursemaid to attend to her every whim: dandruff had to be brushed off her shoulders or her towel had to be handed to her when standing in the bath despite the fact that she could easily reach it. 'SISTA! We need you to be with us when we have drinks in the foyer before DINNA!' So, greatly embarrassed I stood in full uniform sipping my sherry as the rich and famous came in through the revolving doors, wishing the floor would swallow me up! She appeared to bask in the glory of having her own nurse in attendance! My only fear was that some hierarchy in the nursing profession should walk in and find me drinking in uniform in public.

The next day I called on the hotel doctor who was caring for her. I told him I could bear it no longer and apologised for leaving after such a short time. 'Sister,' he said, 'I don't blame you; you have stayed longer than any of the other nurses she has had. Thank you very much for your patience!' And I left.

Another job I was given by Coward's was to nurse at the house of Orpen, the painter, in Weybridge. It was a difficult case which was made easier under the watchful eye of the GP, Dr Lankaster. The other nursing sister I worked with, Ruth Conley, from Australia, and I became good friends and shared the day and night nursing needed between us. In our time off-duty we used to go for long walks along the riverside. Sadly our patient died, but the family invited us to stay on, at their expense, until the funeral was over.

Whenever I had extra time on my hands, Coward's was to be a very reliable standby for employment throughout the rest of my nursing career.

In February 1949 I was selected to play in my first matches for the East of England Lacrosse Team: one match was against the Midlands and another at Brighton against Roedean Girls' School. Some time later I was invited to join the England Lacrosse team for a weekend of trials at Bournemouth. I went and hugely enjoyed it but I never did, in fact, play for them.

On June 11th my brother married Eileen Hay in the lovely St Mary's Church in Westerham; a very happy day with the reception in her parents' beautiful garden.

In July I again played in the Frinton-on-Sea Open tournament but I was beaten in the first round by 6-0,6-3!

An application to join the Royal Choral Society (RCS) brought me a letter from the secretary, Mr Patient, inviting me to attend an audition at the Royal College of Music. I was auditioned by the organist Arnold Greer and Mr Patient. On 18th October 1949 I received a card telling me I was now a member: Number 130; left soprano; row 5; seat 36. What organisation. I loved every moment of my time with the RCS. Janet Theobald, who was to become a close friend, auditioned at the same time and was given a seat next to mine. We frequently reminisce about the wonderful times we had with the RCS. We rehearsed in the Royal College of Music and gave concerts in either the Royal Albert Hall or the Royal Festival Hall under the baton of Sir Malcolm Sargent. My favourites were the *Messiah, The Dream of Gerontius* and the *Christmas Carol Concerts*. In that year I did a lot of singing, which was something that continued throughout the years ahead as I also sang at several music festivals. But work was calling and my time 'off' had ended.

It seemed incongruous to be living a life which included (as well as work) tennis, swimming and mixed hockey matches. There were times when I could not join in but in between 'painful' days I took part in everything. Our best effort was in the Inter Hospital Swimming Gala on 27th September 1945, which was held at the Marshall Street Baths in London, where five of us, all nurses representing UCH, won six cups and a shield! We were amazed and exhausted.

Hockey matches were played in Regent's Park. We played with

'mixed teams' composed of doctors, nurses, students and ancillary staff. Before we could start we had to collect the goal posts from a hut, slot them into holes in the ground and return them after we'd finished! I had no idea life was so complicated. (I hope things have improved as we approach the 2012 Olympics!)

We played tennis matches too. The one I mainly remember was against the Middlesex Hospital. Their one court was situated in a central courtyard surrounded by hospital buildings. After matches we were spoiled with *gorgeous* home-made cream teas and cakes. UCH did not rise to such opulence: so, in my role as captain, I went to see the Matron, Mrs Jackson, and asked her if we could not do better than thick bread and butter and jam, which were the teas *we* provided. She smiled and said she would see what she could do. From then on our teas greatly improved. I went to thank her.

In the 1940s Wimbledon Tennis continued as best it could. One player, Gussie Moran, nicknamed 'Gorgeous Gussie', was famous for the pretty lacy white pants she wore under her very short dresses. I was so taken with them that I bought some pants and attached some frilly white lace round mine. But I'm afraid I couldn't compete with her looks (or her tennis!), though I'm sure I played better tennis as a result!

It wasn't often that anything exciting happened but once, when I came off night duty, I changed and went for a walk. I was just passing Heals shop, opposite Warren Street tube station in Tottenham Court Road, when I happened to glance at a man selling fruit from a barrow. He was looking around as though searching for someone. I crossed Tottenham Court Road and, approaching the tube station, I looked back. As I looked, I saw a woman come up to him and between them, from under her jumper, they exchanged a hand gun and hid it under his coat. I went into the phone box and dialled 999. Within seconds a police car came to a stop in the road at the side of the station entrance hall. A policeman came in and, seeing me standing on my own, came over to me. 'Are you Miss Vlasto, Madam?' I said I was. He then asked if we could be seen by the person in question: when I said we could, he moved me to where we could not be seen talking and asked me to point him out. He then walked quietly to the police car, which was already on the move and, getting hold of me, asked me to get into the back; then he told the driver to go across both lanes of traffic to pull up at the side of the barrow. A second police car drove up behind us; the driver got out and stopped the traffic. All the traffic on Tottenham Court Road was stopped. The cars around us screeched to a halt! As they pulled up the policemen jumped out of their doors and, from behind the man, took an arm each, turned him around and pushed him into the back of the car – beside me! I was terrified and was very relieved when the driver opened my side of the door and told me to 'get out' which I did with great speed! The police said they would be in touch with me. True to their word, the next day they told me that they had found the gun on him and had taken him to be charged at the police station but gave no further information. They thanked me for calling them and then left. I was to hear no more.

Chapter Five

In the 1940s, I forget exactly when, I had met Lulu Dukes (Marie Rambert's younger daughter) when taking class at the Mercury Theatre, Nottinghill Gate, and talking about the theatre, she mentioned that there was an audition for a soprano soloist in *Oklahoma* at Theatre Royal, Drury Lane, London. It was about to go on tour; would I be interested? I can't think what possessed me to apply (goodness knows what would have happened to my nursing career!) but I did and was given an audition date by the Department of National Services and Entertainment which was set up during the war for the entertainment of troops and others.

I joined the group of would-be singers after my audition card had been checked and waited my turn, clutching my music nervously. I soon realised that I hadn't the remotest chance of being accepted when I heard all the loud, proficient, mature voices that were being heard. My little soprano voice, untrained in those days, can barely have reached the judges sitting in the middle of the stalls let alone the seats in the balcony! We were to return March 20th to learn the results. I managed to get my off-duty time to allow me to attend but told no one where I was going. Greatly relieved that I wasn't selected, I joined the 'Thank you for coming' group and made for the stage door as fast as I could. 'See you tomorrow,' someone called out to me, then someone else said the same. It was only then that I realised how these wretched people were traipsing around from one audition to another, with all the difficulty of travel brought about by the war, in the hope of getting work. I felt guilty and embarrassed that I had a safe job and a salary to go back to. I waved goodbye.

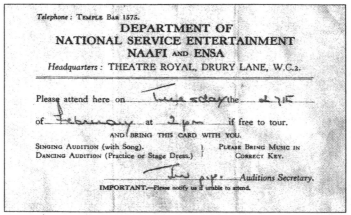

My audition entry card for *Oklahoma*.

Having found an article with photos in the *Nursing Mirror*, August 9th 1947, relating to the fact that UCH had bought the Grafton Hotel on Warren Street, I remember how it was to be a new nurses' home. My impression was that it was much more spacious and up-market than our Huntley Street home.

At last, in October 1949, I received a letter from UCH to say I could go back to work. On my return I was sent to do three months TB nursing (which we were required to do as part of our training) at the King Edward VII Sanatorium at Midhurst in Surrey. My 'set' had already done their time there and this was to be the one occasion when I really felt I had been left behind away from my friends.

With my colleagues being in London I felt somewhat alone in my off-duty time but I was considerably more relaxed and free, and so I took to playing the chapel organ (although I had never played one before!) which faced out in a V formation, with no walls along one side, overlooking the gardens, woods and beautiful countryside. No one seemed to mind my practising, or if they did, they were kind enough not to tell me. I also hired a horse from some Midhurst stables and went riding, by myself, in the surrounding countryside. Riding through the woods was quite magical.

Being fond of milk I was delighted to be told we could drink as much as we liked, (local cows provided for us) and we fed extremely well also. Such a change from the paucity of food elsewhere but we needed protection from the highly infectious tubercular organism. It was hard not to be conscious of coughing and spitting and we felt the patients' discomfort and embarrassment. When the weather was nice, all the wards' doors opened out onto the terrace.

The nursing was similar to that which we had done at UCH in one of our wards caring for TB patients. 'Spit-pots', as we irreverently referred to them, had to be collected, cleaned and replaced daily. Mucus stuck to the enamel sides and was difficult to clean. It was not a very pleasant job but, nevertheless, an important one. Afterwards, just as before, going over to the dining room for lunch with the smell of fish pervading the air (despite being called whale-meat) was just about the final straw and many of our plates found their way into the centre of the table, uneaten, despite our hunger.

Once, when on night duty, one of the other nurses (unknown to me) had draped herself in a sheet wearing a white mask and heaving herself up into the loft started moaning, appearing and disappearing into the dark hole. Even the night sister, arriving on her rounds, saw the funny side.

Another time, when very tired, one of the night nurses put a red blanket down in the bath, took a pillow off the shelf and said, 'Vlasto, warn me when Night Sister arrives.' We carried on with our duties. There was a squeak as the ward door opened. Before we could move Sister started walking up the ward in the direction of the bathroom. I was speechless but my colleague called out, 'Sister, could you come and look at a patient for me?' That was a near miss. When it was my turn, I went sound asleep not noticing that the tap was dripping onto my toes and had soaked the blanket and I hadn't even woken up! We *were* tired. I returned from Midhurst to UCH in January 1950 and was sent to work on a surgical ward, pleased to be back in London again.

At the end of March I joined Putney Ladies Lacrosse Club, attending their first post war AGM. I then played for them for some time and also for Reigate Ladies but the trouble with my back meant that I could not always be available; also I could not always get my days off to coincide with practices and matches.

It was great returning to UCH and I threw myself back into

work. For my last few months I was to work in a special ward set aside for the examination of doctors taking MD examinations and senior doctors taking more advanced exams. In a mock set-up, six 'acting patients', who were mainly past patients with specific chronic ailments, spent the day in beds along two sides of the 'ward'. The doctor had to examine the patients and report their findings and make a diagnosis. I was the only member of the nursing staff there and worked alongside the examining doctors and specialists, providing whatever assistance was needed. This was interesting work as I much enjoyed looking after the 'patients' and the doctors. I had to keep reminding the patients to be true with their answers but, at the same time, not to lead the examinees into the correct diagnosis! Occasional hints were given, such as a rather loud cough when the examiner had forgotten to check their chest sounds or the odd moan when he had not palpated their abdomen which would probably have helped him (there were few female doctors) to get the correct diagnosis. Their meals were sent up from the kitchen and they jumped out of bed and sat at a communal table before jumping back in for the afternoon session. They were old hands at this.

I did not realise it at the time, but later it became obvious, that the Matron was aware of my back problems and had decided to take me off heavy duties. I was told I was chosen for this role as they had noticed how good I was at dealing with people. Perhaps this was in part true; anyway, I like to think so.

Before I left UCH we had started an eight hour shift system which made a great difference. Not only did we work fewer hours but three different shifts meant we could have some varied 'down' time. During one of these times, while working in the Obstetric Hospital which was part of UCH, I wrote this rather risqué poem which I have kept since 1950:

> There was a dame called Mrs Blow,
> On May 1st she had a Colpo
> As midnight struck she rang for a po',
> And was distressed she could not go.
>
> So up the stairs I flew for Sister
> And by bad timing I just missed her
> Eventually she, I found,
> Was out upon her midnight round.

With frozen hands she poked her tum
But still the urine would not come
The night nurse being too far gone
Produced a syringe and omnopom.

The moral of this you will find
To catheterise is such a bind.
Therefore, when you get on duty
Be sure the houseman charts a beauty!

Our final State Registered Nurse exams loomed ahead as did our hospital exams. I was horrified when, taking my practical exam (along with another colleague), we were asked to treat the patient, who was lying in the bed in front of us, for severe shock. The instruction was, 'The patient has collapsed in bed. Deal with it nurses.' Unfortunately I was at the bottom end of the bed. The obvious treatment was to tilt the bed back so that the blood would go to the head (the area of most need) while my colleague would give oxygen at the other end. I lifted the bed, kicking the bed blocks under the wheels on each side as I did so. At that moment I felt excruciating tearing pain in my back and believe, now, that I must have torn ligaments which had further aggravated my existing back problems. Unfortunately in those days, we only had x-rays of bones as opposed to the scanners now which can show detail of tissue and nerve damage. It was thought that I was depressed but I am sure it was a misdiagnosis.

Despite having had a spinal fusion, I was forced to leave UCH because of the many disturbances there had been in my training. I think the hospital must have considered me to be a liability by now! And I left on August 21st 1950. I never worked the extra year as a staff nurse or passed my hospital exam and was quite inconsolable about this. But I did get the SRN (State Registered Nurse) Certificate and qualified as a fully fledged nurse. However, thankfully, I enjoyed many years of nursing and nursing-related work throughout my life. My problems seem, in retrospect, so small compared with those three nurses in my set who contracted poliomyelitis, and I often think of them.

After leaving UCH I saw an advertisement for a Staff Nurse at the National Heart Hospital in Westmoreland Street in London and applied for the post. I was accepted but only worked there for

Soldiers bringing gifts to children in hospital. The 'V's on the light shades were made by the nurses.

RED CROSS & ST. JOHN WAR ORGANISATION

HOSPITAL PASS

NAME ....
RANK ....
TIME : FROM ....
TO ....
DATE ....
SIGNED ....
H 889   B & D LTD [ITEM]

To Nurse Valesco
With our best wishes
for a Happy Xmas.
From The Tired Nurses.
• • • Xmas 1944
MERRY CHRISTMAS

Good wishes from
The Tired Nurses.

Commandant Mrs
Berdoe Wilkinson
on left.

Set 86 on their first day of the PTS at UCH. I am middle row far right.

My UCH employment card and UCH as it was in my father's time.

WADS – performance of *No Medals*. I'm sitting on the arm of settee.
(Reproduced by permission of *Sevenoaks Chronicle*.)

Self with UCH colleagues at a wedding – note the fashion!

Triumphant UCH nurses' swimming team

I took photo of some of the English Lacrosse Team during trials at Bournemouth. Captain Margaret Boyd at front left.

Compulsory Identity Card

My brother and Eileen Hay on their wedding day.

My sister Helen and her husband Aidan Long.

Chapel at Midhurst Sanatorium, where I played the organ, 1948.

My sister Christian living in Karachi.

UCH Nurses' Home when we were there.
(Reproduced by permission of *Nursing Times*.)

Myself with the poster I made.
(Photo by G.B. Murdie.)

My leaving party at CHUB.
(Photo by G.B. Murdie.)

Singing with Nanaimo Choral Society, representing Wales!

Self on lawn in front of
Nanaimo Hospital

With Ann and Grace Hendy
who were not able to be at the
farewell party.

On Emmie at Wheatland HR Ranch,
Wyoming, 1952, with cousins
Robert and Steven Mitchell.

Myself as Sister at
Frigidaire.

Frigidaire Factory at Colindale
in the 1950s.

Self and colleague at
Frigidaire.

Elisabeth Lane in Trafalgar Square; me in picture on the right.
On our way from Charing Cross Hospital to our room
in Craven Street, 1953.

Cast of
the BBC
programme
To Save a Life.
I am on right of
second row
back.

An incident from the
programme *To Save a
Life*. I am the nurse.

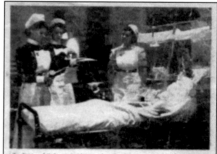

In my UCH uniform for the
filming

Standing in front of St Martin-
in-the-Field, Charing Cross
Hospital is on the left.

Outside the
Royal Albert Hall
where I was singing
in all the
posted events.

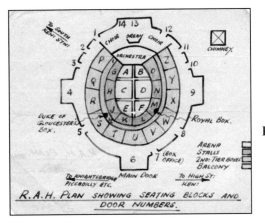

Mr Patient's
drawing of the
entrances to the
Royal Albert Hall.

THE BRITISH BROADCASTING CORPORATION

Broadcasting House, London, W.1

TELEPHONE: LANGHAM 4468   TELEGRAMS AND CABLES: BROADCASTS, TELEX, LONDON

Date as Postmark

ST. MARTIN'S SINGERS

MOST URGENT. Please ring my office as early as
possible today and say whether or not you could
manage a 'live' broadcast of "The Way to
Heaven's Door" on Sunday next, October 31st.
Faulty Recording.

W. D. K. B.

An indication of what's next in my hectic life!

a short time before being sent to the country branch on night duty. I was not really happy there and on returning to the London branch I walked round to the Television Offices on Marylebone High Street still wearing my uniform. There I spoke to the man on duty at the entrance. I told him I would like to speak to someone about my chance of getting some acting work and was it possible that they *might* just talk to me? He took me inside the entrance hall and spoke to a lady in a small reception box, telling her of my request. She then asked me to wait a minute while she contacted Robert Barr. The man turned to me and said, 'Good – he's the one you want to see. He's a really nice man, very kind and I'll bet he sees you.'

The lady who had been on the phone turned to me and said, 'His secretary would like to speak to you,' and handed me the phone. Stammeringly I began to apologise for this very unusual way of approaching someone. She reassured me and said she was sure he would be really sorry to have missed me but she would tell him I had called and was sure he would like to meet me. Incredible! Such courtesy and kindness! She said she would ring me and took my number. Two days later she did!

Apparently she had told Robert Barr that she had found my voice so 'gorgeous' that he *had* to see me. This is what he told me over a cup of tea in his office a week later. We chatted for some time and then he said he would see if there was a part for me in one of his productions but he couldn't promise anything. A short while later he rang me and asked if I would be interested in advising on the nursing procedures in a production of a play he was producing called *Casualty Ward* and that I could have a small part in it for which I was to receive the princely sum of 8 guineas for the programme. I still have the receipt, dated 13 June 1951. This gave me the impetus and excuse I needed to leave the hospital and I duly gave notice and began looking for an agency where I could do some private nursing to keep my bank manager happy.

At this time, 2nd September 1951, when singing in the Marylebone Church Choir, I had met an actress, Ann Elliott, who kindly offered me a bed in her little basement flat in Upper Harley Street – a stone's throw from Regent's Park. This enabled me to look for work in London and I again worked for Coward's Nursing Co-op.

97

e

TELEVISION (Talks)

THE BRITISH BROADCASTING CORPORATION

Broadcasting House, London, W.I

TELEPHONE : LANGHAM 4468.   TELEGRAMS : BROADCASTS, TELEX, LONDON

Our Reference: 01/PC/MCB

13th June, 1951........... 19......

DEAR Madam,   appear

We invite you to ~~speak and broadcast~~(s) in our television programmes as detailed below upon the conditions printed overleaf.   If you accept, kindly sign and return the attached confirmation sheet, or reply otherwise, as soon as possible.   (See condition 1 overleaf.)

Title...."Casualty Ward"...Producer - Robert Barr (Wel: 4424)............

Date(s) : Rehearsal(s) June 18th m 23rd.................... Broadcast.......25th June, 1951.

Time : Rehearsal(s) 10.30 m 5.30 p.m.................... Broadcast...9 m 10 p.m...........

Place Rehearsals....Gt. Cumberland Hall, Bryanston St., W.1. Transmission
                                                        Alexandra Palace.

Fee Eight guineas (£8.8.0.)..
       To appear as Nurse

Letters addressed to speakers c/o the BBC will be forwarded, but for statistical purposes the letters may be opened before being forwarded unless we are notified of any objection. Letters marked "Personal" are forwarded unopened.

Miss Nancy Vlasto,
24 Porchester Terrace,   Yours faithfully,
W.2.
                                        THE BRITISH BROADCASTING CORPORATION

                                        Holland Bennett

JMH   Programme Contracts Department

A confirmatory note from the BBC for my role in *Casualty Ward*.

Further singing opportunities came my way when Colin Ratcliffe ARCM formed The United Hospital Festival Choir which I and my friend Janet Theobald joined. We sang in many concerts, including several at the new Festival Hall on the South Bank. Anyone working in the field of healthcare was eligible to be a member, so we had doctors, nurses, physiotherapists, radiographers, and dentists, among others, all wearing our respective uniforms. There were hundreds of us and I believe we made quite a good sound!

Chapter Six

I became restless and anxious to travel the world and decided to go and find work in Canada, which I had enjoyed very much on my earlier visit. In the 1950s British visitors could only take £10 currency into the country and had to be 'vouched for' by someone there who would agree to be financially responsible for them. In this case my uncle George Croil in Vancouver kindly wrote a letter saying he would be responsible for any financial problems I might have.

On October 13th 1951, at the start of my travels, I went as a 'nursing companion' with an elderly lady who was travelling to New York to stay with her daughter in Scarsdale; I would stay there for two nights. Mrs Carder (now deceased) had been married to an important executive of a major oil company, but he had recently died and she was now quite frail. She was given the use of the oil company's flat, which overlooked St James's Palace in London, for the one night before travelling. We shared a room and, as I was too excited to sleep, I spent much of the night looking out of the window and watching the Guardsmen marching up and down outside the Palace by the lights of the lamp above.

On the following morning we caught a train to the Southampton docks. We came face-to-face with a sleek and beautiful liner, RMS *Media*, ready waiting for us at the dockside. We watched our luggage being hoisted into the air and swung across to the centre of the ship and gently disappearing into the hold. We were piped aboard and were greeted by a smart uniformed sailor.

Once Mrs Carder's name was mentioned I was conscious that we received exceptional attention by all the staff (she was definitely a VIP!). I found this somewhat embarrassing but decided to make sure I enjoyed it all as I was unlikely to experience it again.

On reading the beautifully designed Cunard booklet, I noticed that among the list of the passengers, I had a line all to myself, being the only one with a surname beginning with *V*. On board were twelve gynaecologists, one of them was Timothy Flew, the senior gynaecologist at University College Hospital with whom I had worked as a nurse.

As was my usual habit, I put my name down on the purser's list to take part in a table tennis tournament and prayed that the sea would not be too rough. I am not a good sailor! After a few rounds and a week later, I found myself in the final and won the first prize of a very attractive '*Media*' powder compact with a little cup – a lovely surprise.

We arrived on the Hudson River and passed the Statue of Liberty on Saturday 20th October on a beautiful day, a bright sun was shining out of the blue sky and glorious reds and oranges of leaves were floating down from the trees.

We landed in New York at 5.45pm to find a dock strike in progress. It took two hours to unload the luggage from the hold. I arranged for my trunk and army grip to be sent through to Vancouver and booked my berth on the train to Montreal on the Monday's 10.30pm train.

Mrs Carder's family took us on a wonderful drive around the area of Scarsdale. The trees were turning crimson and looked as though they were on fire.

The day I left New York I first went into the city and found Drake Hotel, where I visited an elderly friend of the family. (Sadly she committed suicide, naked, on the railway line a year or so later.) From there I phoned the American Nurses' Association and they arranged for me to visit the New York Hospital. Everywhere I went television was much in evidence (far more than in the UK at that time) which I found quite irresistible!

Arriving in the hospital in the afternoon, I was shown all over the massive building by three nursing sisters, one of whom was from Brooklyn, one from Norway and the other lived locally. They gave me dozens of pamphlets and a book of nursing statistics which I found very interesting. For example, the hospital had 1,000 beds and there were 500 nursing staff. Each patient had their own equipment and fridge locker beside them. Every private room was en-suite (unheard of here in those days). There were 30 operating theatres doing approximately 60 operations daily. There was a large sterilising room where all dressing and instruments were autoclaved (we were still boiling our instruments at that time). Rubber gloves were mended and powdered in special containers with an arm sleeve for the person working there. I left the hospital that day in the company of the three nursing sisters and they took me on a sightseeing tour of Radio City and the Fifth Avenue shops before I took my leave.

A male acquaintance I had met on the ship, met me as arranged in the Canadian National Railway building in Fifth Avenue to collect my ticket for the following day which would cover the trip from Montreal to Vancouver, and *horrors* we found the place closed! Inside we could see a man cleaning the office. We made signs to him and he unlocked the door. On hearing of my predicament and after some time and serious persuasion, he managed to find someone I could talk to. My luck was in. It happened to be the head man at the office, a Mr Plait, the general passengers' agent. He took off his hat and coat and set about making up all my tickets. He then paid for our bus fares to the Grand Central Station and over the phone asked the man at the ticket office there to help me all he could. He asked me to contact him if I ever returned this way. I was impressed by the courtesy and kindness of this American gentleman.

My friend then took me all over New York City using buses and subways. We went up the Empire State Building, staying there about half an hour looking for landmarks such as the United Nations building. Then we visited a modern art exhibition. After this we went back to his hotel, The Wellington, for supper. We then went for a long walk through Central Park. I felt that I would not have liked to have done this on my own. At 10.30pm he saw me on to my train to Montreal and so I took my leave of the USA.

My sleeper was adequate although I was far too excited and nosey to keep my eyes from peeping out of the window into the darkness as the country raced by. It seemed almost sacrilegious to be travelling by night and missing the scenery outside. At night the seats are pulled down to make sleepers.

We pulled into Montreal station at 9.15am. I was expecting to be met by a cousin of my mother's, Lloyd Croil, to whom I had written a letter asking if he could possibly meet me as I only had one day in Montreal and would like to meet him and his wife. I searched the station but found no male standing around looking for me, so my heart sank somewhat. I had a letter of introduction from the Royal College of Nursing in London asking anyone to help me should I contact them. So armed with this letter and leaving my case in the left luggage, I set off up the main street. The first important thing to do was to find some breakfast. I saw a Woolworths and enjoyed my first Canadian meal of toasted muffin and jam and a hot chocolate drink – bliss!

Now I felt ready to face a day on my own in a strange city. As I emerged from Woolworths I stopped the first lady I met walking towards me in the street and asked if she could direct me to the Nursing Association. She seemed slightly hesitant as she asked me why I wanted to go there. I then told her the story about my cousin and showed her my letter of introduction from the Royal College of Nursing. 'Well you stopped the right person,' she said. Incredibly it turned out that she was a doctor, a Mrs John Stewart Henry. On reading the letter, she took me back to her home at 3057 Cedar Avenue, Montreal and told me she actually worked at the Royal Victoria Hospital. She then proceeded to give me several cards of introduction to doctors and nurses at the hospital. After this she asked if I would like to have lunch with her as she felt my cousin would be very distressed if he knew I was here only for the day. She managed to persuade me. She had a lovely house on the side of a hill leading out of Montreal. She then rang my cousin only to find they did not know I was coming and arranged for them to pick me up at tea time.

After lunch my benefactor took me to the hospital where I was shown all around before returning to her house. There I was met by my cousin Lloyd Croil and his wife. They were so excited to see me and I them. They took me to their home and then back to the station for the 8.20pm train with a large box of chocolates and biscuits, which were to be my sustenance for the next four days.

My parents had generously prepaid one meal a day to the Canadian National Railway (CNR), so they were sure I would not starve during my four day journey through Canada! As it turned out it was a very good thing they did, although I was greatly helped by some fellow travellers. Two independent and charming middle-aged businessmen, noticing I wasn't going into most meals in the buffet car, questioned me and found out why. From then on they took it in turns to pay for my breakfast and lunch until they reached their respective destinations. I managed to get their addresses and was able to write and thank them for their generosity and kindness.

It took three days to cross from the west to the east of Canada – a journey of such beauty I'll never forget. There were miles of wheat growing where three and four combine-harvesters travelled across the massive plains, side by side. It reminded me of the Trooping the Colour ceremony in Central London when the inside soldier marks time while the outside ones march with full strides to turn the corners in a large full sweep round. Then as we approached the snow capped Rocky Mountains, we passed rushing rivers and dark green forests. Beds on Canadian and American trains lie from front to back (not side to side as ours are) which is much more comfortable as one sways from side to side. Bliss!

This was when I made my first 'faux pas'! There was a very courteous, tall, handsome railway sleeper attendant looking after our every need and as we approached the Rocky Mountains, which were expected to come into view about 5am, I asked him if he would kindly 'Knock me up in the morning' to see them. I was quite surprised by his delayed response and his large eyes which appeared to grow even larger, before he said, 'Yes Ma'am.' It was only some time later, when I was quoting the incident to my family, they said, 'Nance, you *didn't*, did you?' Apparently 'knocking someone up' has a totally different meaning in Canada! After passing through Banff, Longlac and Winnipeg we encountered snow blizzards and it was bitterly cold – as we discovered when we dismounted from the train to stretch our legs on the platform – the temperature was 10° below freezing. The scenery was stunning, with snow-laden forests and ice covered lakes.

When passing through Jasper I bought a postcard of beautiful Mount Edith Cavell which I have to this day. I can find no words to describe the true beauty of the Canadian scenery, so varied and alive with dark forests, sparkling rivers, lakes and lofty snow clad mountains.

I slept for eight hours nightly in my bunk, over the three nights it took to cross Canada. At Kamloops junction a taxi awaited me (paid for by CNR) to take me to Kamloops where we arrived on October 27th at 1am. There, I sat in a warm waiting room till the train came in to take me to Kelowna. The train ran alongside beautiful lakes, and yet again a charming young man treated me to breakfast and did his best to make me 'believe' and have 'everlasting salvation'. I thought he was a salesman but perhaps he was a preacher in disguise.

At Kamloops my Uncle Tom Croil, with his lovely spaniel 'Chief', was on the platform to greet me. He took me to the Royal Arms Hotel, where we chatted, shopped and had lunch. Then he drove me in his Pontiac to Summerland. We drove alongside the Okanagan Lake where the red leaves of the maple trees were reflected in the water like blood and the sun shone down on us. We spent the fortnight driving around; visiting my uncle's friends, out to garden parties (the sun always seemed to shine) and fishing in the lake from his little boat with an outboard motor. The McCleods, friends of my uncle, had kindly booked rooms for us at the family resort and convention centre called Fairmont Hot Springs. It is in the Columbia River valley in south eastern British Columbia. The rooms overlooked the amazing hot springs pool with the steam rising from the surface while snow and mountains were all around us. It was a wonderful relaxing time before settling down to find work. On the evening of my last day in Summerland, I went to give blood at the Transfusion Centre only to find that the nurse, Anne Hayes, whom I knew from UCH, was in charge of the unit. What an amazing coincidence!

On November 8th 1951, I arrived at Vancouver station at 11am where I was collected by my Uncle George and Aunt Ailsa Croil. After lunch, I went to see Miss Wright, a senior nursing officer. She told me that without a Canadian Nursing Certificate I would not be able to work in a teaching hospital unless I took the BC (British Columbia) examination. I told her I did not wish to sit yet another exam and would happily work in any hospital. She took a note of my uncle's address and said she would be in touch.

I had hoped to find opportunities in broadcasting and *were* I not to find enough nursing work, would be happy to make this my main method of earning money. I took a bus into the centre of Vancouver and went to the enquiry desk of the Canadian Broadcasting Corporation. I made an appointment for the following day with a drama producer to see what opportunities there might be for me. Having done this I went to another building, to a Dr Trite's office to whom I had been given a recommendation by Dr Henry in Montreal. I met several other doctors, Kinsman, Whitelaw and Mathews, who were all most helpful. From there I went to the Vancouver General Hospital and saw Miss King, the Matron. She spent two hours showing me all over the hospital which was most interesting and I would have liked to work there. It was a one-thousand-five-hundred bed hospital and very busy, but again, it required my having a BC qualification.

I returned to my uncle and aunt's house. In the evening I went with their daughter Barbara to a Guide enrolment meeting, talked with Guides and Guiders and met two Sea Ranger Commodores. Guides are the same the world over! I am very proud to have been one. And seeing the Guides in their smart uniforms reminded me of a photo I had seen in the newspaper of Uncle George who had just been awarded an OBE (Order of the British Empire) to add to his CBE, which he had received from the king himself in London.

Later, I was offered an audition at the Canadian Broadcasting Corporation (CBC), which I passed with good marks, but they did not feel they could give me enough work with my English accent! However, I was recommended for professional radio work where it would not have been of significance.

The next day my uncle took me on a boat trip to Deep Cove. Then we visited my other cousin, Ailsa, and her family in North Vancouver and drove back down the coast road and through Stanley Park watching the *Nanaimo* boat (formerly known as *Princess of Nanaimo*) coming in from Prospect Point.

On November 16th I accepted the post of staff nurse for general duties at the Nanaimo General Hospital on Vancouver Island. I remember going to the shops and buying two white nylon uniform dresses which cost $9 for two, which I thought was exceedingly good value, and some white stockings and shoes (being the accepted mode of a nurse's dress). I also went to CBC radio station to tell them I had found a job but was still interested in broadcasting. Bill Buckingham, Ray Whitehouse and Ted Levac all helped me and I had an interview with two script writers in the Vancouver Hotel.

On the 20th I sailed to Vancouver Island in the *Princess of Nanaimo*, seen off by my Aunt and Uncle. The sea was calm and there were islands everywhere. At the Nanaimo dock I took a taxi up to the hospital which could be seen on a distant hillside overlooking the small town. The houses were mainly made of wood and had been owned by miners, Nanaimo having been a mining town for many years.

Miss Kelly, the Matron, met me and took me to a miner's house where I was to have a room until one became vacant at the hospital. At the nurses' home, just at the back of the hospital, I was made most welcome and, hearing that I was a singer, I was asked if I would sing at a nurse's wedding the next week! I did.

And so I began nursing at the Nanaimo General. We were woken at 6.15, breakfast was at 6.40 and we went on duty at 7am. I started work on what was called the old men's ward. I remember some of the patients quite well. Two old men, who were brothers, were driving a cart with a team of horses, when a lady hooted a horn behind them. The horses bolted and one of the men put out his foot to take the jerk and the board fell through in front. Both men dropped between the horses and the wheels and were dragged along with the cart and one of them, my patient, broke his leg and fell sideways. The press reported that both were said to be recovering but his brother had now developed chicken-pox!

On my first afternoon off, I went down to meet the manager of CHUB, the local radio station in Nanaimo. They were very welcoming and, having already heard from the Vancouver CBC, they thought they might be able to give me some part-time work and if so, would phone me at the hospital, but, he told me there was no money with which to pay me! I told him I didn't mind, I had a job and it would be good experience for me.

That evening in the nurses' home, there was what they called a 'shower' which is a gathering of friends to bring presents for the person celebrating a birthday or wedding. One of the nurses was getting married and we were all celebrating! Drinks, especially beer, flowed freely in the home and their boyfriends also used to drop in and out quite frequently. Most of them were 'loggers' in the forests around Nanaimo. We had great fun. A dear old dog used to make his home with us and these naughty men used to give him beer to drink and he would dance around or lie on his back pawing the air and singing. I found this somewhat distressing and said so; they rarely did it again.

On the 25th I went down to St Paul's, the Anglican church, and met the vicar Rev Albert Hendy and the organist Ray Hutchcroft and practised *Ave Maria* in the church for the wedding. It was a beautiful little church and its parishioners were very friendly people who were extremely kind to me. Albert's wife Eleanor was particularly welcoming and I became very fond of their two little girls, Ann and Grace. I nursed Ann in the hospital when she developed pneumonia and used to babysit with them both when their parents wanted to go out and my duties allowed it.

During my journey from England, particularly on the boat crossing, I had handmade several hundred Christmas cards and thought I could sell them to make some much needed money. One day I went into a very small café, the Esquire, and meeting the owners Alf and Angie McKee, I discovered they had come over from England some years before and they were really pleased to have personal news from 'home'. From that day we became firm friends and they were exceptionally good to me; they would never let me pay for any food or drinks I had at their café. When they heard about my Christmas cards they insisted on putting them up for sale in their café and then (I'm sure they persuaded them) all their friends bought them! They were a wonderful couple and I was devastated later when their café caught fire. I was rehearsing with the Nanaimo Choral Society when we heard fire engines racing past and could smell smoke. As we left the building we could see smoke coming from a building in the high street. I ran along and to my horror saw the café on fire and firemen going in with hoses. I stood nearby to see if I could be of any help and to find out if Alf and Angie were still inside. Then I heard that Angie had gone to have a rest in the Malaspina Hotel and left something frying on the gas flame. Alf had gone to see if she was feeling better. I was very relieved. I tried to help a fire officer who had collapsed in the street from smoke inhalation. As I sat on the ground beside him a press reporter came up and took a photo of us both which went into the local paper stating that 'Pinky was helping' – why Pinky?

I had only been working at the hospital for a short time when

107

I got a phone call from CHUB. They wanted to talk to me. I went down in my free time and saw Chuck. 'Would you be interested in producing and presenting a children's programme? You will be free to do it however you want. We have never had one and I am sure it will be very popular.' *Would I?* There was nothing I would have liked better!

We agreed that I would start the next day. HEAVENS! What had I let myself in for? I went into a hospital office, put some paper into the typewriter and started typing for the first time ever, and wrote my first script. Make an opening slogan, choose music to precede and end the programme, write a script, decide on a book to read, write instructions for the radio engineer, then type all that I had written, then GO TO BED!

The next day I went on duty, did my shift and then went down to CHUB, gave the script to the engineer and then started going into the studio. As I was about to open the door, the engineer said, 'Heh! What are we going to call you?'

'I've no idea,' I replied. 'Not Miss Vlasto, not Nancy, what shall we call me?'

'Pinky,' he said, 'you are wearing a pink cardigan – hurry up there is just one minute to go!' I went into the studio, sat down at the microphone and watched my cue to start. Nerve-wracking!

The music we had chosen for the programme was coming through the speakers and then I was cued in with the words which were to become my routine introduction: 'Draw up your chairs little boys and girls and make yourself at home. Glue your ears to your radio, for this programme's all your own.' And I was off! This was the pattern of broadcasting every weekday from December 18th 1951 for a quarter of an hour, always introduced as Pinky. This name was to follow me wherever I went. When my hospital work coincided with the time of my broadcast, I used to record it the day before, after I had finished my programme that day.

After leaving a dance ball one evening I forgot to pick up my little handbag. In the morning I called in at the RCMP (Royal Canadian Mounted Police) – no, they hadn't received anything. Then onto the Nanaimo Free Press – no, they hadn't received anything; why not put it in an advert? So they put in an article asking if anyone had seen it and that it belonged to 'Pinky' at the Nanaimo Hospital. They told me that I was only known by the name Pinky in the town so that was the best name to use. I got it back!

Having the freedom to present this programme as I wished, I did my best to engage the children with the wider community and we made scrapbooks as gifts to various children's hospitals in the hope of lifting their spirits while confined to bed.

In December I nursed in the maternity ward. I was rather out of my depth here, never having done midwifery training in England, but there were other nurses who had. This was followed by a time in the children's ward.

On days off I often took a cabin in the night boat across to Vancouver. On December 14th I was invited by Miss Palliser of the School of Nursing in Vancouver to attend the candlelight capping ceremony. This was a delightful moment when the nurses received their first caps after leaving training school. The nurses involved sang songs, played the piano and read poems all by candlelight, which ended in the singing of *God Save the King* and them receiving their caps from the matron. A truly memorable occasion which I thought we might emulate in Britain.

I joined the choir of St Paul's Church and sang there whenever I was off-duty on Sundays, sometimes doing the solos. On December 23rd I sang the solo *'Come unto me all ye that labour'* from *Messiah* at the carol service. On Christmas Eve we sang carols all around the hospital wards carrying candles which were in glass containers wrapped around with red paper.

Christmas telegrams came from my parents and family which made me feel very homesick but were very welcome. Up to this time I had been troubled with continuing pain from my back but now it was becoming increasingly severe; lifting patients and making beds was difficult. I was given injections by my own doctor but the nursing was so heavy and demanding that they had little effect.

I now went on night duty which was from 12 midnight to 8am (three eight hour shifts). I used to relieve the night sister Mary Holmes (to remain my friend till this day). On the first night we had an emergency laparotomy, a haemorrhaging woman and a diabetic coma. I realised that we were in business in a big way!

The view of the town and harbour was a magical picture under a heavy fall of snow. The surrounding area was so peaceful and calm and the only sound was the hooting of the train announcing itself as it approached the town. I had to walk down this snowy hill every day to do my broadcast and then back up again to the nurses' home. It was excellent exercise, though the thought of it now makes me wonder how I did it! I certainly lost weight, which was a good thing.

On December 31st 1951 I attended a lecture by the Nanaimo Civil Defence on 'Atomic Warfare: Precautions and Nursing Procedures', which indicated the fear of atomic warfare in all countries. We saw the New Year in standing on our ward balcony overlooking the sea and harbour in the distance. Snow muffled the sound of parties going on in the streets and nearby houses and the ships' hooters pierced the cold night air.

Early in January 1952 I went to Cooks to see if I could change my six months round trip ticket (kindly given to me by my parents) to extend my stay until June and travel back through the west coast of America, where lived cousins of my mother's, and via Wyoming to catch the *Media* again from New York. This they agreed to do. I was delighted and extended my work permit up to June 13th.

And so my work and broadcast routine continued. Having made many friends, my social life was full and satisfying. Singing with the Nanaimo Choral Society took me from one end of the island to the other and many towns in between. I was invited to do many of the solos and even represented Wales at one of our concerts! Thankfully we sported daffodils, NOT leeks, on our evening dress clothes.

Choral Group Well Received At Ladysmith

LADYSMITH, May 1. — The Nanaimo Choral Society, a choir of some 60 voices, presented a rare musical treat to the citizens of Ladysmith in its second concert appearance here at First United Church Wednesday night.

A capacity audience demonstrated by their applause full appreciation of the fine choral and solo work presented under the direction of Catherine Alexander, A.T.C.M.

Accompanist was Ethel Findlay, A.T.C.M.; assistant accompanist, Hilda M. Nuttall, A.T.C.M.

E. W. Forward, former choirmaster of the church, expressed appreciation and said he was particularly pleased with two numbers by Handel: "Largo," sung by Nancy Vlasto, and "O, Thou That Tellest," from the Messiah, solo by Ethel Findlay.

The choir was sponsored here by the junior women's auxiliary, and president Mrs. W. J. Seaton presented corsages. A social hour followed.

I began inviting children to take part in my programme, interviewing them and encouraging them to sing or play their instruments; I think I enjoyed it as much as they did! I also sent messages to children on their birthdays. I ran competitions such as 'Road Safety' and got the 'Mounties' (mounted police), who had an office in Nanaimo, to come and give out the prizes. I had no trouble getting these prizes

110

because, as soon as firms heard about my programme, free books and toys arrived from everywhere in the hope that I would advertise their companies. In January, I received a letter from the manager of CHUB thanking me for the programme and telling me that he had received many compliments about it. At the studio a lady had written from Vancouver to congratulate me on my readings from *Winnie the Pooh,* all of which did my ego good as this was my first effort in creating a programme!

Sample of one many letters I received from children.

On the eve of my birthday the Programmes Manager of CHUB told me that mine was 'one of the best programmes we have on air at the moment'. That was the nicest birthday present anyone could have had. I felt quite cheerful. The radio station made records in the church of two of my solos which they gave to me as a present. I'd never had that done before!

February 6th brought the terrible news of the death of King George VI. I referred to this in my programme that day and our thoughts were with Princess Elizabeth, now Queen Elizabeth.

I spent ten days in bed with back pain. My Uncle George and Aunt Ailsa came over from Vancouver to take me back to see a specialist there. They kept me in bed at their home for a week. I was then allowed to return to Nanaimo but not to work for another week. So I resumed my usual round of nursing, broadcasting and singing and was so happy to be back.

On March 18th 1952 there was a terrible accident on the Port Alberni Road at Parksville. A truck laden with logs crashed into the Port Alberni stores; the truck smashed into the Mickey Dress store and the trailer and logs slewed round into the Shelldrake Jeweller's Store propping up the building which came down on top of them. Six people were injured, four of them seriously, and we were warned at the hospital, via the local radio, to be ready to receive them. The local radio was most useful in alerting us to imminent admissions.

One time a lady had been cleaning a coat with spirit on top of her ironing board. As she rubbed it vigorously there was an enormous explosion and she was blown through a plate glass window onto the lawn outside. She was badly burnt all over her body. We received warning via the radio as we worked in A&E and immediately filled a bath with tepid salted water. As she was brought in we put her straight into the bath so her entire body was submerged. I remember her red hot face was so swollen it covered her lips, eyes and nose so she could hardly breathe. I 'specialled' her for some time, much of the nursing being done on an inflatable mattress and through tubes out of various orifices. She never complained and was an example to us. I believe it was about five months later that she walked out of our hospital somewhat scarred but alive.

Because of our proximity to the forests many of our casualties were injured by falling from tall trees, being cut or having limbs amputated by chain saws. While I was there a group of us were taken into the woods by one of the men working there and given a demonstration of felling trees 'top rigging' which were to be turned into telegraph posts. Ed Herman was one of them and he was very proud that he had been chosen, on an earlier visit, to accompany the King and Queen and to demonstrate top rigging.

Another of my patients was a hermit. When in the Canadian army in 1918, he was hit on the back of his neck with a rifle butt which cracked a vertebra. He suffered endless headaches after this but discharged himself from the hospital before much could be done to help him. He didn't have any small talk but what he did say was quite profound and informed. He was a fascinating gentleman.

Many of our patients were indigenous Indians, some of whom lived in reserves up in the woods bordering the town. One day I found a patient sitting in the basin in his room and using it as a toilet. Clearing up defecation material was just one of the nurse's endless duties but I was very quick to show him the way to the toilet! One of my Indian patients was a very dear, polite and delightful man – Walter Fraser. He was aged 42 but sadly he died. I was deeply affected by this as I became very fond of him.

I got an appointment with the RCMP to have a learners' driving test (before I was allowed to start driving a car). I had to put an X as an answer to the questions, sit on a seat and put the brakes on, which showed a red light, and take an eye test. I was told I was 'average': 'some old men over eighty have been known to do worse.' It cost one dollar. Then I had my first driving lesson with a gentleman friend. We drove to Wellington and back in his ten thousand dollar car. I was terrified but excited.

In May I wrote a slogan for the Nanaimo Free Press competition to encourage people to raise money for the funding of the Blood Transfusion Unit. I won! It was this: 'Every cent you give helps others to live!' I still have the cutting announcing the fact that I won it. But if there *was* an award I never received it!

Albert and Eleanor's little girl, Ann, was brought in with pneumonia, diarrhoea and vomiting and was very ill, and the next day her sister Grace, too, had the same symptoms. I was glad to be allowed to nurse them. They soon recovered with the use of penicillin (which had come into use during the war).

On another day that month I found myself in charge of a ward with eighteen children, four of whom were 'bottle babies', and other patients. I wonder, now, how I coped with just one nurse's aide to help me.

On May 26th I had a surprise visit from my two uncles, George and Tom, who 'sat in' on my afternoon broadcast. I believe they found it quite interesting. Then they took off to join their family at Yellow Point on Vancouver Island.

My last working day at the hospital was on June 9th 1952. In the afternoon my doctor, Dr McLean, his wife and their little girl, Barbie, took me to Port Alberni for the day and a picnic lunch in the woods at Little Qualicum. I was sad to say goodbye; he had been very good to me.

My colleagues, who had been such good friends and such fun to be with, made sure they gave me a good 'send-off' party. As darkness descended, they took me down to the sea where there was a raft several hundred yards out in Departure Bay. There, by the shore, was a large motor boat with flags and bunting and messages hanging from all possible places. All around the edge, the entire circumference of the boat, were grape fruits cut in half, like a yellow ribbon. This was a reference to my liking grapefruit when they were all drinking beer which I loathed! We all got on to the boat and set off for the raft. The sea was a little choppy but we thought it would be fun to get onto the raft and – with our gramophone playing records – we could dance on its large wooden surface. We got the little dinghy free and held it tight to the side of the boat. Four of the ladies got in and the attached rope was gently run out against the choppy sea. They got on to the raft and sent the dinghy back to the boat. Three others and I were just stepping into it and I had just put my camera into the boat when it started to overturn. Madly we grabbed the arms of two of the ladies who were being sucked under the boat by the swirling tide and pulled them back on board. But my precious camera (which was full of photos) disappeared into the dark waters. I was very sad. We tried again and eventually got all of us onto the raft and there we danced by the light of the moon. My colleagues drank beer and I ate grapefruit! What a wonderful send-off. I have never forgotten it.

On the day of my final broadcast the CHUB staff invited me to join a party as I was rounding off my last session. They had invited all the parents and youngsters who had written in or taken part in my programmes. I was so touched. The triplet boys had made some pink earrings and a brooch out of some stiff card and added silver stars, which I put on and wore during the party, and kept in my precious box for more than sixty years! Their wonderful cards and letters told me that my efforts had all been worthwhile and I knew they, and I, would miss each other. Many years later, I was told that after I had left no one else had ever taken on a children's programme which was sad to hear.

My colleagues at CHUB kindly presented me with a photo of all the children at 'Kiddies Korner', as they called it. Among them, listed on the back of the photo, are Ken Milne, Lynn Porter, Gary Porter, Jackie Barley, Jill Hurford, the Marshall triplets, Larry Krutko, Gloria Krutko, Nicky Krutko and Judy Carmichael. Although Anne and Grace Hendy were not present on the day of the photo shoot, I had a chance to see them again when I went back to Nanaimo in 2004; sadly their parents had died earlier. I also stayed with Jill Hurford briefly.

Then I was invited to a beach picnic with the Choral Society who wished to give me yet another send-off! We had a wonderful picnic, drinks, cooked 'weiners' (sausages) and toasted marshmallows round a wood fire on the beach. We sang songs and chatted. Then Mr Kelly made a farewell speech and told me they were getting me a book of poems written by a disabled lady, a native of Nanaimo; they would send it to me as it had not yet arrived.

A friend of Mr Westwood kindly drove me to Victoria to say my farewells to my cousins Ann and David. Three hours later I caught the bus back to Nanaimo, a three-hour trip and a beautiful drive with glimpses of the sea all the way.

The St Paul's church choir gave me a wooden model of the Nanaimo Bastion at a party after the last Sunday service.

On Friday, 13th June 1952 I left Nanaimo, and I must admit to shedding tears, as did my friends, and set out for Seattle.

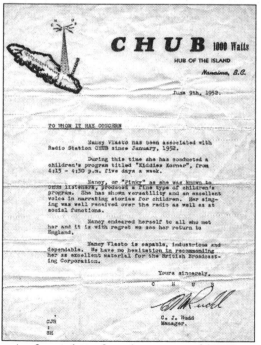

A reference letter from the manager of CHUB.

Chapter Seven

I visited my uncle for one last time before leaving Vancouver, and boarded a train to Seattle where my mother's cousins Elizabeth and Don Peterson lived. It was a most comfortable train. There was a running commentary telling us what we were seeing as we passed through the countryside which was most interesting. In the corridor outside the carriage was a large container from which we could get ice cold water. About an hour and half later, we passed Bellingham and saw our first American flag. Dozens of oil containers passed us by and on one I noticed a sign 'Milwaukee' on it; this was where my mother was born. There were enormous fields of strawberries alongside the track. I went through the train to the lunch car, a super deluxe compartment only found on the new 'streamliner' of this route.

We arrived in Seattle in the state of Washington at 1pm where I was met by Elizabeth, or 'Honey' as she was known to us, and her son Steven. They said they saw someone carrying three suitcases and guessed it was me! They took me to my first drive-in snack bar and then we drove about 60 miles in and around Seattle. It was a beautiful city, hilly and surrounded by sea and lakes.

We went to the Boeing factory to pick up her husband Don. The factory employed twenty thousand people and Don was an engineer there. We drove around the hills to look down on the planes – the then new jet plane was much in evidence.

Then driving across a floating bridge we arrived at their home at North East, 14th Street, Bellevue. The view from the terrace overlooking the city was breathtaking, especially as the lights went on and sparkled like diamonds in the darkness.

The next day we swam in the very cold lake, but fortunately the sun was quite hot! Honey took me to Frederick store ('the best store in Seattle') where I was amazed by how modern it was, with nylon everywhere. In the evening Don took me to see my first baseball game 'The Seattle Rainiers', we shouted ourselves hoarse! I seemed to spend a lot of time eating delicious ice cream.

On June 27th my cousins saw me off on the 9.20 train to Warlock. I had four very friendly porters in my carriage. One of them got off the train with me to buy some chocolate and for me to send an air letter card home. He remarked over his shoulder, 'Man, you'll sure wear yourself out!'

Here another cousin met me and drove me to his parents' home in Tacoma. Emma and Pud were exceptional people. They had arranged a quite wonderful trip to show me all there was to see down the west coast of California as far as the Mexican border. It was absolutely fascinating. Every day gorgeous hot sun shone down on us and we travelled many miles in their comfortable air-conditioned car. Everywhere we went we ate strawberries and cream and ice cream. My poor figure; but I was in my element!

For those who know it, or have a map in front of you, we were on a long drive via Kosmos, White Pass, over the mountain to Yakima (160 miles). We arrived at Toppenish at 6pm and spent the night in a lovely motel (two double beds, shower and toilet cost $8.85). After supper out, we went to what appeared to be a mainly Indian town and saw a crazy American movie.

After a large breakfast of ham, eggs, hot cakes and coffee, we set off from Toppenish and went via Goldendale to Maryhill. There we visited an old castle (I was told that the Queen of Romania had 'lent a hand'). A certain Tim Hill had built this as his dream house with a glorious view down the Colombia River. There were massive granite mountains and views for miles. He was hoping to be a landlord, with servants, and to have tenants who would make vineyards and generally cultivate the land along the banks of the river. However this never came to pass and he turned it into a museum. There was an interesting collection of works of art, particularly from Romania, Greece and India.

We then drove on and stopped at Bonneville Dam in Oregon

(the third largest in the world in 1952) and watched the salmon, and other fish, jumping up the swift running water to the spawning ground in the calm lake at the top. They were counted by an electric 'counter' as they swam across over the top of a special platform. Once the spawn developed into fish they swam down to the sea and remained there for four years when the whole cycle started again. I found this fascinating to observe. (How lucky we are in these days to have so much detail of nature brought into our homes via television.) Then we drove back the four hundred miles home.

The next day I was asked to sing a solo, *The Holy City,* at their Presbyterian church in Toledo and then met some of the congregation. Afterwards, my cousin Pud let me drive his jeep to where his coal seams were on his property. Until quite recently I had a small piece of coal I had pick-axed out of the ground. I'm quite sad I have lost the only evidence that, for one day, I became a miner!

I was driven to Portland which took two hours, spent the night there and then got onto a train – the Shasta Daylight – a wonderful train which was most comfortable. Superb scenery lined the way to Oakland Pier, from where I went on to San Francisco by ferry over moonlit water under the Oakland Bay Bridge. I took two street cars, lugging my two cases! People were very helpful and got me to the YWCA where, thank goodness, I had made reservations. It was now 1am. Everyone else turning up was being turned away.

The next morning July 2nd I had breakfast at a coffee bar across the road with a ticket provided by the YWCA. After this I went to the St Francis Hotel on Union Square and took a three hour coach tour of the city. It was most interesting; we visited the Mission Dolores founded in 1776. The church is a hundred and fourteen feet long, twenty-two feet wide and the walls four feet thick. The roof is made of the original timber and tiles. The timeless beams of rough hewn redwood lashed together with rawhide. They used vegetable colours to decorate the ceilings. It was all most attractive. On the way we passed down streets where there were luxury homes costing thirty thousand dollars (in 1952!), a visit to Twin Peaks gave us a wonderful view of the attractive city below, then to Fisherman's Wharf which ended a most enjoyable tour. I loved San Francisco.

I next caught the train to Los Angeles where not one, but seven, of my mother's cousins welcomed me at the station.

Eula and Shivas Mitchell told me I had 'a Mitchell look' about me! My impressions were of sun and palm trees as we approached their home. That evening they took me to the planetarium (one of five in the world at that time); the title of the talk and accompanying filmed back drop of the sky was 'Journey to the Moon'. We went up onto the ramparts to see Los Angeles spread out below us. Back home we watched Florence Chadwick (who swam across the English Channel both ways) swimming a twenty-three mile crossing here.

The next day the family took me to Forest Lawn Memorial Park. It covered a vast area and contained several churches of varying denominations. There were flowers everywhere and beautifully manicured lawns. It was frivolously called a place for 'hatch, match and dispatch' for one could – for a large fee – pre-pay one's christening, marriage and funeral! We saw a dramatic revealing of a reproduction of the painting The Last Supper; with soft music played as the velvet curtains draped across it opened. I found this too sentimental and commercial and it rather spoilt my feelings for the beauty of the site which was on a cliff overlooking Los Angeles.

While shopping in LA, I was fascinated by the wealth of goods in the shops, compared with the dearth of goods in England, and bought three nylon dresses to take home with me! England was still very short of attractive clothing and I was mesmerised by what I was seeing here. I was taken to the Henry E. Huntington library, museum, art gallery and garden and a 'posh' shop called Bullocks Wiltshire where we had a delicious lunch with a mannequin (fashion) show thrown in. During a drive all around Beverley Hills, we saw the luxurious film stars' homes and passed rows of orange and lemon trees. Most nights we went to barbecues; I do not believe I had heard of them in Britain in those days.

My family took me to a television show in one of the studios at Hollywood. We stood for an hour at the front of a queue and got good seats. It was in a 'Bandstand' show with clever and amusing acts. On the way home we went to the Chinese Movie Theatre where all the famous film stars had signed their names and left the imprint of their feet and hands in a slab of pavement in front of the building.

119

On July 7th my uncle went to the police station to try to trace his dog which had been missing for some time. The police handed him the dog's collar as it had been run over; we were all very sad. The next day was a hot sunny morning with a heavy mist. My uncle came into my room to say that he had arranged for us to go and visit the RKO film studio (he was, I think, involved in a professional way with them). We arrived there and were taken to have lunch in the cafeteria where we joined the 'stars' and everyone and anyone working in the studios. We saw several stars including Jane Russell. A young man took us around the 'shops' and showed us everything that went on in the background. We saw the miniature ape that was used in the film *King Kong* and were then taken onto the set where they were shooting the film and stood right bedside Robert Newton and Linda Darnell. The former had, apparently, been so drunk and unable to rehearse because of it, that they paid his then girlfriend two thousand dollars every week for her to sit by him, on the set, to stop him going out to get a drink. Two weeks before we were there he had married her, but there she was, flirting from one actor to another, combing and waving their hair as if she had done it all her life and she really thought she was being of use!

After watching for about fifteen minutes we looked around the back drops and off-the-scene actions. Each of the stars had their own caravan around the set where they retired after each shoot. The policemen at the gate had taken my camera and I retrieved it as we took our leave. As we left I realised that I still had a strong desire to have something to do with drama (as I did with ballet) in the years ahead.

My uncle had booked us into a motel apartment right on the beach at Laguna called The River Apartments. It was modern, equipped with everything one could need, and had a balcony protruding over the sea which pounded on the beach below.

As a sea mist descended upon us, we drove to La Jolla (pronounced La Hoya). We drove past vast oil fields along the coast on either side of the road. In La Jolla I swam in the Pacific for the first time, plunging in on the waves which rolled up onto the golden sands. There was always a lifeguard keeping watch. Unfortunately as we approached the Mexican border I realised I did not have my passport with me, so we were unable to cross the border, but beyond the check point I could see a man sitting outside his house, his sombrero over his face, with his donkey beside him. It would have made a wonderful painting.

We spent a night in the Fairhill Apartment Motel and then on July 10th turned the car round homewards. On the way we called in on a family friend who had a house in the centre of her eleven hundred acre ranch of orange and lemon trees. Her Mexican cook made us a Mexican meal using rice as the basic food with avocadoes followed by peaches and cream and cake. I simply dared not stand on the scales during my trip! Afterwards I picked an orange, a grapefruit and a lemon to take home to my mother as a 'thank you' for her having such wonderful cousins who were so good to me.

Back in Los Angeles my uncle drove me to the top of Mount Wilson overlooking the city. There was a wonderful view with all the lights twinkling. We looked through a twelve-inch telescope and saw Mars travelling across the lens at a good speed. After we returned home my family had yet another treat for me. They took me to the Greek open air theatre to see the Russian Ballet of Monte Carlo dancing the *Nutcracker*, *Swan Lake* and *Scheherazade*; most enjoyable. The next day I posted a parcel of clothes home but I can't remember if they were mine to save me carrying them or a gift for my family to surprise them.

On July 12th a farewell party was given for me to which sixteen members of the family came. Before leaving England I had been told that this 'get together' of the family was going to take place. So I got a big bag and filled it with sixteen small, cheap and fun gifts for everyone to have and dressed them all up in attractive paper. They all took turns in putting their hands in the bag and taking a gift out, they were then allowed to exchange them with someone else if they wanted. I remember that one was a pair of frilly knickers which caused much amusement when one of the men opened it! We played charades, exchanged photos, and I read out a letter from my mother to her American family. The next day I went to the station to take the Streamliner to Cheyenne in Wyoming, to yet another cousin! This was a long and enjoyable trip.

We went past hot dry land, large rounded boulders, cacti and palm trees, then through the San Bernadine Mountains, Afton Canyon and other places to Death Valley during the evening. As my back, which had given me continued trouble throughout the

121

f

week of my journey, had become very painful, I decided to pay for a sleeper which cost me five dollars for the extra rail fare, though I never understood why, and six dollars for the sleeper. It was well worth it though the train ride was far from smooth.

We passed through Las Vegas, Salt Lake City, Ogden and Green River. There was snow just east of Green River the day before, but this day the sun was warm despite a breeze, which was quite cool, coming from the mountain. After tea in the restaurant, the train arrived in Cheyenne at 6.30pm July 14th.

My cousin's daughter met me at the station and drove me to the Wheatland HR Ranch just as a beautiful sunset embraced the grassy plains and moors. Jean suddenly said, 'Well what do you know, there's A CAR!' We only passed four during the seventy mile drive! On arriving at the ranch my Mitchell cousins were on the veranda with their grandsons Robert, Steven and baby Scott. Horses were standing lazily tied up to the wooden veranda. This visit was one that I treasure daily in my heart. It was a very relaxed home with very gentle and kind people and the boys were a great joy to me. Every day they would arrive before breakfast and call up to my window to tell me my horse, Emmie, was ready for me. I'd throw on my bathing costume and a pair of jeans and dash downstairs where the boys were on their ponies at the front door. Then we set out riding over the fields and alongside the river, jumping off and throwing ourselves into the water whenever we felt like it. They were such fun to be with.

One morning we watched family members, Boy and Robert Mitchell, 'lassoing' young calves. This involved lassoing them, then jumping off the horse which stops and backs up pulling the rope tight. The cowboy then slips the noose over one front leg and brings the two hind legs up and ropes them together. I never really liked watching this but got more used to it when I saw it happening at rodeos I attended.

On another occasion when we were out riding, the ranch dog, Lassie, was in a fight, right beside us, for fifteen minutes with a racoon. It looked as though the racoon was badly hurt so I dismounted and finished it off with a stick; Lassie was bleeding from her ear, nose and jaw and I think she would have been killed.

While at the ranch, the temperature hovered around 100°F. One day we went to a rodeo at Gering, Nebraska. It began at 8pm and there was thunder and flashes of lightning all the time. Once it stopped, the show began. I was completely absorbed by everything going on. Two of my cousins, who were cowboys, took part in it riding bucking broncos. It was a hundred and twenty miles each way, but there was hardly a car in sight!

We went trout fishing in a nearby stream, the catch of which we had for meals, and the boys and I continued riding and swimming. I was in seventh heaven! I sent my parents a postcard from Chugwater, a town which lies in south-eastern Wyoming. I was told it was so named because, in the olden days, cattle used to be rounded up and forced over the edge to their death, making a chug sound as they broke their necks, presumably to save them having to kill the animals individually. To my relief, I was assured that they no longer did this!

On July 21st the family took me to the station where I caught the City of Portland train to Chicago. I wanted to try and take part in the radio programme 'Welcome Travellers' for which I had heard I would receive some payment. Someone meets the train at Chicago and whips you off to the studio where you are interviewed. Unfortunately we were too late. I had very little money, so, having the rest of the day to kill before catching my train to New York, I went out to catch a bus to go to the studios. I saw a taxi parked nearby and asked him which bus went near it. He said, 'You're English aren't you?' I said yes. 'Well then, get in, I'll take you.' I told him I couldn't afford a cab and again asked about the bus. After going on like this for a while, I said, 'Thank you but I have warned you I will not be able to pay you.' He said, 'I heard you, that's okay.' So I got in and he proceeded to drive me all around Chicago pointing out to me the direction of Milwaukee and giving me a running commentary. He was a fountain of knowledge, especially the 'juicy' bits. Once, looking at the hoarding outside one of the cinemas which showed a rather naked woman, he said, 'My! She's sure got a mean shimmie on!' Having found the studio closed, he then duly took me back to the station. I was extremely grateful to him and asked him to give me his address. He then rather spoilt everything by saying, 'You couldn't spend another night in Chicago before you leave?' I guessed what he was after, but explained that my ship was waiting for me in New York. . . saved by the bell! On returning home, I sent him a Tootles tie with a letter of gratitude but did not give him my address. And so I took my last train to New York.

In New York I went to the YMCA by yellow cab with my, now, four cases. The temperature was in the 90s. I spent the morning trying to track down Angela Dukes (Marie Rambert's daughter) but was unlucky. I tried five different ballet schools. One of them, Ballet Theatre School, had known Marie Rambert before the Mercury Theatre days. In the evening I went to an NBC television show which wasn't very good.

It was extremely hot that night in my YMCA room. My night clothes were soaked through. The next day I went to NBC studios in Radio City again and they took my name and address in case they wanted to contact me that day for an interview but, as I was leaving for England the next day, July 25th, it was highly unlikely there would be time for this. This day I took a bus to Altmans where I had a delicious breakfast of bananas and cream and coffee and toast. I bought sixty dollars and five cents worth of canned foods and ordered them to be sent to the ship at the docks. These were to take back to my family to supplement the shortage of food.

I had lunch with a friend in the very smart Drake Hotel and then went to the Courtland White Star office to try and get a lower berth in my cabin. As mentioned earlier I was returning home by the *Media*, the same ship I arrived in from England. I then walked to 292 Madison Avenue and queued for one hour to get a sailing permit (this was to save me time the next morning). In Times Square I saw a film which featured Michael Wilding and Anna Neagle. I was impressed that buses only cost ten cents to go anywhere but twelve cents in Fifth Avenue! A friend remarked to me, 'New York is luxurious without any of the comforts.'

At 8.30am I got up and took a taxi to the docks, Pier 90, and there was the beautiful *Media* ready and waiting for me. I had to book a deck chair and a seat in the dining room and found that evening I had been put at the Chief Purser's table. It was an interesting mix of people; among them a couple who were racing-car fans, a couple in the antiques business and a couple who were spiritualists. Conversation at the table was fascinating. The first day out the sea was quite rough. I am not a good sailor!

There was never a dull moment throughout the trip. Every day we were issued with a card giving our programme of events, such as the *Media*'s orchestra mid-morning music, deck games, news broadcast, tote on unit figure of the day's run, cocktail hour, horse riding and dancing time. One evening I was invited to sing with the orchestra. This was quite an experience for which I was awarded a 'special prize'.

On August 1st 1952 we sighted the coast of Ireland and so, nine days and three thousand and ninety-seven miles later from when we left New York, on Saturday, August 2nd we docked at Liverpool. From here I took the train to London. I noticed that everyone else got into a 1st class compartment except me! I got into a filthy little 3rd class carriage at the very end of the train; there were two very pleasant railwaymen and another man in the shipping business with whom I had an interesting conversation.

As the train pulled into the station, I saw my parents and Helen who had come to meet me and we all drove home to Westerham. So came to an end a very happy and wonderful period of my life which I shall never forget and an experience for which I will always be grateful.

Chapter Eight

Returning from my time in Canada and America I found a letter from Robert Barr awaiting me. It was to ask me if I would like to take part in a second television play he was producing, this time to have a larger acting role. It was to be called *To Save a Life* and rehearsals would start in September. Although I had written to apply for a post at Charing Cross Hospital in London I had no immediate plans and I was delighted to be given this opportunity. I had, of course, to join the actors' union Equity which, on the strength of my broadcasting experiences, I was informed had been accepted.

In the meantime, Robert Barr, on hearing that I was not in full time work, told me he had a good friend who was in senior management at the Frigidaire factory in Colindale, London, whom he knew was needing someone as holiday relief to run the factory surgery. Would I be interested? I told him I would be, since Charing Cross Hospital had not yet replied.

Within three days I had been interviewed at Frigidaire and accepted as a temporary placement. My job involved keeping the surgery stock in good order, doing a 'round' of the factory every morning to check on the welfare of the workers and to warn them of any potential hazards, running daily surgery times, treating minor injuries and ailments and assisting the doctor on his visits. I also talked with the workers so that we could know each other. I had to 'clock in' as did all the workers and found it quite intimidating.

The surgery where I saw my patients was small, with a waiting room, and approached by steps leading up from the factory floor. In the middle of the building there was a slope and a covered way where an ambulance could draw up right alongside. Everywhere around the factory lay stacks of sheets of metal with razor sharp edges. These filled me with horror! They were to be the cause of many of the injuries that came to my surgery.

The factory had an excellent system for first aid emergencies. Every day there was a team on call. When the emergency bell rang throughout the factory, one of the team would down tools and run to the surgery; the other one would go straight to the ambulance and drive it round. They would then dash around to the nearest hospital with the injured worker, thus saving many lives in the process – an excellent organisation. It was an experience I was glad to have.

I was shaken by an incident when one day a worker was brought up to me with a severely injured arm – sheet metal, as usual, was the culprit – and he was bleeding badly. His haemorrhaging was so violent that blood had squirted all over the surgery walls. After he had gone to hospital in our ambulance, and wanting to save any unpleasantness for the waiting patients, I started to wash the blood off the wall. 'I wouldn't do that if I were you, sister,' said a voice. When I asked why not he told me that, 'All the cleaning staff might come out on strike!' That was my first experience of union action on the job! What had we come to?

I worked at the factory for a month in October before I heard from the Matron at Charing Cross Hospital to say I would start there on December 8th. The gentleman who had appointed me seemed quite sad when I told him I was moving on, and gave me a very kind complimentary letter of reference. And so my short appointment at Frigidaire came to an end. In some ways I was really quite sorry to be leaving there; it had been an interesting and enlightening experience to work in a factory, so totally different from anything else I had done.

During this time I was in the throes of all the rehearsals for *To Save a Life* which were held in a large room at 60 Paddington Street over the period 24th November to 3rd December. Studio rehearsal was held on 4th December for the live transmission the following day. It was so good to work with many of the same cast who were also in the *Casualty Ward* production.

Programmes were still transmitted *live* so there was no room for errors! This put considerable pressure on the actors and all concerned with the production of the programme. The day the live programme went out from Crystal Palace on December 5th 1952, I was playing a nurse looking after a sick little boy who was lying in an oxygen tent, so he was surrounded by the clear plastic sides of the tent and the oxygen entered through a hole in the corner. Suddenly a cry went up from the props lady, 'Where's the cylinder key?' We all scrabbled around on the floor under the bed to find it. We could hear the 'cue in' music beginning to fade over the intercom and the call 'Two minutes!' rang out. I noticed the little boy was getting quite distressed, turning very red in the face. The countdown began '10, 9, 8, 7, 6. . .' and at '5' someone called out 'Here it is!" and handed it to me. I jumped out of the way of the cameras and turned on the cylinder, closing the open flaps of the tent as I did so, and letting in the oxygen just as the word 'ACTION!' rang out. I know I was breathing heavily as the camera closed in behind me! Apart from this, I thoroughly enjoyed the experience. Good reviews in the papers the next day must have been rewarding for Robert Barr who was a much respected producer.

On returning home I found a letter from Gordon Smith, the Drama Booking Agent Manager for the BBC. It said, 'Mr Gielgud has asked me to arrange a booking for you.' On October 28th I received a letter stating that an audition would be held at Broadcasting House and would include the use of dialects. Following the 'features' audition the report was sent to me 'we considered your performances interesting but, unfortunately, not entirely suitable for our normal programme purposes.' I was quite disappointed.

Around this time my cousin Ellen Mitchell came over from America to stay with me. I thought she might enjoy seeing around the country by hitch-hiking, my favourite way of getting around. So we set off to hitch-hike to Wales. We travelled via Cardiff, going over the Brecon Beacons and back via Windsor, where we had lunch in a pub at the bottom of a hill leading to the castle. As we left we almost bumped into a ruddy looking gentleman and asked him the best way to get to the main entrance of the castle. He told us how to get there and suggested we asked for a certain gentleman, whom he was sure would be able to help us.

We approached the armed soldiers at the entrance – very dishevelled and with rucksacks on our backs – and asked where we would find this gentleman. His house was pointed out to us within the castle walls. To our amazement a large, brightly painted model crown was over the top of the front door. We looked in dismay and debated whether we should ring the bell. In our carefree, happy mood we decided to take the risk and chance our luck.

A charming lady opened the door, smilingly taking in the sight of these two travel-weary, dishevelled women, and said, 'Hello can I help you?' We did our best to back out and apologised for bothering her, but as soon as we mentioned the name of the gentleman at the pub, she invited us in and sat us down by the lovely crackling fire in the beautiful sitting room. She appeared genuinely pleased and interested to meet us, especially when she found that my cousin came from America. She rang through to her husband who was in the castle and asked him to come to meet us and invited us to have tea with them. After a wonderful tea (we were hungry from our travels) and a chance to wash, he showed us all round the castle; my cousin was thrilled. We talked for some time before we left to hitch our way back home. It had been an amazing and happy encounter and we wrote to thank them on our return.

My application as Staff Nurse in the Diagnostic X-ray Department at Charing Cross had been accepted following a visit to the Department and an interview with the Matron. I remember feeling somewhat 'uncomfortable' when looking around the Department – it seemed so far away from my idea of nursing, as I had known it.

I met someone who was to become a long-time friend, Elisabeth Lane, who was the Staff Nurse in the Radiotherapy Department which was on the floor above mine. We discovered that we both wanted to 'live out' and not in the nurses' home in Hampstead and decided to find a room nearby to share. Having got permission to live outside the hospital as long as we were near enough to be on call, if needed, we started looking.

In no time at all we found a room at the top of a house in Craven Street, number 35, a five minute walk from the hospital. It was near St Martin-in-the-Fields and the street ran down the side of the station and parallel to Northumberland Avenue, down to the Thames. Every time a train pulled in or out of Charing Cross Station the house shook! It was built right beside the 'Arches' where long flights of narrow steps at both ends lead down through a tunnel under the railway lines above.

At the far end of the tunnel was a little flower shop which sold, among other things, tiny bunches of mixed flowers, which we thought may have been from the cast-offs of Covent Garden nearby (Covent Garden used to be near Trafalgar Square behind the hospital). These we sometimes bought as gifts or to cheer up our little room. At that time life was incredibly drab and grey, even plates and cups were plain white, no colour being allowed to decorate them. I used to buy little pots of oil paints and paint flowers and leaves onto my china and glass.

Our cosy room was tiny, with a bed on each side and a table in the middle with two chairs, and a cooker in the corner. To our great joy there was an open coal fire in the wall; I was not sure if it had been used recently but Elisabeth and I arranged for the coalman to call. We discovered an old basin-stand with an empty cupboard underneath right outside our door on the landing, just perfect for pouring the coal through the basin hole and taking it out through the door!

Another convenience we discovered, on the first day, was a tiny shop called John Garvey at the top of the steps right beneath our window. I think he sold most things anybody could have wanted. My ration book shows just how much we used it. One of us would go down and do the shopping, putting it in a basket to which we had tied a rope. The other would haul it back up to our window above. I wish all shopping was that simple!

R.B.1
16
SERIAL NO. 1
MINISTRY OF FOOD
BQ 499949
1953-1954

RATION BOOK

Surname VLASTO   Initials M A

Address 35 CRAVEN STREET
LONDON. W.C.2.

IF FOUND RETURN TO ANY FOOD OFFICE

F.O. CODE No.
4A

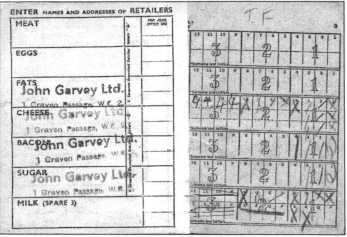

Inside the ration book – showing shopping from John Garvey.

So we were all set for a happy time ahead and we enjoyed every minute of our stay there. Our caretaker/landlord sat in his room, door open, just to the right of the front door. He only had one leg and seemed to sit there all day, every day, reading his paper, only looking up when we came in or out. He was a very friendly and helpful man, even allowing me to keep my bike in the narrow passage. (Something I am sure I would not be allowed to do in the years to come under the umbrella of Health and Safety!)

Elisabeth and I walked to and from the hospital, passing through Trafalgar Square to get there, parting to go to our various departments. Although this was a training hospital we were entirely independent.

One day in December 1952, as I was passing the church of St Martin-in-the-Fields on my way home from the hospital, I heard some beautiful singing coming from the crypt beneath the church and wandered down the old stone steps to see what was going on. I found a group of around twenty mixed-voice singers who were being conducted by a gentleman. They were all in mufti and were producing the most lovely sounds as I stood in a corner to listen.

One of the choir members saw me and drew me to the attention of the conductor, who I was to find out was the Rev. W.D. Kennedy Bell, or KB as he was known. He was the Director of Overseas Religious Broadcasts for the BBC as well as being presenter for the Temple Church in London. He immediately called out, 'Come in! Can you sing?' I said, 'Yes.' Without hesitation he said, 'Come and join us.'

That is how I came to join this wonderful choir 'The St Martin Singers' which gave me many years of joy singing an endless amount of wonderful music. The standard was high and sight reading essential as we were continuously singing different music. This was handed out to us at rehearsals by the choir secretary Mrs Loveday, affectionately know to the singers as 'Mum'.

We gave recitals all over the country, be it in little country parish churches, cathedrals, private homes, or even prisons. At Christmas we always gave a recital and sang carols in a students' residential home called Cumberland Lodge at Windsor, as always this was a happy visit. Although the weather was cold, the building and the welcome were as warm as ever and we loved singing in these beautiful surroundings. Mainly we sang the Overseas Religious Broadcast Services of the BBC, usually broadcast from the Maida Vale Studios. All money earned was, by common consensus, used to pay for any expenses incurred, such as music, travel and lodgings.

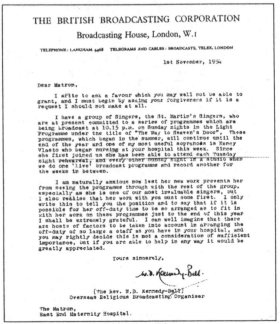

My hectic life!

132

An interesting thing the Singers did in this year was to give a concert in Holloway Prison for Women in London. I was horrified to see warders, as they were then known, walking up and down between the rows of prisoners, keys on chains hanging from their belts and watching the prisoners all the time. I was conscious of a total silence, eyes looking at the floor and blank white faces devoid of any animation. Someone suggested that they were listening intently; I think they were bored stiff and couldn't make head nor tail of what we were doing singing there. I hope I am wrong.

During one of our other visits to a church in the country, having climbed off the bus, we went into the church for a rehearsal and were invited to tea with the Vicar and his wife after the recital. I was cooking flu and frantically swallowing aspirins and blowing my nose. The house was invaded by beautiful Burmese kittens. I adore all animals and was completely captivated by these gorgeous little beasts. I decided to buy one at great expense to take back with me. I chose one, later to be christened Cindy, and when the time came to return home I hugged her in my scarf and under my coat. I began itching and scratching and only then did I remember I was allergic to cat fur! Between that and feeling more and more ill with the fast developing flu, I began to realise what a mistake I had made! Added to which I should have remembered there was a rule in my digs that there would be no animals in the house. When I arrived home I went straight to bed and snuggled up with the kitten. To my horror I heard the footsteps of the landlady coming my way. I hastily drew my suitcase towards me, popped her in and shut the lid. I said a little prayer that she wouldn't 'meow' when the landlady came in. My prayer was answered and after checking that all was well the landlady went away. It was then that I realised I couldn't possibly keep the kitten, so I rang my sister Helen telling her of my plight and asking if she'd like a present of a kitten. To my great relief she said she would and agreed to come and get her. She was to become a great family pet in the Long family and died at the ripe old age of sixteen years, according to my nephew David. He and his brother and sister had all grown up with Cindy as a family 'member' and were greatly saddened at her going.

Once, when I was a patient in Guy's Hospital, the 'Singers' came and gave a short recital for all the patients which was much appreciated. And a few of us sang at short services held in the wards at Charing Cross Hospital.

Though it is a great sorrow to me that not only was I never able to sing with them again but, in particular, to know that 'KB', 'Mum' and many others of the group at that time are no longer with us. I am left with treasured memories.

Daily, my work in the X-ray Department continued; caring for patients in the waiting room and during more complex X-ray procedures such as bronchial, kidney and heart examinations, as well as the more embarrassing bowel investigations when I felt I was most able to give comfort and reassurance. Because the remaining staff were all radiographers and radiologists I felt a bit out on a limb as the only nurse. The radiographers were very friendly but I sensed that the senior one felt that they did not need a nurse in the department, saying to me one day, 'We never had one *before!*'

I looked past this condescending remark as there were more imminently exciting events occurring outside the four walls of our hospital! Our Princess Elizabeth was to be crowned Queen. It would be a long procession with all the horses and troops. How could we best view it all and from what vantage point? I happened to see a small notice at the News Reel Cinema at the top of our road on Trafalgar Square. We could see the filming of the entire event from the procession leaving Buckingham Palace to its return. Included also, there was a packed lunch and use of toilets. All this for £2.50 each! We couldn't believe it and bought three tickets. I rang my cousin Kirsty in Edinburgh and invited her down to join us. We put up a camp bed between ours and set the alarm for a six o'clock call, determined not to miss any of the day!

After dressing and gulping down our breakfast, we set off for the two minute walk up our road and into the cinema. The weather was awful, cold and wet. The streets were lined with people, many of whom had been out all night, and they were already drenched.

We entered an almost empty cinema, warm and comfortable, and there was a picture on the screen showing the crowds up the Mall and all the flags and bunting decorating the streets. And there we sat, warm and dry, yet seeing everything that was happening for about six hours. Another bonus was the toilets! We

134

wondered how the crowds in the streets were faring, trying to keep their viewing places yet find the nearest loo and join the queue!

Then out came the royal coaches flanked by beautiful shining horses and the sound of their hooves clattering on the sand-strewn roads. The excitement was almost tangible; the voices of thousands thundered out as each coach passed by. Princess Elizabeth was lit up inside the coach, a truly magical vision. She waved sedately but with a smile; she must have been anticipating all the things she had to do during the complex ceremony in Westminster Abbey but, I imagine, believed that the people were happy about her accession to the throne and were supporting her with their presence despite the rain.

The ceremony was moving and bathed in the most gorgeous musical sounds one could imagine. Elisabeth, Kirsty and I commented that only in Britain could such a wonderful event as this be staged. Possibly not true, but we enjoyed the euphoria we were experiencing! I heard later that the Peers present put their sandwiches inside their coronets so that they could be eaten at the appropriate moment during the rehearsals!

As the service drew to an end, the rain stopped, the sun came out and the procession set off round Parliament Square. We decided to leave the cinema and join the crowds at the junction of Whitehall, Trafalgar Square and the Mall and saw the entire procession pass by and move up the road to Buckingham Palace. We then returned to our seats in the cinema and saw all the close-up scenes around the Palace. We had an excellent packed lunch and afterwards walked the two minutes back home.

That evening, as the one before, the streets heaved with people talking, jostling, laughing and soaking up the atmosphere and excitement of the day. We joined the crowds around Buckingham Palace and cheered and waved as the new Queen Elizabeth II and her husband Philip came out onto the balcony.

My cousin returned to Scotland and Elisabeth and I went back to our usual routine.

My work at Charing Cross Hospital was to assist the doctors at any procedures requiring nursing help, to equip the X-ray Department with any medicines and materials needed, such as barium, and to care for the welfare of the patients while they were in the department.

One of my patients turned out to be a Police Commander, who

wanting to thank me for my care, invited me down to Scotland Yard (at that time on the Thames Embankment) and showed me around their 'Horror Museum'. This he duly did, and I found it fascinating if not somewhat gruesome.

Covent Garden lay at the back of the hospital and marketeers used to throw out onto the street any fruit or flowers they had not sold by late in the afternoon. They invited us to go and collect any we would like to have. The theatres, too, were exceptionally good to us. Any tickets unsold by about 4pm for the evening performance were pinned to the nurses' home board and could be used by any of us. Being very fond of the theatre I often went with friends and we splashed out on coffee and ice cream as we hadn't had to pay for our tickets. I became quite an 'authority' on which plays were good and which I didn't like, and friends and family would ring me up to see if I had been to a particular play. I am still grateful for this wonderful time. We were, of course, the hospital to which actors and actresses were sent in event of need; most of the theatres were situated around Charing Cross Road and we were their nearest hospital.

One day I went with a friend in her car to see a ballet at the theatre at Covent Garden. After it ended we had a light meal in a café nearby. Leaving the café, we walked up past the back entrance and saw several boxes of peaches put out with the rubbish. My eyes popped out of my head. Looking into the boxes the fruit looked only slightly bruised, so I picked up two boxes and started walking with them, beside my friend, back to the car. Who should come towards us but a policeman in uniform! I gave him a broad smile and then walked on as though nothing had happened. We arrived at the car. It was then that I realised I had left my keys on the table in the café. We pushed the boxes along the ground under the car and retraced our steps. As we passed the entrance with the boxes again I took a mental note of where they were, passed the policeman who was standing at the corner and retrieved my keys, thankfully, from the café. So, back past the policeman (with my, I hoped, disarming smile), then again as I reached the entrance, I slipped another two boxes from the pile and hurriedly got back to the car. There, after checking that my 'friendly' policeman was not in sight, I retrieved the other two trays from under the car, threw them all into the back of it and my friend drove off as fast as we could! I still quake at the thought of it all! For, even though they had been put out to be collected with the rubbish, I still felt as thought I had 'stolen' them. Even now I have feelings of guilt! The peaches were perfect, but we knew we were taking a risk. How did we know that the dog next door had not peed on them? *WHY* had they been thrown out? We shared them between us; they were gorgeous!

These funny and amusing escapades were very welcome and necessary to keep my sanity as, although I quite enjoyed my time working at Charing Cross, it never really satisfied me. I missed the 'hands-on' personal care of the ward patients and, after two years, became quite restless.

Earlier in January 1953 I had an interview for *In Town Tonight* with producer Peter Duncan. A phone call from the BBC said they were interested in my visit to Canada and could they phone me the next day and ask me questions over the phone. They would then write a script from what they had learned from our conversation. Later I would be invited to go into the studio to broadcast a live interview, which was scripted. When the day arrived on Saturday 17th January and on entering the studio, I discovered that other guests being interviewed were Mademoiselle from Armentière; John Mills the film star and his wife; Billy Wright, the well-known England footballer; and the flea trainer, 'Professor Alfred Testo', from the circus at Olympia where he was giving performances. He gave us a magnifying glass, which he produced from his pocket, and we were able to see his fleas performing aerobatics on a fine thread, balancing along it, turning in circles and throwing themselves in somersaults without ever falling off. It was quite fascinating. Gusta Kruse, an elephant trainer was also on the programme. Two days later I received a letter telling me the broadcast had been recorded and I could purchase a record (78 rpm) if I wished. I did, and still have it to this day!

On my way out of the building I took the lift down and found that the Mills were also going down in it. I smiled at them but they didn't respond and appeared to deliberately avoid eye contact. I think their standing in society made them wary of relating to other people who were out of the 'safety zone' of their professional colleagues and work environment, but it did make me feel somewhat uncomfortable.

A letter from Colin Ratcliffe arrived inviting Janet Theobald and me to take part in performances of Coleridge Taylor's *Hiawatha* at the Royal Albert Hall. What fun! There was no hesitation in accepting. He had formed The London Coronation Choir using his United Hospital Choir members and adding to them members from many choral and operatic societies from the greater London area, which formed the choir of Indians. It was an enormous venture which was much enjoyed by all those taking part. We wore precious little in the way of clothing and rolled around hugging our blankets as the drips of sweat fell from our bodies, supposedly shivering with the 'cold and ice of winter' around us. The song *Onaway Awake Beloved* sung by Chibiabu is one that I shall always remember, and the words of Longfellow's *Song of Hiawatha* are, I believe, some of the most beautiful ever written.

Rehearsals began in a hall in West London, eventually transferring to the Royal Albert Hall in Kensington. We enjoyed every minute of the rehearsals. The part of Hiawatha was taken by Gordon Clinton who ran into trouble during the rehearsals.

138

Noticing I was a nurse, he asked if I could help him because the beads he had to wear were rubbing on his chest and causing him great discomfort. We went into his dressing room and he showed me his beautiful hairy chest which was covered in red, sore blisters. How on earth he had managed to sing at all I shall never know.

The next night, in the interval at the rehearsal, I took dressings and antiseptic cream with me and dressed his wounds. This I continued to do every night following the first performance until we had done the final performance. Daringly, I asked him if he gave singing lessons. A week later he started the training of my voice. During the years to come I also studied with David Galliver (a well-known tenor) and Fabian Smith, Professor of Singing at the Guildhall School of Music.

On the days of the performances (from June 29th to July 11th 1953) we gave nightly shows and two on Saturdays. We used to take a No. 9 red bus to the Albert Hall dressed as Red Indians with full make-up on. We felt distinctly out of place and wondered what the passengers must have thought of us.

My parents took a box at one performance and several of the family came to join them. I was saddened that they had apparently laughed their way through the entire programme and thought it was hilariously funny; they didn't appear to have appreciated either the words or the music much. Such a shame.

I wonder how many of the general public appreciate what an absolute warren of corridors, entrances and exits there are at the back of the Albert Hall! People pop up like rabbits out of their holes to see where they are in relation to the stage. I never *DID* find out if I was facing north, south, east or west when I was back there. Very confusing, and I had a terrible time to find my way within the Hall itself. On mentioning this to Mr Patient, the secretary of the Royal Choral Society, he kindly drew a diagram to help me. This might be useful for any reader going to a concert there and appears within the photographic sections of this book.

By the end of 1953 I had formed a small choir; we called ourselves the 'Charing Cross Singers' and among other things we sang at the Nuffield Centre for the Forces in Trafalgar Square and the Royal Empire Society in Northumberland Avenue.

Several months later I took part in the Commonwealth Pageant in April put on by Ralph Reader, John Snagg and Colin Ratcliffe with the London Concordia Choir. This pageant of nursing was held at the Royal Albert Hall which showed the work carried out by nurses through the ages from pre-Roman to the present day.

1954 found me still living in Craven Street and working in the X-ray Department. I received a card informing me that I was now a member of the United Hospital Festival Choir. I regularly attended rehearsals after work for the various choirs I was singing with and, in particular at this time, getting ready for another performance of *Hiawatha*, which was due to be performed again by the London Concordia Choir in the Royal Albert Hall on June 17th. This was the second year we were to perform this. Again rehearsals were great fun and Janet and I had a good laugh during them. Once again the words of Coleridge Taylor were hard to sing seriously when lying under blankets in the arena, dripping with heat and at the same time singing about the cold and frosty winter!

On the actual day of the first of several performances we were to give, we were greeted at the stage door at the rear of the building by distraught faces; *all* the performances had been cancelled due to insufficient tickets being sold. Everyone was totally devastated. The decision had just been taken following an emergency meeting and even the soloists (who, of course, along with the orchestra, had all to be paid) did not know until they turned up at the same time as we did. Everyone was in shock and we turned around and wended our dejected way homewards. I have frequently looked back on this time and wondered what had happened? I can only think that having performed it the year before, it was possibly too soon to play it again and, unlike previous years, it was not so well known or even in vogue at this time. It is a rather slow moving show.

On a weekend at Betsoms with my parents, my sister Christian arrived with the shocking news that she had decided to move to Pakistan with a man called Ghulam Abbas, whom she had met in London. I was on the stairs and heard everything that was going on. I could hear the distress in my parents' voices as they sought to understand what was happening. They then asked for more information as to how she met him and his home circumstances. The answers they got did nothing to placate their fears. I have to remember that, at that time, travel was rare and racial intermarriage was frowned upon and not even recognised. Only time passing and the knowledge that they had married in Karachi enabled my parents to accept the situation.

I was the only one of my family who would go to see her off at the station. Two of her friends were also there and, seeing my distress, they took me for a cup of tea in the café. It was not until ten years later when I went to Karachi for the first time that I realised that Christian was happy being married to Ghulam Abbas, adored her children and was well-suited to the lifestyle and culture there. She thrived in Karachi despite the tragedies that were to befall her much-loved family.

My restlessness grew at Charing Cross Hospital and needing a change, I decided to write a letter of resignation and on July 31st 1954, at the age of 28, I left. I took a few weeks off work before moving on to the next part of my life.

My singing lessons continued with Gordon Clinton. One day he asked me if I would like to take advantage of a lift to Edinburgh with the Elizabethan Singers comprised of himself, John Whitworth (counter tenor), Renee Soames (tenor) and Elizabeth Jerome (I hope I have got her name correctly). It was great fun. I was invited to sing with them when they sang for some of the guests in a hotel where we spent a night on the way.

By now, remembering the embarrassing fact that I was not trained in midwifery when acting as relief Night Sister at the Nanaimo General Hospital, I was sure it was high time I trained to be a midwife and I *did* love babies!

I searched the Nursing Times Advertisements for suitable training hospitals which had a vacancy for trainee midwives and decided to apply to the East End Maternity Hospital in Commercial Road in East London, whose authority was the Stepney Group Management Committee (this hospital closed in 1968). There I was to train for six months to achieve Part I of the Central Midwives Board examination which would be taken in May 1955. I was accepted and started my training there on November 18th 1954.

Many months were to pass happily, working very hard in our friendly little hospital. The building, as far as I remember, consisted of two Victorian houses joined together. The antenatal mothers were able to go out and sit in the delightful little garden at the back and chat to each other over cups of tea, until the birth became imminent. It was all very unhurried and the atmosphere as relaxed as possible. They had a chance to get to know the nurses as they passed to and fro among them. Many were in their dressing gowns and their visitors were able to join them there.

As I was still living with Elisabeth in our little Charing Cross room, I had to ride my bike, daily, through the streets of London in the early hours of the morning and back through the dark evenings with the light from my tiny front lamp directed on the street in front of me. One day we decided to have an evening party in our little room. To save ourselves running up and down the stairs all evening, we left a note on the door saying 'Welcome! Come on up to the top of the stairs!' This worked beautifully but after everyone had gone home and we were settling down to sleep, I suddenly remembered that the note was still there. I shot down the stairs to retrieve it before we turned Craven Street into a red light district!

I found different ways of getting through London to Commercial Road but my favourite way was along the Thames Embankment, between the law courts and then past St Paul's Cathedral. And then either by Mansion House, Bank, Cheapside, Leadenhall Street, Threadneedle Street or Cornhill and Aldgate High Street – as the mood took me – then into Commercial Road. The roads held no fear for me as the level of traffic in those days was somewhat lower than today.

Evidence of the war was still everywhere: damaged houses, large craters and wild flowers bravely peeping out of every crevice to find the light.

At the hospital we were to learn that a midwife's role was not a 9-5 job. We worked extremely hard but found it very rewarding. I think there are few more wonderful sights than row upon row of little babies wrapped up in pure white sheets and sleeping peacefully. However, if only *one* of them woke up and started screaming (and could they scream!) most of the others joined in the chorus.

We had delightful sisters in charge of us. One, I remember in particular, who, when we were on night duty, used to allow us to have about three-quarters of an hour to rest, lying on the very hard floor of our sitting room and pulling down a cushion for a pillow. We were so tired that we slept flat out the moment we lay down until we were woken to allow the others to have their turn. We really appreciated this but I was never to have such luxury again! I remember a night when one of the sisters threw a pillow to us at the bottom of the stairs and, throwing it back, we started a hilarious 'catching' game, and had to be sure that the patients couldn't hear our stifled laughter.

Exams loomed ever nearer and we had to fill in charts to show how many babies we had delivered plus details of examinations made, any complications and what postnatal care we had given.

We passed Part I of the CMB (Central Midwives Board) and I decided to continue and train for Part II. This allowed midwives to deliver without a doctor present if it was a normal delivery. I applied to the Lady Rayleigh District Nurses' Training Home at Forest Gate in Beachcroft Road, Leytonstone, right in the middle of the East End of London. There I was joined by a friend, Margaret New, and a new colleague Betty Holt, and we worked there together for six months.

As I was required to 'live in' I sadly parted company with my friend Elisabeth and our lovely little room. I still have fond memories of living in the Charing Cross area and Elisabeth and I have kept in contact for the past fifty years by phone and letter.

Janet and I still managed to get together for special occasions as can be seen by photos taken outside the Queen Elizabeth Hall where we were singing with the Royal Choral Society. Later it was with great regret I decided to retire from the RCS because of my working hours nursing after passing my Part II exams.

On arriving at the Lady Rayleigh Home in September 1955, I was greeted by a rather formidable Superintendent-in-Charge, Miss Wearn, and was shown to my room. This was to be a very interesting experience in my life and I think I grew in stature (probably in more ways than one!) and during the six months of the CMB Part II training, I really began to feel quite secure in myself, which had not always been the case.

Part of our work was in patients' homes and some of the time was spent in the Forest Gate Hospital, Forest Lane. We travelled around on bikes carrying with us everything we needed to do our work. Strapped to our bicycles, in a black bag, we carried, among other things, Minit portable gas and air and money in case the electric meter ran out, as it often did. Sometimes we were lucky and the senior midwife went ahead in her car taking the heavier items with her.

Once we had completed the second part of the training, we

were qualified to practise unsupervised as midwives, only calling for help from a doctor if we were concerned or if certain serious conditions presented themselves. I enjoyed this independence and, thankfully, managed to pass the Part II exam.

On one such 'independent' occasion I was called out at night to a lady who was in labour. I think she must have been as surprised by its arrival as we were, as I don't believe she had had any prenatal visits. It was a very poor, dirty and dimly lit old Victorian terrace house and her ten other children were all sitting on different steps of the steep staircase leading up to her room. I delivered the baby but there was no cot to put him in. I pulled out a drawer and put layers of newspaper on the bottom and then wrapped him in a worn blanket. After clearing everything up I went out onto the landing and was confronted by a very drunk husband who was returning from the pub. I gave him the news and hastily left, assuring him I would return the next day. I hoped the children would get to bed.

My ego was boosted by a letter from the Matron of East End Maternity Hospital inviting me to return there as a staff midwife after I had completed my midwifery training at Leytonstone. However, as Leytonstone was also a District Nurses' Training School and I had already been accepted for that course, I decided to stay on and train in district nursing. I started the six months of training which I enjoyed immensely. Nursing people in their own home was a joy and gave me great satisfaction; sometimes we became good friends. I was told my commencing salary would be £350 per annum less emoluments £153 per annum plus a cycle allowance (priceless!) for 3,500 miles per annum.

The nurses' home was always in need of money for smooth running and extra comforts, so I decided to try my hand at hairdressing. To my surprise the nurses (who rarely found the time to go to a hairdresser) lined up for me to try my cutting and washing skills. I was amazed that they used to come back for more and that I wasn't 'sued for damages'! This raised quite a lot of money for the Home and I had learnt yet another skill, even if it was by trial and error!

One day when out on my bike, with my black bag on the back, on my way to visit a patient, I stopped. A horse rider came alongside me. We had a chat and it turned out that she was going to university and wanted someone to exercise her horse for her. I

In Charing Cross uniform.

The Elizabethan Singers,
Gordon Clinton is in the middle.

Margaret New, Elisabeth Lane
and self outside the
Royal Albert Hall.

Janet Theobald and self –
the Royal Choral Society.

Singing
Elijah at
the Royal
Festival
Hall.

East End Maternity Hospital, which I am
told is no longer there.

Margaret New in the
garden behind EEMH.

Me at the back of
EEMH.

Mothers awaiting arrival of their babies
at East End Maternity Hospital.

Daph and Bunny at entrance
to 7 Park Road, Surbiton.

Growing tomatoes on our
balcony, 1957.

Myself playing tennis at Surbiton
Lawn Tennis Club.

I borrowed the props from the table in the left picture for the
costume in the right which won the Butlin's
Fancy Dress Competition!

Singing on the River
Avon.

Wearing my new coat
from Rhodes.

At the Cairo Pyramids.

Friends and customers at Emma Mayo's mannequin show.

Presents from parents and
children when I left
Tolworth Infants' School.

At ENT surgeon Kenneth
Rotter's party in Hampton.

Grove House
at Froebel
College.

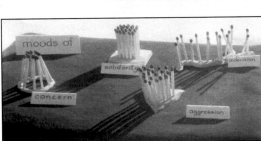

Example of Mood
and Movement
for my final
dissertation.

En route to
Spain, our two
tents and car
loaded up.

Myself, Su and Janet
outside Rouen Cathedral.

At the campsite Aire-sur-l'Adour,
1975.

Aidan, Helen,
Mum and I
on the bench
donated to
the people of
Oxted.

Leading some children from Lindon Bennett School on the day of the Queen's Jubilee, 1977.

Tent and loaded car on Glencoe campsite. Eileen having a restful read.

At Eileen Conway's with Mum's school friend Nellie Adam in Elgin on our camping trip.

could not believe my luck, nor she, and we arranged that I would call in the next day and meet her mother and familiarise myself with her horse and tack, and also so that she could satisfy herself that I knew how to ride! From then on, during my months of training, I used to go to the house, tell her mother I was taking the horse out and go for wonderful rides in Epping Forest nearby.

It happened that, at the time, I was going daily to give a shoe and boot mender his injection of insulin. One day he asked me if I knew of anyone who could make use of a beautiful pair of leather riding boots which someone had forgotten to collect over a year ago. I don't think he knew that I was riding at the time, but I told him about my doing so and that I would love to give them as a gift to thank the girl for trusting me to care for and ride her horse. When I gave them to her she was absolutely delighted as they fitted her perfectly. I told her who had given them to me and she said she would call in and thank him. What a happy ending!

I became quite fond of many of my patients and was thoroughly spoilt by them; boxes of chocolates and many other small gifts were generously given despite my protestation. One particular gift I have never forgotten, I used to bath and care for a middle-aged lady who was quite ill with rheumatic fever. On my last visit to her, having completed my training, she asked me to sit down beside her. She then told me to climb up to the top of a bedroom cupboard where I would find a paper bag. 'It looks like nothing on earth but it means a lot to me and I'd like you to have it.' I climbed up on a chair and inside the bag was a collection of loose bits of metal. 'Bring it here,' she said. With difficulty she pulled them out and handed them to me. 'This used to be my favourite lamp shade. It only needs soldering and you will see the beautiful shape it is. I want you to have it.' I had this collection of metal for nearly sixty years though I never managed to turn it into a lampshade. I know it is ridiculous but I hadn't the heart to throw it away! This epitomises my philosophy of treasuring the small and unostentatious things in life.

On completing my six months' training as a district nurse and with all these trainings under my belt, and with a mind to move from the East End of London, I decided to apply to train as a health visitor, an area of nursing which would make use of my previous trainings, yet would be very different in many ways. There was a vacancy for a trainee health visitor with the Surrey

145

g

County Council. It was linked with Brooklands College at Weybridge. I applied and was accepted to start my training in September 1956.

The Medical Officer of Health for the Borough of Kingston upon Thames was Dr Greenwood. As I had no idea of the area I rang and asked him whether he knew of any lodgings where I could stay while I was training. The next day he rang to tell me that a lady in the house opposite to his own, at No. 7 Park Road in Surbiton, took in lodgers and had a vacancy. My friend, Betty Holt, whom I had met when in Leytonstone, also applied to Kingston at the same time as I did, so we decided to cut costs and share 'digs'. We thought this sounded promising and decided to look into it.

Throughout our training time, Margaret New and I had talked about travelling the world, hitch-hiking everywhere and, having arrived at a certain place, we would use our nursing skills to raise money for the next stage of our 'journey'. My parents were horrified at the thought of my travelling the world in this way! To that end I bought a specially textured Nook camping tent (cost me £19 at the time) which was supposedly rot-proof and called 'non-l'eau' for protection in extreme weather. Sadly I was let down as Margaret decided that she wouldn't join me after all. I was devastated and had to revise all my plans. My precious tent ended its days when I donated it to a recent Pakistan earthquake appeal. But all this is well in the past and Margaret (now Mrs Hess) and I are still in contact from her home in New Zealand.

Chapter Nine

In January1956 we rang Mrs Daphne Hamilton (now deceased) and she was happy to rent us a room at the front on the top floor of her house in Park Road. She had her sister Bunny and sister-in-law, Jimmy, living there with her, among other lodgers. They lived downstairs where wonderful paintings of their families hung from the walls and their rooms were adorned with elegant furniture, and one sensed they had come through better and more privileged times. Betty and I had a happy year there as we trained to be health visitors.

One of the lodgers, an elderly lady, Miss Wright (we all called her 'Wrighty'), renting the room next to ours was a chain-smoker and we spent our time trying to get rid of the smell of smoke which pervaded our room!

Our room had a window leading onto a small roof over the top of Daph's bay-windowed bedroom below. We used to sit out there to do our studying and I grew boxes of tomatoes and wall flowers around the edges. Daph was a delightful and tolerant landlady and never complained about my antics. The three ladies were wonderful characters of whom I became very fond. One minute they were up ladders cleaning and painting the house in paint-stained trousers and the next they drove off in their old 'banger' dressed in their best clothes, hat and gloves, off to the races! Miss Wright, too, was an avid race fan and sat in her room listening to her radio to see if she had won any of her bets.

I caused a real furore in the house when I decided to get a

television and told Daph about it. She said she was worried that it would use more electricity so I checked with an electrician and assured her I would turn our light off when using it, which satisfied her. I was amused when gradually, as the days passed by, all three ladies and our neighbour, Wrighty, piled into the room to watch the races with their betting papers at the ready. The events in this house were an entertainment in themselves and deserve a book of their own!

Our health visitor training began with lectures in a building in Kingston and then moved into our local clinic, South Place in Surbiton. My trainer was Miss Davies, a very Welsh and very kind lady. We got around on our bikes but occasionally I got a lift in her little car, visiting mothers in their homes. The doctor with whom we worked was Dr Pearce.

I much enjoyed the home visits we made to assess very new born babies and the baby clinics we staffed. The babies were gorgeous and I always enjoyed the consultations we had with the mothers and trying to encourage and help them with any problems they might have. I think we were able to give them practical advice at a time when they most needed it. We were also 'school nurses' and visited the local schools checking the children's welfare, vaccinations and immunisations, and particularly looking for sight, hearing and head lice problems. Differentiating nits (lice eggs) from dandruff was quite an art! We also ran relaxation classes for antenatal mothers which was one of my favourite duties.

On April 15th, 16th and 17th in 1957 we went to the Royal Society of Health building at 90 Buckingham Palace Road in London where we sat the Health Visitor Royal Society of Health examination. There were seventy-six candidates at the time Betty and I took them – sixty-one passed. Thankfully we were among them. The results were displayed to the public on a board outside the building on 27th April.

During this time I continued singing in music festivals, concerts and with the Surbiton Oratorio Society, and still had my weekly singing lessons with David Galliver at his home in Banstead. My life was full and happily so, with many activities. I continued going up to London to sing with the St Martin Singers and managed to get to most of the rehearsals, concerts and recordings though this was quite tiring at the end of a day's work.

Finding time to do all this, not to mention sports, was quite a challenge!

In the winter I played lacrosse with Putney Ladies, Reigate and Redhill Ladies and with the East of England team, for whom I also played several matches. I was invited to take part in the trials for the England Team but never, in fact, played for them.

It was with some great trepidation that at the age of 31 I decided to take a course of driving lessons and was terrified most of the time! I used to pray that the traffic lights wouldn't turn red as I approached them or that the car in front of me wouldn't decide to stop! One day, when driving through the centre of Kingston with my instructor, he told me to stop at the side of the road as he wanted to talk to me. I did so and, turning around to face him, managed to rest my arm on the door handle. The door flew open. Of course there *had* to be a cyclist passing just at that moment. I knocked his handle bar and he fell off. I felt physically sick and, getting out of the car, approached him very apologetically. As we were near the police station I went there with him to report the accident and to wash the slight graze he had on his arm. Following this, there was a court case at the Kingston Magistrates Court which the AA attended on my behalf. Thankfully, the case was discharged as an unfortunate accident and on payment of four shillings I was discharged. That event didn't do anything to calm my nerves and I didn't drive again for several years. I continued riding my bike to work and in and around Surbiton.

I was still playing tennis most evenings and weekends and after scouring every other road in Surbiton discovered that the Surbiton Lawn Tennis Club was in the road next to mine! I played for the 2nd and, occasionally, the 1st team. One of the most enjoyable matches I played was against Oxford University, though I can't remember if we won or lost. The club became my second home and I was often to be found there. It was a place where I made many friends. Volunteer members used to give their time to the club serving teas with delicious sandwiches and cakes. I used to love sitting beside the courts having tea at a table while watching the play going on. I was grateful too, that it had a bath for the use of members as I was only allowed a bath once a week on a certain day at a certain time at our 'digs'; so many were there in the house and only one bathroom! After tennis I would occasionally swim in the Lagoon pool off Raeburn Avenue, in

Surbiton, which had been built in 1933. It was wonderful to have this facility, plus a small pool for young children, a sandpit and tennis courts. Sadly the pool developed cracks which were never repaired and it closed much later in 1979. I really missed being able to lie along the terraces lining the sides and sunbathe after the day's work was done. I hoped that, one day, public appeals would get it back but it is now covered by buildings and all hope gone. The journalist and writer June Sampson has written about this in her book *Kingston and Surbiton Old and New (1992)*, published by Mark Davison, with accompanying photos which brought back to me these happy memories.

At the tennis club I became a committee member and for a short time, about two years, took over responsibility for the junior members. In the summer of 1957 I entered the Open Surrey Championship at our club, somewhat brazenly, I think! I only managed to get five games out of the two sets played – not exactly Wimbledon standard. Nowadays a much higher standard of play is required for the 'open' entrants but I am very glad to have had the experience. There are more 'levels' now to group players of various abilities. Much more sensible.

In my free time I joined the Volunteer Care Scheme where we chose to be a Duty Officer who answered the phone to requests for help from members of the public, or a Visitor visiting people who needed help, or as a Case Mover carrying the 'Care Scheme case' daily from one Duty Officer's house to the next on duty. Later I became a committee member and Vice-Chairman over several years.

At first, following my health visitor training, I was appointed as health visitor and school nurse starting at South Place Clinic in Surbiton. I moved to Roselands Clinic in New Malden. Daily, I rode my bike over to Roselands, where I had a desk in the office. Then after dealing with phone calls, writing up notes and filing cards I would cycle over to my visiting area of New Malden and Worcester Park. Some days, when it rained, I was soaked through by the time I had reached my area and I can't believe I was a very welcome guest at my families' homes! It was thought to have been as a result of this that I developed pneumonia and spent some time in Surbiton Hospital. My GP, Dr A.D. MacArthur (now deceased) wrote a letter to the Medical Officer of Health for Kingston, suggesting that health visitors should receive a petrol allowance to enable them to use cars for their work. This was how it came about, shortly after, that health visitors got a petrol allowance, paid by the mile, during their working day.

My area covered the roads between the A3 and as far as Green Lane in Worcester Park. These were some of the happiest days in my nursing life. In the 1960s we cared for the whole family, from infancy to the elderly. We got to know antenatal mothers in our area and then took over from the midwives after ten days postnatally. Mothers could ask for help at any time during the day and were encouraged to attend our Baby Clinic for check-ups on their general health, weighing and advice on feeding and sleeping (since that, it seems, is what all babies do!). Despite being childless myself I seemed to have an affinity with babies and children.

A new clinic was being built much closer to my area at the Manor Drive, Worcester Park, Surrey, which was where I was to work from 1957-1969, where I would later end my days as a health visitor. There was a pub right behind our building and stables across the road where I used to sometimes visit the horses. It was quite a highly populated area with a mix of private housing and council flats. I continued working in my health visiting area and as a school nurse attached to Malden Manor Infants and Junior Schools. Here, I gave my first lesson to a class on health education. During this time I started a club for mothers, holding meetings at the clinic and inviting speakers from all areas of life. It was called the Manor Drive Clinic Club, later to become Malden Green Ladies Club. This club thrived and on occasions I had been invited back to visit them as a guest, and in 1986 I was invited back to their 21st Birthday celebration as founding member, at Manor Parochial School in Worcester Park. Sadly they closed in 2008.

My living situation had changed. From Park Road I had moved into a room at 8 Oakhill Road in Surbiton which I was to share with a friend and colleague, Edith. It was a charming little semi-basement room with a kitchen between my room and her room. Mine overlooked the little back garden, half of it being below the level of my room and a step leading up to the window on the other half (rather like a stage) on which rested my bed. The garden flowers leant in towards the warmth of my room and lit and framed the windows. The squirrels too, used to pop in to see me, dropping down onto the window sill and sitting themselves comfortably on the bowl of fruit while they surveyed the land around them before tucking into the fruit they had selected. There was a full-length cupboard door in the corner which cleverly hid a wash basin but Edith and I shared the kitchen and toilet. We also had our own front door onto Oakhill Crescent which kept us very private and self-contained. I was very happy there.

One day my parents, who were visiting me, said that they thought it was time I had a flat of my own and kindly helped me to purchase a ground floor flat in a new block, just being built on the other side of the road. This was to become No. 17 Russell Court, Oakhill Crescent. I was thrilled to have my first home and much enjoyed using my savings to furnish it along with some 'bits' my mother gave me. The first thing I did was to look for a dog. I had long wanted one. When visiting my sister Helen in Brasted in Kent one day, a neighbour came in with a tiny dachshund puppy on a lead. He was adorable and I asked from where she had got him and whether there were any others of the litter left. She thought there was one black and tan bitch left. I went straight to the phone and within two hours I had driven, with a friend, to Sevenoaks, returning with another adorable puppy. She was to be called 'Mandy', her kennel name being 'Amanda Baby Doll'. Anyone owning a dachshund will know what wonderful, fascinating, comical and loving creatures they are. She came everywhere with me, for, by now, I was the proud owner of a Ford 'Popular' car, given to me by my parents, and she used to curl up among the blankets and was the centre of attention of the mothers I visited and the children outside the school gates. When I was doing a clinic the mothers used to report to me on Mandy's welfare as they looked in through my car windows on their arrival.

She was to have three litters of puppies in the following years, and they, too, used to come in the car on my rounds tucked up in a blanket, having drinks from their mother's milk bar and, once inoculated, going for little walks in the local park. Needless to say, they ended up in several homes in the district around the clinic and they were frequently seen trotting around the locality.

Mind you, they are very useful animals too. One day, when I was leading a relaxation class for antenatal mothers, I was trying to explain how they might relax. I got the bright idea of bringing

Mandy in and, sitting her on my lap, flicked her paw up which then, because she had no control over it, flopped down again. It worked a treat and she caused great laughter and they soon got the message.

I remember one occasion when there was an embarrassing moment when cycling to give a talk on *Bathing a Baby*, I stuck the naked doll into the bag at the side of my front wheels with the legs sticking out in the air. The looks of horror I got from people in passing cars had to be seen to be believed. It was quite hilarious! Could they possibly have thought it was a real baby?

Home visits were important and we got to know our families very well, often becoming good friends, and even fifty years later, still keep in touch. One family I got to know very well consisted of a young school girl, Hazel, her parents Connie and Gerald (he was wheelchair bound) and her grandparents. They all lived together and I was privileged to look after them all. I am still in touch with Hazel and her husband Mick and their children.

Young children's sight and hearing were tested by health visitors both when they were babies and again at school, any concerns being referred to a doctor. I found this work very rewarding and was pleased when the local doctors, unaware that I had just made the decision to leave health visiting, invited me to become their first 'practice' health visitor. I felt pleased to have been the one they chose to work with them and was really quite sad that I would not be able to have the experience of working in a GP practice.

In November I was asked by the Kingston Health and Welfare Department to give talks at the Malden Adult Education Centre on *Prevention of Accidents in the Home*. I did this on several occasions. I also joined the Samaritans doing duties at the Kingston Centre in St Andrew's Road, Surbiton for a few years. I had to stop doing this when, at that time, we were all to be required to take our share of night duty; but living alone and with dogs in my flat there was no way I could continue!

At Christmas time I got some friends together and sang carols in the streets of Surbiton and the station forecourt in aid of St Dunstan's, a charity for men and women blinded on war service. A year later, I was sad to receive a letter from St Dunstan's thanking me for past help but saying they were no longer accepting money collected by carol singers at Christmas. I believe this is no longer the case.

I continued singing with the Surbiton Oratorio Society (whose name was changed to Kingston Choral Society) and the Kingston Chamber Music Society. Concerts with the latter kept me busy at this time and favourite works were to be *The Shepherd on the Rock* by Schubert and Claude Monteverdi's *Beatus Vir.*

Every year, I used to enter the Kingston and Surbiton Music Festival. They were always very well organised and were staffed by friendly, caring people. I believe we were all very nervous but I went in for them primarily to hear the helpful criticisms from the various adjudicators. Most years the comments varied, which was useful because when you heard different people saying the same thing about a problem they had with your voice, one realised that it was a fact and something to work on!

I also entered the 'Bible reading' category which often had some somewhat unpronounceable names in it. This discipline was to be a help to me when later I did the Bible reading on Sundays in my church.

For some years I sang the solos for the annual Festival of Hymns run by the New Malden Association for Old People's Welfare. Groups from all over the borough came together by foot, car or bus-load to sing well-known hymns. Surbiton too held festivals, though not of hymns, and I sat on the committee for several years.

May 1959 Surbiton Lawn Tennis Club Championship: I was beaten in the first round by the eventual semi-finalist, Miss E Parssmore, 6-1 6-3, who was beaten by Margaret Court 7-5 6-2. I felt better after learning this!

Severe back pains during the summer had me carted off to New Cross Hospital and after several weeks returned to Westerham to recuperate.

Chapter Ten

The St Martin Singers had, for some time, been anticipating a visit to Oberammergau to attend the open-air Passion Play, held every ten years. 1960 was to be the year; all paid for by the professional fees deposited into our account. We had a most wonderful visit to Austria and I have never forgotten the almost 'fairy tale' feel over the three days we were away. We flew to Munich and from there a bus took us to several places where we gave pre-arranged recitals at one or two churches, including the Basilika at Innsbruck, where the collection went towards paying for damage caused during the war. Our next port of call was the village of Fürstenfeldbrück up in the mountains with a fast flowing river running down the side of the hotel where we stayed. A few of us braved the cold and walked up the side of the river, then swam down with it till we arrived parallel to our hotel and jumped out.

Next we arrived at Oberammergau where we were each welcomed by the different families with whom we were to stay. All the actors lived, or had been born, in this town and the men could be seen walking or cycling through the streets, their long hair (grown especially for the occasion) flowing behind them. The married couple who owned the house where I stayed were taking part in the play. He was a carpenter and carved for me a beautiful little calf standing on its front feet with its hind legs in the air. He did this while sitting on the end of my bed, in one evening, and refused to take any money for it. I found the

Austrian people both courteous and friendly. As I have mentioned earlier our expenses were paid out of our fund so we could just enjoy ourselves.

The play was superb. The stage was open to the sky and thankfully there was no rain to soak the actors. Sadly, half way through, an incident in the row just in front of me was very distressing and affected us all. An American gentleman, sitting beside his wife, suddenly lurched forward, unconscious, to the ground and was promptly attended to by the First Aiders on duty. I fear he had had a severe heart attack and was taken from the theatre by stretcher. My heart went out to his poor wife! They had come all this way from America especially to see the play, and we wished we could do something to console or help her but of course we couldn't.

On returning to London, life for the Singers went on as usual including recording a service from the chapel of the Tower of London (officially known as Her Majesty's Royal Palace and Fortress) for the BBC. We also sang a service in the chapel of the Chelsea Pensioners' Hospital in London and occasional services at Southwark Cathedral. These were unique and interesting experiences which we much enjoyed. I had been trying for some time to get an audition at the BBC for radio drama productions. It wasn't to be until August 1967 that I received a letter inviting me to an audition. Despite passing it I never heard any more!

This year the St Martin Singers, at my request, came down to St Mary's Church in Westerham to give a recital in aid of a charity they were supporting. I sent a letter to Lady Churchill who lived at Chartwell in Westerham telling her of the concert and asking if she would care to attend. Unfortunately, she informed me by letter that she could not. My sister Helen laid on a tea back at her house and we all went there before returning to London.

One day when I was visiting my family in Oxted I met a lady who turned out to be Miss Mary Callister who was the headmistress of St Michael's School in Limpsfield, Surrey. During our conversation she asked if I would give a talk at her school on the work of a health visitor. I gladly accepted and on May 9th 1962 I duly arrived at the school. To my horror, as I was ushered into the school hall, what looked like hundreds of young girls stood up in one movement, with a *WHOOSH*, while I was escorted up to the front. There was silence – which seemed to last a lifetime – until I realised I had to do something about the situation and asked them to sit down! What an incredible reception. They were so well behaved and listened so attentively that I would like to think it was because they were genuinely interested in the subject. Anyway, over the years I gave many talks in schools on various subjects.

In my role as health visitor I was invited along with a GP, a marriage guidance counsellor and two head teachers to sit on a panel in the New Malden Institute to answer questions relating to family problems which I found most interesting.

In January 1963 I took and passed the Family Planning Association's exam and began working one day a week with the doctor at South Place Clinic after my day's work as health visitor.

During the year I attended the Holiday Course of Surrey County Music Association at Gipsy Hill College on Kingston Hill, and as usual loved every minute of it. It was organised by Norman Askew, Fabian Smith and Roy Hickman, who were tutors that year. (Later, in April 1972, attending the AGM in Kingston, I was elected as representative for Surbiton.)

A 'bee in my bonnet' kept me wanting to visit a Butlin's Holiday Camp and see what it was like and find out why they were so popular. So I rang and booked myself into the Clacton Butlin's for the Easter weekend. It was to be a most interesting three days. I quite liked the little 'rabbit warren' rooms each of which contained a bed, dressing table and drawer and a place for hanging clothes. The thinness of the wall between each of the 'cabins' did not allow for much privacy (it was quite amazing what went on all night!) and *YES* we were woken by the loud speaker telling us 'WAKEY WAKEY'! It was time to get up for breakfast. I didn't mind this because the food was excellent and there were no set places where we had to sit, so I met many people and learnt a lot from talking with them.

I was amazed at how they produced literally thousands of breakfasts, lunches and dinners, each with two sittings, and the more I thought about it the more I wanted to find out how they managed it. So I asked if I could see around the kitchen. They immediately arranged for me to do so and it really was one of the most interesting things I have done. Everywhere was spotless, all the staff working at full speed in clean aprons, caps over their hair and machines doing nearly all the work, rumbling the skins off potatoes, slicing carrots and so on. The gentleman showing me around said, 'There is one thing that machines cannot do which is one person's job, can you guess what it is?' I couldn't. We arrived in a part of the vast kitchen and there was a man sitting on a stool in front of a milk churn. On one side there was a huge basket of eggs and on the other a basket for the egg shells. His essential job was to crack one egg at a time, smelling it before tipping the inside out into the churn. As he pointed out to me, 'The last of these hundreds of eggs could be the only bad one; put it in there and the whole lot becomes useless. We have no means of testing for the smell of bad eggs.' Yes, his job was *definitely* essential.

There was plenty to see and do and I particularly enjoyed the children's competitions on land and in the pool. Someone drew my attention to the poster announcing there would be a fancy dress competition that night. Although I had nothing suitable to wear I decided to join in.

Looking around the dining room table I took a bread basket, some serviettes, several corks (from the little bottles of wine we were given) and two of the wine bottles. I hung the bottles from my ears, hung the corks around the edges of the bread basket which I wore on my head and 'inked in' music notes and treble and bass clefs on the serviettes and pinned them to my skirt, and went as 'wine, woman and song'.

To my amazement, despite competition from the many people who entered (some of whom had bought ready-made costumes with them), I won the first prize and was made to stand on a stool while the local press took photos! I never did see the local paper as I was leaving the next day, but they kindly sent me two photos.

During the early summer my friend Marion Milford, a well-known singer, put my name forward to David Calcutt who was the conductor of a group called the Avon Singers. This group gave an annual recital from a boat in the River Avon. On Whit Monday we weighed anchor at the foot of a sloping lawn from a pub, the *Rose and Crown* at West Harnham, where a large audience sat with their drinks. This was all in aid of charity for the restoration of the ancient Priory. It was fortunately a beautiful and calm evening. We were told our voices carried far across the fields to Salisbury Cathedral. Indeed it was a delightful opportunity to be making music with such excellent musicians. We slept at the Priory owned by M.D. Clayton and the organiser was Bill

Oxenbury. I see from my list of 'must haves' were midge repellent, torch, cushion, hot water bottle and music. Note the order of priority!

In December the Chatsworth Christian Choir, conductor George Delderfield, invited me to sing the soprano solos of the *Messiah* at St Saviour Church, Coppleston Road, Denmark Park SE15. I was very chuffed to have been invited to do this as I was not yet used to finding myself in front of a public audience. This was my first advertised professional performance. However, there was a problem. . . I always seemed to have trouble finding a loo! And here was yet *another* church without one. So after a brief rehearsal I crept out in the dark and shamefully squatted down among the graves, just praying for forgiveness and that no one would come round to the back of the church. I was in luck and breathed a sigh of relief as I went back in for the start of the performance.

I made my first visit, albeit brief, to see my sister in Karachi, Pakistan in 1964 on my own. My parents kindly agreed to look after my dog for me. I flew out with British Airways and was met by my sister Christian, Abbas her husband and their four children Kamran, Mariam, Neelofer and Kauser. In true British fashion I gave my brother-in-law (whom I had only met once before) a hug and a kiss and I sensed I had done a forbidden thing in his Muslim country. Afterwards I apologised if I had embarrassed him or the family. There was very much less integration of British and Asians at that time and we were less aware of each other's customs.

Everything was strange to me: the buildings, the clothes, the sights and smells. In those days rivers of manure ran down the gutters of the roads and camels stalked around the streets spitting left, right and centre. The colourful paintings on the sides of the buses and vans were in cheerful contrast to the brown of the sandy roads and buildings and I was quite mesmerised by it all. The family had wanted me to see the snake charmer who earned his money visiting homes in the area. He came and sat cross-legged on the gravel in the garden. It was quite amazing to see the snake rise as he played his (far from tuneful) pipe. I had seen this on film but in the flesh it was much more entertaining. I'm still not sure what 'treat' was given to train them to do this – doubtless an unexpecting mouse or two.

159

My brother-in-law Ghulam Abbas was a well know writer and my sister broadcast on the local radio station in the late evening on some nights. She had asked me to take some music and sing and be interviewed for the radio station and also to sing at the school where she was teaching. I had no idea what songs to take and foolishly thought that the good old English song *The British Grenadiers* might be suitable. I'm quite sure it wasn't! I only know that the old dusty piano hidden in the corner of the studio was to be used to play my accompaniment and that some of the notes were at least two tones out of tune! It sounded like the 'honky tonks' of olden days and was almost impossible to sing to but I did my best. At the school the children politely applauded but I'm sure they couldn't make head nor tail of me. They gave me two beautiful hand-sewn head rest covers for my chairs which I am still using. I then had a recorded interview at the radio station which was quite heavily censored.

I much enjoyed getting to know Kish's family and, when I left on 9th January, they all came down to the docks to see me off. I had decided to return by sea just 'to ring the changes'. The enormous RMS *Caledonia* was there to meet us, having come from Bombay. When I boarded it, I stood beside the rails waving to the family and watching food being thrown from the ship to the wild dogs below on the dock. There was a cacophony of sounds of people trying to sell their wares on the quayside. Sometimes lines of rope, which were tied to the ship were dropped down to the quay and the goods being bought were attached to them and hauled up on board. A young boy would be sent onto the ship to collect the money.

My family gave me a beautiful leaving present, a hand-painted round lampshade made from a camel's bladder! I can still feel and hear the sound the lampshade made as it rolled from one side of my cabin to the other as the seas got rougher and rougher! It is still in use today in my front hall, none the worse for the experience.

As we arrived at the Red Sea our ship docked for a short stay at the Port of Aden where we were allowed to disembark and buy goods from people selling their wares from wooden tables along the quayside. I bought a little radio which has lasted me for many years. I was fascinated how the language changed as we moved from one radio area to the next. We were offered a sightseeing trip by coach through Cairo and to see the pyramids. This was an offer I could not refuse and paid the extra few pounds for the privilege. We travelled up the Red Sea, lying on the deck with the sandy land on either side of us until we arrived at the place where our specially chartered coach was waiting to take us to Cairo. Here those who had paid for the extra excursion disembarked and joined the coach. Driving parallel alongside our ship, I was aware of the disproportionate size of the massive bulk of the liner compared with our tiny coach.

In the city we went for a snack in a restaurant where a belly dancer did her bit and we all had the questionable pleasure of her sitting on our laps with her arm around our shoulders. Anyway, it was just another experience! Then we went to the pyramids where we were offered a ride on a camel. This I couldn't refuse (though it didn't do my back much good!) and I still can't forget the arrogant look of a camel and loved it when they showed their 'spitting' characters!

We returned to the ship which, by now, had sailed up to the port at the top of the Nile where it meets the Mediterranean Sea. We boarded it as a most stunning crimson sky accompanied the sinking of the setting sun; it was quite breathtakingly beautiful and I stood looking at it for some time.

We were supposed to be stopping at Cyprus and to be able to spend some time on land, however, due to local unrest as well as a terrible storm and rough sea the crew decided it would not be safe to do so. It was a pity as it would have been an interesting visit. So we sailed on through rough seas, when almost everyone was ill with seasickness, including some of the sailors, to our next port of call which was to be Gibraltar.

We all got off at Gibraltar and went our separate ways. I went up through the town to see the soldiers changing the guard at the barracks. I was amazed to see the police and soldiers in British uniforms. Everyone seemed to speak English which was a help. Walking along the rocky ramparts I encountered the mischievous monkeys who were always on the lookout for food. I didn't have any and perhaps that is why one of them whisked my scarf from around my neck and tantalisingly dangled it over the precipice. Just as I reached out to snatch it back, he let go and it dropped far below. I wondered who would go down every evening to gather up all the treasures that had landed down there! The passengers all returned to the ship as it left for Southampton but I made for the airport as I had to get back to work the next day and the ship would not get me back in time. Eighteen years earlier I had nursed Sir Ralph Eastwood, who was the Governor General of Gibraltar, when he was a patient at University College Hospital. Although I tried to find him, I was unsuccessful and made my way to the airport.

Letter of thanks from Sir Ralph Eastwood.

I went home to see my parents and to retrieve my dog Mandy, all of whom I missed, and then drove back to my flat in Surbiton. My parents were very kind and gave me money for a Morris Minor which cost £446. Later Mandy was to produce two puppies on my bed! One I called Hector and the other I called Flood because I left the tap running in the kitchen and the water was everywhere!

To finish off 1964, I completed giving a course of twelve lectures on Home Nursing for MEFAS. As we couldn't find an examiner, I had to examine my own students!

On January 30th 1965 Churchill died at age 90. His funeral was at St Paul's Cathedral and I went to his lying-in-state at Westminster Hall. Four guardsmen stood, heads bowed at the four corners of the coffin, as streams of people passed slowly by paying their respect. His body was taken up the Thames by boat. The cranes all dipped along both embankments in salute as the boat passed by. It was an emotional time and many were in tears.

March 21st of this year was very special to me. It was the only time my mother and Margaret Channon (my music teacher from school days) came to hear one of our concerts. I was singing the soprano song *Shepherd on the Rock* by Schubert and also, with a small groupm *Zögend Leise*. My friend Pat Bayliff was the contralto soloist.

I notice that I attended two Miniature Dachshund Club Championship shows in 1966 and 1967. In one of them, at the suggestion of my vet, I entered Mandy (listed as Amanda Baby Doll) to see how we got on. She must have had her tongue in her cheek as I had not the remotest idea how to show a dog! She sat when she was told to stand, she sat down when she was supposed to walk round the ring and she wouldn't let them look in her mouth. A total disaster! There was much 'tut tutting' from the experts around me! Asking how we had got on, I gave my vet a piece of my mind but she thought it was hilarious.

In June 1966 I was driving up South Lane in New Malden when I saw a crowd gathered around a car and a little boy lying on the grass verge. I stopped my car and ran over to see if I could help, only to find it was one of our little boys from Malden Manor School who had been hit while crossing the road. I started mouth-to-mouth resuscitation but realised that he was already dead. The ambulance arrived and his mother had been fetched from nearby flats and we both went with him to Kingston Hospital where she was told the terrible news. I have never forgotten this dreadful incident and was in communication with the council regarding a possible zebra crossing at the junction where it occurred. I returned to the clinic to recover.

I saw a correspondence course advertised for Teaching English as a Foreign Language (TEFL) for £300. And in order to make further use of my shed in the garden and, because I thought this would be an extra useful qualification, decided to go ahead and enrol. I received a quantity of well-presented printed material giving instructions and explaining the course which was to be held over five instalments of teaching and coursework. I worked very hard during the course and was impressed with the critiques which came back to me, signed by my 'tutor'. It seemed straight forward and legitimate. All correspondence went to a post box address, which did concern me, but because of my many activities it was essential that I did it by correspondence. I would, here, warn *anybody* thinking of doing a correspondence course to look carefully into its legitimacy. I received a letter congratulating me on passing the course and stating that I would be receiving a TEFL certificate. This never arrived. I was very angry as I had spent many hours of work and money to attain this certificate and approached various educational and trading standard experts for advice, only to find that many others had been similarly conned. There was no recourse as there were no addresses.

On two occasions during my free time over this period, I examined the Red Cross VADs (Voluntary Aid Detachment) in their Maternal and Child Welfare exams. They were written papers which consisted of four questions and each VAD was questioned on practical work by myself separately.

I'm not sure if this was the first year that it was implemented but I know I was the first person to sing as soloist during a Festival of Hymns on 28th September 1966, especially organised at Christmas time by the New Malden Old People's Welfare Association in Kingston. Hundreds turned up at the church, some coming by coach and were to do so in the ensuing years. I was so pleased to be asked back each year until eventually Hymn Festivals stopped and, sadly, have never been reintroduced. I never found out why it was – perhaps a change was needed.

Another singing venture came my way. Ladies were invited to join the boys and gentlemen of the Chapel Royal Choir at Hampton Court Palace in September. I had been auditioned by the organist, Norman Askew, at his home where I was put through a nerve-wracking series of tests. In the beginning there were five of us but the only names I remember are Margaret McCleod, Violet Etheridge and Celia Gordon-Clark. We all sang on the cantoris side of the chapel. There was, understandably, great consternation (and not a little resentment) among the residents at the time and permission had to be sought from The Lord Chamberlain before ladies could be appointed. We sang our first service on 25th September 1966 to the apprehension of the local parishioners, whose doubts appeared to have been placated once they heard us sing!

Rehearsals were held at the Palace on Friday nights in a fairly small choir vestry at the side of the chapel. In the wintertime it was very eerie walking through the dark passage leading from the car park to the chapel, only lit by candlelight. It felt as though we were back in Henry VIII's day! We wore crimson robes with hats to match, with white surplices over the robes. There was some consternation when it was realised that the ladies might have to have their own toilet! But in the end it all worked out all right. We were occasionally required to sing at special services and thoroughly enjoyed every moment of our time there.

Of the music itself, what can I say? I have never sung such a variety of beautiful church music either before or since. I felt proud and deeply honoured to be chosen to sing there and much enjoyed the atmosphere and companionship of the choristers and The Gentlemen. They, and the residents and congregation welcomed us most warmly.

One of the choirmen gave me the following ditty which had been written as we were leaving the chapel:

1. As I came thro' Hampton, thro' Hampton, thro' Hampton,
   As I came thro' Hampton, I heard four ladies sing:
   O tuneful may the Chapel go, the Chapel go, the Chapel go,
   O tuneful may the Chapel go, Now they've got ladies in.

2. O who's like my Nancy
   So spry, so true, so bouncy
   She is foremost 'mong the many
   Gay girls of Chapel Royal

Chorus:
   They'll bill and coo so sweetly,
   Or in the service neatly
   They'll bow and march in weekly
   These girls of Chapel Royal

3 They wear odd red bonnets, red bonnets, red bonnets,
   They wear odd red bonnets and robes of crimson hue.
   And tuneful may the Chapel go, the Chapel go, the Chapel go,
   And tuneful may the Chapel go, Now they've got boys anew.

At Christmas time, I treasure the memory of the walk through the gardens to the house of the Queen's representative, Sir Charles Harvey (I believe his title was Chief Steward), to sing carols around a roaring fire in his sitting room, enjoying mulled wine and mince pies! On the last Christmas Eve that we sang in the chapel we had lined up, as usual, at the door leading into the chapel but our leading choir boy, Douglas Read, had failed to turn up in time and Gordon Reynolds pointed to me and said, 'Nancy – SING!' I'll never forget it; I had such an adrenaline rush! He was staring at me waiting for me to sing, so I started *Once in Royal David's City*. As I began, out of the corner of my eye, I saw Douglas appearing. To this day I am not sure whether I am glad or sorry that he didn't turn up in time. I believe it was the first and will probably be the last time this was sung by a woman in the Chapel Royal – what an honour!

On December 14th Norman Askew was returning from holiday in Spain with his wife when he collapsed and died in the plane. A funeral was held at the Chapel Royal on the 21st December, which was a very traumatic service for all concerned.

In January of 1967 I was invited to sing the oratorio soprano solos for *The St Matthew Passion*, along with contralto Pat Bayliff, tenor Alex Barrie and bass Julian Edwards, at St Mary's Church, Hampton in Middlesex.

I was very surprised to receive a letter from Ralph Nicholson (Director of the Surrey County Music Association) inviting me to be the soloist for a couple of days for the performers in the Accompanists Course at Glyn House Ewell in Surrey. These performers were being examined for how well they could accompany music and singers of all types. The performers were allowed to provide their own singer but most didn't. This was a paid job and I was somewhat scared when confronted by music of all kinds and sorts from lieder to opera (in different languages). The accompanists were going to have to be sensitive to everything I did in the way I sang and interpreted the music. This was indeed a challenge for them as well as for me! He told me afterwards I had 'passed with flying colours'. It was a great relief!

In February I disgraced myself by agreeing to sing, from sight, the soprano part in Cavalli's eight part *Laudate Nomen* in a concert in Oxted, Surrey. The music had been sent to me but I had never sung it before and I became completely lost. How on earth the other seven singers kept going I'll never know. I still blush at the thought of it! I felt I had really let the conductor and the other singers down badly.

At work, amongst my health visiting duties I gave a talk on Home Safety for volunteer visitors for the elderly arranged by the Medical Officer of Health. I also gave talks in schools on appropriate clothing and the danger of wearing shoes with too high heels! Standing girls on the tables with one foot wearing a flat sole and the other a very high heeled shoe, I showed them the damage that could be done by forcing the foot forward. I'm not sure how many took note of my demonstration but I could only try!

Spring came with further trouble to my spine when I was admitted to Stanmore Hospital for a spinal fusion. The top of my bed was under a window and I was lucky that I could see the trees and flowerbeds in the mirror hung above my head. Although my back was extremely painful following surgery, I was helped by daily lessons from an artist and a Pitman's typing teacher. It was a bit scary as I had to lie flat on my back and the typewriter was strapped in place on a pulley from the ceiling above my head! I couldn't understand why no other patient in the ward had accepted the offer of 1-1 classes. It was quite wonderful and I am sure helped me through this difficult time.

On my feet again in August, I sang in a concert for the Malden Good Companion Club with piano accompanist Ruth Taylor. We 'paired up' for many concerts and, as always, the rehearsals were the time we enjoyed most, at times being quite hilarious events! Other accompanists, with whom I sang in many concerts and festivals, were Pat Amey and Margaret Brown, especially with the Kingston Chamber Music Club of which we were members.

Previously, Pat Bayliff and I sang the solo parts in many concerts together, winning the duet category in the Kingston Festival in the 1950s. It was always fun to sing with her and I benefited hugely from the experience of attempting to blend with her beautiful, rich contralto voice. On several occasions we sang four of Dvorak's Moravian duets, including a public concert on Kingston Hill.

October saw me on a two-week package holiday to the Greek island of Rhodes with a friend 'Robson' (I forget her Christian name) who was always called 'Robbie', perhaps that's why! It was a lovely island with beautiful sandy beaches and buses to

167

take us to visit local villages and through the countryside. The houses in one of the villages called Paradissi were all painted in different pastel colours and the narrow streets were shaded by vines which stretched from one side of the road to the other. Underneath this canopy, shielded from the strong sun, sat the women on benches beside long tables where they selected and picked the grapes which were being cut down around them. I wished I had my camera with me, but even without a photo the sight is impinged upon my mind. Swimming in the sea there was a joy and I long to return one day. A brief excursion to Marmaris and Kepisi on the Turkish mainland by boat included a visit to a market area where there was much bustle and colour and a ride on a camel on the beach. At least I can say, 'I have been to Turkey'!

Returning to work I took part in giving a course for the New Malden Adult Education Centre on the topic of *Day Care of Children* for the princely sum of £4.45 plus travel expenses.

In December I was again invited by St Mary's Church, Hampton to sing the soprano solos for Bach's Christmas Oratorio along with Janet Flavell (contralto), Paul Taylor (tenor) and John Underhill (bass). Francis Deacon conducted.

When Gordon Reynolds took over the music at the Chapel Royal it became clear that he wanted to go back to boy trebles. He was planning for the choir to join, occasionally, with other Chapel Royal choirs, who only had boy choristers. So the ladies, with great sadness, offered to stand down. Late December 1967 the women choristers hosted a farewell party for the choir in my flat, to which Gordon Reynolds, the Chaplain Reverend Canon FVA Boyse and Sir Charles Harvey came. We were all presented with silver pencils inscribed with *Chapel Royal* and the dates we had sung there.

Shortly after my departure from the Chapel Royal, I drove down after work to take part in the Worthing Music Festival; my friend Bobbie Ellis came with me. We stayed as usual in the lovely Burlington Hotel, our room overlooking the sea front. The adjudicator was the well known soprano Isobel Baillie and I was amazed and thrilled when I was awarded the Chanctonbury Cup for an 'operatic aria', the Johnstone Cup for 'Oratorio', the Blake Cup for 'Classical song' and the Challenge Cup for 'concert performance of a song'. These would, I was told, enable me to compete in the forthcoming South of England Festival.

Following this, I arrived in Purley, with my cups clanking in my suitcase, for my usual lesson with Fabian Smith. I told him I had brought my 'loot' from Worthing. He was delighted and read the examiner's comments with interest and, I think, some surprise! On one other occasion, the examiner was Professor Philip Cranmer from the Queen's University of Belfast who wrote me a letter and said 'your voice was most promising and well worth persevering with'. I am sure that music festivals do the average singer a great deal of good, as long as they recognise that it's an excellent opportunity to sing to an audience and to have a free (well, nearly free) assessment of one's voice qualities.

The time arrived for the South of England Festival. After work I left for Worthing. Sadly, despite travelling by car through snow and icy roads to take part in the festival, it was finally cancelled due to weather conditions and I had to turn round on reaching Worthing and drive all the way back to Surbiton! On the way down I was stuck in miles of traffic, no one could move and I was desperate to find a loo. I saw a field of brussel sprouts across a ditch. I told the driver of the car behind me what I was doing. He said he would be doing the same himself in a short time. It was nearly dark and the car lights of the stationary queue of cars must have had an interesting sight of me squatting in amongst the cold, wet brussel sprouts! The traffic still had not moved when I got back into my car. This was not one of my happiest expeditions!

1968 still found me at Russell Court in my last year as a health visitor.

Up to this time I had not affiliated myself regularly with a local church but in April I attended St Mark's Church in Surbiton, where I sang in the choir for a short time before going to St Andrew's in the town centre, where I was to sing in the choir for many years. I became a member of the PCC (Parish Church Council) and the organiser of the advertising in the Parish Magazine, which involved visiting shops etc and renewing their desire to advertise with us. I very much enjoyed doing this but found the physical requirements were becoming too difficult.

I underwent another spinal fusion and while having my surgery received a letter and a large bunch of flowers at the hospital from the Chapel Royal. Once recovered, I was appointed to give a talk for the Royal Borough of Kingston by Dr John C Birchell, the Medical Officer of Health, in a syllabus of a course for *Visitors to*

169

h

the Elderly at the New Malden Education Centre. In December I also gave talks on the *Day Care of Children* and *Accidents in the Home*.

There were severe floods in Hampton and Molesey this year. I remember well that I put on my wellington boots and went down in my car to see if I could do anything to help. As I went along Summer Road in Thames Ditton towards the A309 I found two boys doing the front crawl up the road, which was by now a running river. One look was enough; I realised there was nothing I could do and wading through the water got back in my car and went home again.

June 1969. Nancy Cooley, a young schoolgirl and a talented musical friend of mine, asked me to sing three of her songs in the Molesey Festival. She also performed with me at a concert in 1973. She was an amazingly accomplished composer for one so young and I am sure must have gone on to become an outstanding musician.

In November Malden and Coombe Old People's Welfare Association invited me to serve on their Executive Committee as a co-opted member.

I did the greatest amount of singing in the 1960s, both amateur and professional. Noted at the back of this book is a list of some of the singing I took part in for anyone who shares my passion.

Towards the end of this decade an interesting event happened one day whilst visiting Barclays Bank in Worcester Park and talking to the Bank Manager. His phone rang and his conversation went something like this: 'Oh dear, only this morning? What can we do? There's no time to find anyone else!' He looked so distraught and I, feeling so sorry for him (I had no idea what had happened), pointed to myself and whispered, 'Can I be of help?' He asked the caller to 'wait a minute', then turned to me saying, 'The speaker we had booked has had to go away and can't give the talk at our Rotary Club dinner.' 'When is it?' I asked. 'Tomorrow,' he replied. 'On what subject?' I asked. 'World Understanding,' he said looking despairingly at me. With appalling arrogance and with ideas flashing through my mind I said, 'I'll do it.' He gaped at me and said, 'Really?' I nodded. He removed his hand covering the phone and said, 'It's OK, I've got a speaker.' It was only then that I realised what I had let myself in for! On asking who the speaker was to have been, the reply was,

'The Iranian Ambassador.' I could have crawled under the table. In the end I decided to use my experiences of travelling to many countries and recount the help and kindness I had received, and hoped this would be one way of conveying the idea of 'world unity'. The evening of the talk arrived and after sherry and a gorgeous three-course meal with wine, I was well 'oiled' to embark on this dangerous mission. It must have been accepted judging by the barrage of questions that followed, and I departed before they held their Rotarian Meeting, greatly relieved and quite elated. This took place in March 1969 at the Rotary Club in Cheam.

Chapter Eleven

Allow me to share with you a poem written by a fellow health visitor titled *The Lay of the Government Lady*, published in the *Nursing Times*:

> Anna Maria Sophia Jones, was just a bundle of skin and bones,
> The sort of woman you often meet,
> With knobbeldy fingers and large flat feet;
> Her hair was dragged behind in a bunch,
> And she had dinner when you had lunch.
>
> The Government lady came to the door,
> With printed leaflets, dozens and more –
> She spoke to Maria, firmly and long,
> And all that Maria did was wrong.
> She oughtn't to peel potatoes and boil them,
> To peel potatoes was only to spoil them.
> She oughtn't to waste the pods of the pea,
> She oughtn't to stew and stew her tea;
> She oughtn't to feed her baby on breads
> Before it had ever a tooth in its head!
>
> (Anna Maria, mother of five,
> Three were dead but two were alive,
> Always HAD given her baby bread
> Before it had ever a tooth in its head.)
> She oughtn't to spend her money on drink
> She oughtn't to stuff up the drain of the sink;

She oughtn't to shut out the air and the light,
She oughtn't to shut up the windows at night;
(Anna Maria Sophia Jones,
Always fastened her windows 'click',
Air in the bedroom made her sick!)

She oughtn't to buy herself ready-made clothes
She oughtn't – she oughtn't – Oh! Goodness knows
But Anna Maria had spirit within her
The spirit saw what was right she went and did it,
And then, if needs was, afterwards hid it.
Anna Maria Sophia Jones asked in dull and colourless tones
The government Lady to walk inside –
Opened the door of the passage wide
Took a chopper and hit her hard,
Buried the body in the yard.
                                    Anonymous

One of my health visiting experiences was when a dear old lady was dying and she begged me to take and look after her canary and an aspidistra plant; I really couldn't refuse. After she died, sadly the aspidistra died on me later and I found someone who was very lonely and delighted to be given the canary. What a relief!

Throughout my time as a health visitor I had been plagued by back pain, which at times became so painful I had to lie on my bed to ease it. Nothing wrong could be seen on X-rays and I was treated for depression. Anyone who knew me would know I was not a depressive; there was far too much going on in my life which I was enjoying but the pain followed me wherever I went. I had to give up playing tennis which quite broke my heart. Friends were very supportive and I much appreciated their kindness but at this time I was having more time off sick and concerned that I was letting my colleagues at work down.

I realised that climbing up and down the lengthy flights of stairs in the many flats of my area was in fact not a very wise thing to be doing. I started wondering where I should go in the world of work that might be less physically demanding.

In September 1969 I retired from the Health Department of Kingston upon Thames and was given a leaving party at the Manor Drive Clinic by sixty-five colleagues, and received a book

173

titled *Companion to Music*, from the Medical Offices of Health, which I am still using to this day, but sadly, much of it is grossly out of date! I have maintained my interest in this area ever since leaving and am still in contact with a few of the parents.

I had much enjoyed giving talks to people of all ages and seemed to have no problem in holding their attention, so my thoughts went to teaching young children and I decided to look around and see where my chances in teacher education might lie. This was to be a major change in my life; after twenty-seven years in nursing I was to become a qualified teacher.

I was invited for an interview at Gipsy Hill College for Teacher Training on Kingston Hill. I was interviewed by the principal, who, on hearing how highly qualified I was as a nurse, told me that she was sorry but she did not think it would be right to take me from the nursing profession. I was amazed at this. I thought it was for *me* to make that decision! As it turned out I was glad she didn't accept me.

I looked around and found that there was a teacher training college called Froebel in Roehampton. I wrote to the college and was invited for an interview.

The Froebel Institute was founded in 1892 for the training of teachers and the education of children. In years to come this was to be part of Roehampton University. To this day the National Froebel Foundation and the Froebel Research Committee continue to keep alive Friedrich Froebel's philosophy for the teaching of children.

As I drove in through the lower gate I saw a group of young ladies crawling around on their hands and knees in the grass with magnifying glasses. I thought this looked like the place for me! Driving through the beautiful grounds, I was aware of gorgeous old gnarled trees, acres of grassland and, approaching the college building, saw a most beautiful Edwardian house and beyond it a rose garden above a large lake. I thought I was dreaming and knew this was where I wanted to be. Importantly, there were plenty of trees under which I could park my car to keep Mandy and Picky cool when they would come with me. Picky was one of Mandy's puppies.

I was interviewed by a member of staff in a very friendly and relaxed way and thought I had probably been accepted, *but* there had to be an exam to see if I would manage the course. I had

174

always been terrified of exams and on the day I crept in, scared stiff I was going to have to do maths sums! In the event I thoroughly enjoyed it. The questions were such as 'What did Mr Brown say to the housekeeper when he called at the house?' On the desk were four copies of books. It took only intelligence and an inquisitive mind to find the answers (both of which, I *think*, I have my share) and I passed! Three years were to go by like a few weeks and I enjoyed every day I spent there.

I was 43 and excited at the prospect of starting my training as a teacher. Only shortly before I had been responsible for overseeing the health of over 300 families, babies, school children, elderly people and the mentally handicapped, as they were then called. I held clinics and was the school nurse for a junior and an infant school and a visitor to various nursery schools. Suddenly I had found my freedom (I thought!) feeling the yoke was off my back and experiencing a great sense of release.

So it was that in September 1969, I drove up the front drive, off Roehampton Lane, and turned into the car park in a secluded area surrounded by trees where I hoped my dogs would be sheltered and reasonably happy. I entered the beautiful Grove House and was directed to the hall further down the drive, where we were to be addressed, in a somewhat school-like manner, by the principal of Froebel, Miss Molly Brearley. Whispered comments around me suggested that the students, practically all female, were unhappy at being talked to 'like schoolgirls'. Most of them had only recently left school and were eager to move into a different adult world whereas I was quite enjoying returning to the ethos of my younger days! To my amazement some just walked out of the hall!

We were required to attend some lectures such as Child Development, the Life and Ideology of Friedrich Froebel, English and Maths. But we were able to choose two other subjects, I chose Art and Music. For my main subject I had great difficulty choosing between Dance and Drama, mainly because of my past physical problems and my worry about memorising drama scripts. So I opted out of Drama, chose Dance and spent a wonderful three years studying *Laban Dance and Movement*. Rudolph Laban (1879-1958) used time, weight, direction of movement and the relation of the body to the space around it. The

175

course was held in the beautiful Michaelis Hall, a very large studio overlooking the Roehampton golf course. Here I used to arrive early in the morning, driving through Richmond Park, and practised my dances.

Mollie Davies was my main tutor, who patiently saw me through the best and the worst times. During this time I tore knee ligaments and had to have surgery on my knee, when at the same time receiving the news that my brother Pogy had died following surgery for cancer of the lungs. Mollie and Jill Williams, another tutor, made it possible for me to attend his funeral in Devon by kindly driving me up to Paddington Station to join my family on the train and meeting me at the station and returning me to hospital in Surbiton.

It was also not easy at the age of 43 to slot into a group of 18 and 19 year olds and, although I tried very hard to fit in, at times I felt rather like an outcast. I was to find out that I was going to be 'granny' to the other students. For the first few days these young ladies got up to offer their seats to me with a certain amount of deference, it wasn't until I said, 'I am one of you,' and wore trousers and the Froebel jumper and scarf, that they finally began to accept me. Some of the girls were very kind to me and invited me to their rooms but as I had to care for my dogs most of my free time was spent taking them out of the car and walking them around the grounds out of sight of the principal's room! After lectures were over I had to drive back home to Surbiton, about half an hour's drive, and do my shopping, cleaning and deal with the mail and everything else one has to do at home.

The Royal Borough of Kingston had paid to train me as a health visitor. I was now only eligible to have a grant towards education fees. So, for the three years I was at Froebel I got no help with a living allowance. Thus it was that I set about finding how I could finance myself to pay for my bills, rates, food, petrol, car expenses, etc. This had to be done during my free time after college and at the weekends when I was not writing or preparing for my studies or singing in concerts! I fitted in any paid work as best I could.

The first opportunity that came along was cleaning the flat of a friend, who was my vet. She had dogs with very long hair which I had to gather up from all corners of the flat. Then I heard that the Surbiton Tennis Club needed someone to clean the ladies

176

changing room and toilets. I took on this job which suited me well; I could take my dog and radio with me and took my books to study with as well. When I eventually stopped, someone told me that they missed sliding off the polished loo seats! I gave up this job because I had to stay at the college into the evenings as well, so I changed to cleaning cars!

Cleaning cars is quite an enjoyable and rewarding occupation and I started cleaning the college staff cars. One day the principal came out as I was cleaning a car near the front door and asked me what I was doing and why. When I told her she asked me if I would clean hers too. I was fond of Miss Brearley. I had once asked her secretary if I could have an appointment to see her. When asked, 'What did you want to see her about?' I answered that I just wanted to meet her. On entering Miss Brearley's room, I was greeted very warmly and when asked why I had wanted to see her, I told her that I had met all my matrons face to face but had never had the chance to talk to her and hoped she didn't mind my doing so. In fact she seemed quite pleased. Many years later, when I visited her in her home, she told me that I was the first student who had ever done so and she was very pleased that I did.

I thought I would try cleaning cars in the street and used to stand outside a hairdresser's in Ewell Road in a white coat, bucket and sponge in my hands, and offered to clean the cars of people going in to have their hair done. This was very successful so I continued doing this while I was at college and my bills were quite well covered.

The success of the car cleaning was largely due to the kindness of a friend, Eileen Haywood (now deceased), who owned a dress shop on the opposite corner, who allowed me to get clean water from her kitchen. Her shop was called *Emma Mayo*. One morning she rang me up and asked if I would like to take part in a mannequin show she was putting on in the Surbiton Assembly Rooms. I thought this sounded great fun and as it was for charity (we raised £124 for the Tolworth Hospital Chapel fund), it was yet one more experience in my life. So, along with other of her friends and customers, I duly walked the red carpet with many quick changes of clothes and much mirth. She kindly allowed us to keep one of the outfits we had worn as a 'thank you' for helping her. I was so glad to have had this experience, especially as I had just gone through several terrible months of dieting. How many times was I to do this in my lifetime; but this time it was mainly so I could get into my dance leotard and avoid acute embarrassment when displaying my far from beautiful figure!

Another of my fundraising activities was to work in the sorting department of the post office in Surbiton at Christmas time. This experience stands out in my memory as doing something quite different from what I had been used to. I enjoyed throwing the envelopes into the right baskets; it reminded me of playing netball!

Quite early on in my first year I arranged with other students of my year to invite a group of elderly people from the Malden Old People's Welfare to a party in the Student Union building. We arranged to borrow wheelchairs from Queen Mary's Hospital across the road and every student took on caring for one of the guests and saw to their every need. We gave them tea and the students entertained them and there was much hilarity. It was a very successful venture.

It was about this time, when in my second year, that I decided to coach tennis. Although not qualified as a tennis coach, I was a reasonably good tennis player and, as a prospectively trained teacher, had no difficulty helping adults and children to play. One of the boys I taught won the junior competition run by the local Kingston Council which thrilled him and me!

I put an advertisement into the local paper and to my surprise I got an immediate response and much enjoyed coaching children and adults on the local council courts. So desperate was I to get some spending money that I sometimes committed terrible sins and charged extortionate rates of 12/- (shillings) per hour for them! One day I woke up to a dark, foggy, dreary, ice cold winter morning and the student, an adult, rang me up asking if I was still teaching that morning. 'Oh yes,' I said cheerily. 'Just wrap up and wear gloves and we'll soon warm up on the court.' By the time she arrived the fog had thickened and we had some difficulty seeing where each one of us was on the other side of the net! I remember her calling out, 'Where are you?' 'I'm over here,' I called back. What a farce! Icicles formed and 'clinked' as they fell to the ground when the balls hit the net. Despite this, with 'gloved' hands, we managed to have a lesson and I gratefully pocketed my fee and booked her in for the following week. . . 'weather permitting'.

At Froebel I chanced to glance at the notice board and saw a request for a student to befriend a young girl in a nearby social services residential home. I volunteered. I visited this young 15 year old girl, Shirley, who at that moment was up in her bedroom with her boyfriend, Peter, sitting on the bed beside her. I was immediately enchanted by them both and sat and chatted with them for some time. Before leaving the building I went into the warden's office. He seemed concerned about their close relationship up in the bedroom! I tried to reassure him, telling him I didn't think he needed to worry (hoping very much that I was right!) and that if he was happy I would like to visit Shirley every week.

Throughout my time at Froebel I continued collecting Shirley in my car and taking her either to Richmond Park or into the grounds of the college, where we talked together about her life and any worries she had. She adored Mandy and Picky who were in the car and used to sit hugging them. I'm sure they were invaluable in helping to heal her turbulent past traumas and gave her some of the love she was so badly needing. We were to have a lasting friendship, to this day, and I was delighted when she and Peter were married and invited me to their wedding, and later were to have a family of children and dogs!

I much enjoyed the many classes we attended, natural sciences, English, French, art and *even* maths. I particularly like to solve practical problems and once when assigned to measure the height of the ceiling without the aid of measuring tools or ladder within the classroom, an idea suddenly struck me. I pulled down the blind and attached a long ball of string to the bottom of it, then allowed it to recoil to the top of the window which was at ceiling height. I then cut off the string at floor level, pulled down the blind again and detached the string, and, popping outside, found a ruler and measured it. I received good marks for my intuition!

I loved the grounds at Froebel, the gorgeous trees, the beautiful architecture of Grove House and the furniture which the students were trusted to look after. In fact I loved the whole of my three years there and have been happy to keep in touch with it through the Michaelis Guild, which I joined on leaving in 1972, but sadly now disbanded. What a privilege it is to be a Froebelian.

An invitation came from Kingston Hospital asking me to sing

179

the soprano solos for Handel's *Messiah*. Their conductor, Charles Kelson, was putting on one performance by the staff from various departments at the hospital and another performance at St Luke's Church nearby. I was delighted to accept. Both concerts appeared to have been very successful and were well attended.

Teaching practice was a nerve-wracking time: preparing lessons for children you had never met and in a school you have never visited before. My hair stood on end at the back of my neck! However, I managed to pass this. We had to do a practice in two different schools teaching children of the age near to that in which we specialised, in my case 5-7 year olds.

In 1970 my first teaching practice was at the Vineyard School in Richmond which I enjoyed very much. It was so delightful being able to drive through Richmond Park from Kingston Gate and out of Richmond Gate. The school was only two minutes from there. My memories of it are of a friendly and purposeful place; I think I am always happy where there are children.

My final teaching practice was in a school which I believe was in Cherry Tree Avenue, West Drayton and it took me about three quarters of an hour to get there by car. One morning I was due to give a talk to a group of children, which was to be assessed, so I dared not be late. On the way along a dual carriage road, a car in front of me, driven by a lady, was weaving from side to side across both the middle and outside lanes. I was mesmerised and thought I must be imagining it but it continued all the way up the road. I had nothing to write the number down on and was so concerned that I should arrive at school on time that I did nothing about it. I have regretted not doing something ever since and can only wonder if she had been asleep, ill or on drugs or whatever else might have caused her to do this. I only hope she didn't have, or cause, an accident further on.

Alongside the practical dance exams we were required to write a dissertation on a subject chosen by ourselves; mine was called 'Mood and Movement', the research for this I much enjoyed, particularly studying the behaviour of the crowds at a Chelsea football match. Final dance exams were held in our beautiful dance hall: groups, duo and solo dances were judged and again I was greatly relieved to pass.

I had visited a lovely school, which I very much liked, in Kingston to do my first year as a probationary teacher there. But

180

because I was waiting to hear if I was eligible to continue with the second part of the degree course, the headteacher (whom I also liked very much) said she could not keep the vacancy open; so I lost my chance to apply there. In the short time remaining I had to apply to another school, and as there was no choice left, I had to take the only one which had not been filled by a student at a local infant school.

Whilst awaiting the result of my application, I found that travelling was a great way to take one's mind off immediate concerns. I was very glad to have had the opportunity to again visit friends and family in Seattle over April. Later, in August, I went to Vancouver and Victoria on Vancouver Island before assuming my responsibilities back in England. I believe it was around this time that I bought my Austin 1300, which I named 'Omti', which was to serve me well in the years to come.

My application was accepted and I did my probationary year at Tolworth Infants School, with a salary of £1700 per annum, from September 1972 with a class of 4-5 year olds whom I thoroughly enjoyed. Some of them could not manage to go to the toilet on their own and others couldn't tie up their shoe laces, so the word 'teaching' took on a multidisciplinary meaning! It was such a pleasure to have them sitting on the floor in front of me when I read to them, or answering questions when they didn't understand something. At the end of my first year here I qualified as a teacher.

On a flight back from a holiday abroad, always mindful of possible teaching aids, I asked the air hostess if she would give me all the used little salt and pepper pots instead of throwing them away. I arrived in the classroom with this exciting parcel and showed them to the children: they showed *me* what they could do with them, stacking them upwards and making patterns with them as well as counting them. I found it quite amazing how cheap and everyday objects could be used in an interesting and original way to hold the attention of young children.

One day, on passing the premises of a printing firm, I noticed a beautiful white book stand (the kind displaying paperback books in shops) and seeing it was standing beside the rubbish bins, I went in to ask if they were throwing it out. They were; 'Help yourself.' I trundled it home along the street to my flat and there I washed the white plastic sections from top to bottom of the eight tiers and into every section I placed the cards I had made. There were four sides to the stand and I used one for maths, one for English, one for writing and spelling and one for reading. Each was graded in difficulty and numbered, so that I could put into my records the stage the child had reached. The children loved it and were keen to go up to the next rung of ability and always had to bring one of their cards and satisfy me that they had understood what was asked of them. So it was that the brighter children ended up near the top and moved on to the next card and the less bright were always working their way upwards and so rewarded for their work. In this way they were able to work at their own pace and to see their progress.

From the beginning, my Froebel training and individual method of teaching was not appreciated by the headteacher, who would have preferred me to teach everything by rote standing at the front of the class with the blackboard. Although I loved teaching the children, it appeared she was determined to make my life unbearable and moved me from my class to another one outside in a nissen hut.

One day, when in the staff room, we were told that we were going to have a visit from an Inspector from London to assess the work being done in the school. I had no fears for, despite the Head's opinion of me and my work, I knew that I was a good teacher and had a great relationship with the children in my class. Miss Feldman came to each of our classrooms and my children behaved beautifully, showing her every area of our classroom and responding to her questions.

The next morning the Head came into the staffroom to tell us of her findings. 'You will like to know that Miss Feldman says the best teacher in the school is Miss Vlasto.' She didn't so much as glance my way! There was a stunned silence. I would have liked the ground to open up under my feet, so embarrassed was I, a probationer, in my first year, among all those teachers of many years. You could have heard a pin drop!

However, her attitude to me did not change. If it had not been for the kindness and emotional support given to me from one of the other teachers, and the support by the Teachers' Union, I think I would have given up any idea of teaching. I spent much of the time in tears which I had to hide from the children. Some of the parents had noticed my distress, despite my efforts to hide it, and came in to offer me their reassurance and concern that I might leave their children. These parents gave me a beautiful red vase full of flowers when I left shortly after; the vase still adorns my house. I was so grateful for their support.

In the end, in desperation, I phoned our Education Department and was invited to go and see them. I drove there and was welcomed with a cup of coffee and understanding. I shall not disclose the conversation I had with them, suffice to say that shortly afterwards, following two years spent at the school, I was moved to Dysart School for Mentally Handicapped Children in Ham (now described as 'Special Needs'). I was to work happily at Dysart for three years from April 1974.

Many years later while collecting for the Pakistan earthquake in 2005 in the Kingston town centre, a lady came up to me and said, 'Do you remember me? No! It was thirty-three years ago! You taught my daughter Nicola at Tolworth Infants School. You were a wonderful teacher, so kind, patient and lovely. Thank you.' It made my day! And I took out a piece of paper from my bag and wrote down what she had said, so amazed was I at her kind words. I was on such a high that, possibly, I didn't drive my scooter around as safely as I should have!

Fortunately, as you will have realised, I had many other interests which helped to put the stresses in my life into context and bring some relief to stressful times! Once in February 1973, when I was rehearsing to sing solos at a wedding in Westerham Parish Church, I experienced a blissful time of music-making. Some of the choirboys came as well to practice the psalm they were going to sing. When I went in the boys were already practising and I was greeted by strains of music from the organ echoing around the church in the darkness and peace and quiet inside. A welcome from the organist and warm acceptance from the ranks of the choirboys (to whom I was a complete stranger) and away we went. Who can ever attempt to describe the deep sense of pleasure that music-making in this fashion can bring! I was acutely conscious of the sympathetic reception I was given and it is an evening I shall long remember.

Dysart was a school on one level, very light and airy and not far from Richmond Park. Again, problems confronted me! The 'Special' Schools, which had originally been the responsibility of the Health Department, became the responsibility of the Education

Department. Teachers took over the role of nurses who were once in charge of the classes. So it was that I was immediately appointed, by the headteacher Betty Mitchell, as 'Teacher in Charge of Special Care'. The unfortunate trained nurse who had run this area over many years suddenly found me, a teacher, in charge of *her* Special Unit. I found it a very embarrassing situation and she was obviously very upset and hurt. An assistant, Joyce, who had worked with her over several years, also found the situation very difficult. I don't think I managed the transition very well, but I just had to carry on as best I could.

The children cared for in my class were mostly very young, from five years upwards. The degree of their needs varied, but a few were unable to sit up or stand and none, at that time, had any speech. Their means of communication was mainly through their expression and their eyes. We encouraged movement in their limbs, particularly their hands. Locating and grasping items on a table in front of them required their concentration. But their attention span was limited and, therefore, many were unable to feed themselves thus requiring individual help at mealtimes, this was also true for daily toileting needs.

Some time later I transferred to the next class called the Nursery. There one or two of the children were able to stand and even walk a little. I enjoyed working in both of these classes and became very fond of the children. One of my responsibilities was taking music and movement for the whole school and the hall provided a good area to hold these sessions. My excellent classroom assistant was Irene Gent.

The headteacher and her deputy put on a wonderful show at Christmas in which all the children took part and to which their parents, families and friends came. Staff and parents pulled together in a wonderful way, making costumes and helping with props and lighting. The shows were surprisingly professional in their presentation.

During the three years I spent at Dysart I was promoted to Scale 2, when Mrs Mitchell was the headteacher, which gave me an increase in salary for the responsibilities which I was already undertaking, being in charge of the nursery and movement classes.

A few of the children at the top end of the school were sent on an activities course at the Crystal Palace Sports Centre in London.

I was one of the staff chosen to accompany them. It is a fascinating place covering a large area. There is an enormous swimming pool, a track, a pitch where hockey and football are played as well as an area for archery and indoor sports such as table tennis. The children much enjoyed their visit but, of course, had to be very closely supervised. The residential building was very unusual with a spiral staircase leading up to separate rooms off the sides at different levels. One teacher supervised two rooms. When we were having meals, the café staff kindly allowed a few of the children to wait on the tables, which they did surprisingly well despite their problems.

Later, I was to attend a course there for teachers, which was even more fun! I had a go at most of the sports; new to me was archery but I did not enjoy it very much as I prefer active games. The swimming pool was a joy and I dived off the board below the top one, being too scared (and maybe wise) to attempt the highest. The table tennis coach was the coach for the England team who told me that, with some coaching, I could probably make the county team. I was astounded! It was somewhat of an anti-climax to return to school, but the course had been stimulating and presented me with several ideas when planning activities for the children.

I went to several concerts at Wigmore Hall in London at this time. One I especially remember is 20th June 1973 when my friend David Johnston was giving a recital, accompanied by Geoffrey Parsons at the piano.

Other musical activities in which I very much enjoyed being involved included working with the Court Opera Group, under the direction of the late Lesley Woolf. My friend Pat Bayliff, who was kind enough to invite me to join her when doing other concerts, suggested to Lesley that I might enjoy singing with them when they performed Verdi's *Il Trovatore*. I eagerly agreed and in 1975 played a nun and a gypsy and had a whale of a time. For one of their productions, *Mignon*, by Ambroise Thomas, I see that my role was 'properties' and I made a wand for one of the singer's props! In February this year I was invited by my cousin Mary McDonald to sing *God Be in My Head* at her wedding in Edinburgh. She was to marry Surgeon Rear Admiral Albert E. Cadman at St Luke's Church.

Summer holiday time arrived. My niece Mariam gave me the

dates she would be free from college and I booked some of my annual leave. The planning started to travel by my Austin 1300 car to Denia in Spain. My sister-in-law's family owned a small house where I was told we could stay. I invited Janet, a friend of mine, and Mariam invited a fellow student friend of hers, to join us. Both accepted and we began to make plans and work out our route. Tickets for the Channel crossing were bought and keys to the house in Denia collected. I bought many tins of baked beans and mince with the thought that they would at least save us from starvation if times became difficult or if we should lose our money or any other calamity. Our cases were tied to the roof along with the two tents.

At last we set off from outside my flat, the poor car groaning beneath the weight. My neighbours waved us off pointing to the wheels and calling out that they could only see half of them, so low in the road were we running. We laughingly said we would have to hurry up and use the tinned food to lessen the weight! I just hoped that no policemen would notice us. Only then did I have 'butterflies' in my stomach. I glanced at the milometer which read 21,277 miles and we noted this so we could calculate the distances we had covered daily.

As the only driver of the four of us, I realised it was vital that I remained fit and alert and that the responsibility was on my shoulders to get us safely there and back. I took out a hefty insurance to try and cover most eventualities and planned our route, noting in the camping book which camps we were to use. The facilities at these varied greatly from one to the other as we were to discover. All had toilets but not all had private washing facilities. Most were situated in scenic areas and some had a games room, table tennis or a small library where books might be borrowed for the duration of the visit. It would all be an exciting voyage of discovery.

We made for Newhaven where we boarded the boat that would make the Channel crossing to Dieppe. The sea was calm and we took turns resting in the cabin we had booked, arriving in France at 6am. All was quiet as the town still slept and we drove off via Louverne where we stopped for a drink of coffee still hot in our thermos. Driving on we came to a garage in Acquigny where we filled up on petrol and bought some fresh bread for breakfast.

One of my favourite stops to explore was Chartres, where we visited the gorgeous cathedral and walked around the attractive town savouring the French atmosphere all around us.

Back in the car we moved on to find the campsite at Vendôme, where we pitched our tents. It was then 1.30pm and after lighting a small fire we heated some mince and beans for lunch. After this we gratefully settled down on our respective camp beds for a siesta. In the evening we wandered around the area talking with others also visiting the camp, mainly backpacking or families on holiday. It was such a relief to be out of the hot stuffy car. Unfortunately my car didn't have air conditioning.

After a breakfast of tea and coffee and the new bread we had bought with the butter and marmalade we had taken with us (though the butter had turned into a liquid in the heat of the car!), we set off. At 7.30 on the morning of the 29th we made for St Marie de Touraine and from there we drove to Angoulême, where between 2 and 3pm we stopped for some lunch – yes more mince and baked beans! At 6pm we camped at Onesse.

The next morning, July 30th, we stowed away our tent beds and sleeping bags and made for San Sebastián where I noted our mileage read 21,903. We were making good progress and so far had had no problems. . . that is up to now! For, as we climbed up the steep Pyrenees mountain roads my fan belt broke, bringing us to a rather sudden halt with smoke billowing from the engine. You may well imagine my horror.

Fortunately, there were many kind young people climbing in the mountains who rushed to see what they could do to help. One young man asked his girlfriend if she could spare the tights she was wearing. She took them off and, opening the bonnet, her boyfriend tied them around the fan belt. To my joy and amazement the engine started again and, pushed by a group of young men and women, we rolled off down the mountainside waving and shouting our thanks to all the good souls who had, literally, saved us.

As we arrived in the valley below, here, strategically placed was a garage. The proprietor was sound asleep in the shade of the nearby trees having his siesta. I believe the area was called Vittoria. We waited for him to wake up as we drank some badly needed water from our bottles and hid in the shade from the searing sun. Once awake the garage owner quickly solved our problem with a new fan belt and we went on our way greatly relieved and ready for whatever might lie ahead.

Little did we know that a thunderstorm of monstrous proportion was about to engulf us as we climbed to Pamplona in the darkness of night. A very good campsite greeted us where we bought an excellent evening meal from their restaurant and relished eating food other than our tinned meat and beans! There was a lovely open air swimming pool which we could just make out in the dark as we parked our car in the lashing storm with streaks of lightning sweeping across us and in the distance below. Sadly, it was too risky to get into the water, although we would have given a lot to throw ourselves into it and refresh ourselves from the dust of the journey. We pitched our tents and fell into a deep sleep.

We woke in the morning to warm sunshine and emerging from our tents, were flabbergasted to find that not only had I parked the car right up to the edge of a cliff but also our tents were perilously close to the cliff edge and we had been completely unaware of it the night before! A narrow escape, I know I offered up a little prayer of thanks as we drove off that morning. We set off at 7.45 ready to face the long hot drive through the desert of Tudela and Zaragoza. We stopped for coffee in a café at Tudela and for lunch in Minalur. (I do hope I have remembered these names correctly; it was a long time ago.) After this we set off to cross the dry barren area of land until we arrived, roasted with the heat and desperate for more fluids, at a bar ranch in Teruel. I drank around six pints of liquid before I fully recovered.

Having refreshed ourselves we left for the final leg of our journey to Denia where we arrived at 11pm, having travelled 1,087 miles since leaving Surbiton. I have never been so glad to reach anywhere! We found the lovely little villa where we were to stay on the hillside overlooking the town and out to the sea. Here a breeze cooled the relentless hot air and after drinks we threw ourselves onto our respective beds and slept through till late the next morning.

We only had ten days to spend as we were due to return by August 13th. We had booked a cabin on the Channel crossing leaving Dieppe at 6.30am to Newhaven. But at this moment our only thoughts were to enjoy the stay in Denia, and after checking our needs for the kitchen, we set off for the market and to get our bearings in relation to the beach.

I have somewhat hazy memories of the days we spent there but two stand out very strongly in my mind. We had only been there a few days when Mariam's friend, who was very fair-skinned, got heat stroke and became quite poorly, only able to lie in her bunk sweating heavily and semi-conscious. I was extremely concerned about her and decided to give her ice cold washes as she lay where she was. Thankfully this, along with iced drinks, reduced her temperature and she gradually recovered, but it was a worrying time and there was nothing a doctor could have done other than what I did.

The other memory is that, for some reason, my niece and I were very keen to have a midnight bathe in the nude! I have no idea what put this thought in our minds but we were quite determined to carry it out. Through my mind went: police, prison, who would drive my car home, booking flights to get the others home. Despite this, when night fell, we set off in the dark to walk down to the beach, our hearts pounding and well aware of the risks we were taking. I still remember the feeling of the cool air on my body and throwing my clothes on the sand as we quietly waded into the water, whispering supportive comments to each other. We splashed as little as possible so as not to draw attention to anyone nearby.

Having swum around for a very short time we made the decision to get out while the going was good and, towelling ourselves and redressing, hastily walked up the beach and through the town back to our friends. I don't know when I have been so relieved to get 'home' safely without having been caught. I am told that there is more leniency in this respect now; I shudder to think of the risk we took then!

And so our time at Denia sadly came to an end and at 7am on August 9th, we set off for our return trip. The car boot was replenished with fresh fruit and vegetables from the market and our water bottles refilled.

Our first stopping place was just outside Valencia, where we had coffee before setting off for a campsite at Zaragoza. The next morning we set off making for a campsite at Aire-sur-l'Adour. En route we stopped for coffee at Huesca and then for lunch at Pau. We reached Aire-sur-l'Adour at 2.15 and set up our tents before looking around the area.

The next day, our usual 7am start found us en route for

189

Perigneux where we began using up our tins of food. At 10.45 we left for Limoges. My car by now was many tins of food lighter and I could feel the difference as I drove along. Unfortunately, on the return journey we did not risk stopping to sightsee the towns as we passed through them, as our time was limited and we daren't risk being late for the ferry if anything should hold us up during our last hours in France.

At Limoges we camped at Lussac les Châteaux. Here we had a somewhat nerve-wracking experience. After we had tucked into our beds for the night our tent flap was suddenly pulled apart and a large burly and very drunk Russian man started trying to get into our tent. We hastily told him where he could go and he stumbled out falling into his own tent two away from ours. A near miss, I think!

Leaving that campsite safely behind us we made for Londun where we had our usual coffee stop and two hours later stopped for lunch at Le Mans. Our last night was spent in the campsite of Beaumont-sur-Sarthe. On leaving the camp we made for Rouen, where we did sightsee and, again, much enjoyed the interesting buildings, markets and meeting and attempting to talk with the people. We now made for the ferry at Dieppe where we found our boat already waiting for its passengers to arrive.

We left Newhaven at 6.30 and drove to Surbiton arriving home at about 8am with the milometer reading 23,980. I am no mathematician but I believe we had driven 2,703 miles on our wonderful journey to Spain but was I glad to get safely home!

On another occasion when Mariam was staying with me, we were invited to a fancy dress party at Kenneth Rotter's house, my father's successor as an ENT surgeon. They lived in Hampton and we were going to drive there. Mariam dressed as a Red Indian and I went as a baby. I wore a long baby's dress with a matching bonnet, a dummy in my mouth and a bib round my neck with a bottle of milk, suitably laced with a more intoxicating liquor, hanging around my waist. It had last been worn by my father!

As I got into the driving seat I commented to Mariam that all we needed was to bump into a policeman on the way! As we approached a roundabout in Thames Ditton what should we see but a policeman in the middle of the road holding up his hand to stop us to tell us the road ahead was closed. His face was a picture as he looked at this large 'baby' driving the car with a Red Indian beside her. I'd like to have been a fly on the wall back at the police station! To crown the evening, the person who answered the door bell when we arrived was dressed as a baby boy wearing nappies and with a dummy in his mouth! I was not very impressed and I spent the evening trying to avoid him as he insisted on following me from room to room. I was quite relieved to get home safely without any more hold ups by the police.

At an Annual General Meeting of the Kingston and District Chamber Music Society (KCMS) on 21st June 1976 I was elected onto the committee. KCMS was a very active group of musicians who played to a very high standard and gave monthly concerts. As a committee member one was responsible for attending monthly meetings and took it in turn to plan the music for the next programme.

In 1977 a vacancy for a Deputy Headteacher's post was advertised for Lindon Bennett School in Hanworth on the other side of the River Thames; it was a special school for junior children with learning difficulties. I applied for it and was sent for an interview at the Civic Centre in the borough of Hounslow on February 21st. The four other interviewees, two were male, and me sat together waiting to be called in. Inside the interview room sat about seven people all of whom asked questions. I really did not believe I would get the job but, to my amazement, I was appointed and called in to meet and shake hands with all of them including my new headteacher, Mr Royce Spickett. I drove home, still in disbelief at what had happened, and called my dog, who was on the seat next to me, 'Deputy Dawg'.

Before starting, I was funded by the Council to follow a one year course in *The Education of Mentally Handicapped Children* at Maria Grey College in the borough of Hounslow. This was a wonderful course and gave me time to recover from my recent stresses. The staff were delightful and my colleagues very friendly. One of them, Rowena, and I still keep in contact. On completion of the course we took the exam for the Diploma in Education of Handicapped Children in 1979 which, thankfully, we passed.

Finally, I arrived at Lindon Bennett School, was welcomed at the staff meeting held on 26th April 1977 and began a new phase in my life. I much valued working here for the next nine years and enjoyed the challenge of my work as a Deputy Head and being responsible for teaching a class of seven children around ten years old.

As part of our day we sat at table with our respective classes, overseeing their meal times and teaching the older children table manners and, because of this, the staff were given daily free lunches which was very good. We were lucky to have our own kitchen, kitchen staff and excellent dinners. Each class had an assistant who worked alongside the teacher. They were important members of the staff and helped the teachers in many ways.

The children were brought to school in coaches or by car. There was a strong sense of being a 'family' linked with the school – teachers, ancillary workers, coach drivers, attendants, the kitchen staff, the school caretaker and the cleaners were all part of the children's life and helped to make their days as happy as possible.

I was lucky to have a piano in my classroom and made full use of it in my teaching. We also had a television which we took turns in using. One summer we watched a few Wimbledon tennis matches. I followed this through by helping the children to 'have a go' with racquets and soft balls with a net strung across our dining room/assembly hall. This turned out to be quite a popular way of getting some exercise and was also an excellent way of aiding hand-eye coordination. We were given a free hand to teach in the way we found best. No two children were the same and all had varying disabilities which had to be considered. We were fortunate in having a flexible headteacher and a very supportive Education Department in the borough of Hounslow.

One of my roles as Deputy Head was to visit parents in their homes; this I much enjoyed (at the same time being very aware of the problems they faced) and was helped by seeing the children's homes and talking with their families. I became the Professional Tutor for the school after attending a course run by the Hounslow Education Department. I also drove the mini-bus, taking the children riding at the Kingston Riding School every week. Earlier I had taken the Advanced Driving Test to improve my driving skills. At the same time I also attended an *Art of Motoring* course run by the Kingston Borough Council. I found this an enormous help and still think back to the advice we were given when driving my car or, as I now have to, riding my mobility scooter.

This was how I stood beside the trees at Robin Hood Gate in Richmond Park. Drivers entering the park were pointing at Blossom and laughing – which is what I hoped would happen.

On the last occasion when I wore Blossom's head which frightened the young children, 1994.

When I was still able to walk unaided, I stopped to talk to our local police.

Myself, Blossom and her new 'Baby Bud' out collecting at Christmas time, 2005.

Muffy joined me,
in basket, and
greatly helped
attract donors.

At Imber Court
Horse Show with
Graham Cole of
The Bill television
programme.

Collecting in
Kingston upon
Thames for
St John's
Ambulance,
1996.

Blossom out riding!
In the company of
local dignitaries.

Most of Set 86
UCH reunion
at Jean Smart's,
1990.

The University
College Hospital
reunion cake.

Self dressed as
Dawn French
in the 'Vicar of
Dibley'.

Mandy and her three puppies, 1966.

Hector, one of Mandy's puppies.

A canary I
inherited from
a dear
old lady.

Karen on the night
she delivered her
four puppies,
1986.

Pixie and Mandy,
Surbiton,
1969.

Mum with Sootie and Pandy,
1979.

Celebrating my 70th birthday
with Muffy, 1996.

Muffy age 15,
in 2000.

Meg and Annie.

Meg and Annie:
'It wasn't us!'

At the Vlasto Arch in Frinton, with Muffy, 1996.

Joyce Griffin and I on either side of the Mayor of Kingston.

At Club St Lucia, our flat is on the left.

Riding the dolphins in Bahia de Naranjo.

Vintage cars in
Havana, mainly
used as taxis.

Picture of
Che Guevara
on building in
Havana.

Self at the
front desk at
New Malden
Police Station.

Outside the
Police Station with
Brian Jackson.

At my Advanced Driving Test, taken in Putney on 4th June 1976, outside the Star and Garter Hotel at the Towpath entrance, I had to negotiate the steep hill leading up to the Lower Richmond Road. I felt this was a test in itself as it required going through all the gears to successfully exit onto the main road. Today, possibly there might be fewer accidents if drivers were required to take an advanced driver's course after, perhaps, three or four years of driving. Perhaps the driver could pay a reasonable fee to cover the costs and have to pass a test to get a new driving licence and they might also be required to produce evidence of a current insurance certificate.

In the summer of 1977, with my friend Eileen Conway, we went by train from Olympia (where we put the car on the train) to Perth, Scotland. From Perth we camped all over Scotland. We pitched our tent wherever we could find a place. On the first night we stayed at the Scone Palace campsite. We spent one night in the Isle of Skye where, as soon as we started cooking, we were bitten to pieces by mosquitoes! In desperation we left our tent and took a room at a nearby hotel for the night. We were aiming for Achiltibuie, a lovely little village overlooking the sea and the Summer Isles and drove through an area of the most gorgeous lochs. The scenery reminded me of the mountainous areas of Canada. We visited the Edinburgh Festival and the Tattoo and enjoyed wandering around all the events being held.

As I write this part of my life, I am aware what freedom I had in being able to walk, run and travel around anywhere I wanted. One can't realise how lucky it is to be able to do this until physical limitations take over. At this time I am only able to walk with crutches and get about with difficulty. Perhaps that is why I am so grateful for the many years I have had of sports and physical activities.

In March 1979 I gave a talk on *My Varied Life* to The Wives Club at All Saints' Church in Hampton. How I ever came to do this I have no idea but perhaps it set me on the path to write this memoir.

In the same month staff and children at Lindon Bennett School marched around the playground to raise money for Dr Barnardo's. On another occasion, we were invited by the WRVS in Hounslow and Hampshire to spend a day in the country. On 22nd June 1979 school staff and local WRVS volunteers accompanied the

193

j

children on the trip. They had a centre at Burlesdon, Hampshire where we joined another group from Ealing.

While I was busy at work, I was telephoned to be told that my father was dying and I immediately took leave from my school. My sister Christian returned to England from her home in Karachi, when she heard that my father had been taken ill and was unlikely to recover and Helen came from Brasted. We three 'girls' sat in the sitting room next door to where my father lay in his bed. Once my mother had gone to bed we took it in turns to keep watch as he neared his end. I find it difficult to forgive myself that I went to sleep during my 'watch' and he slipped away, lying peacefully beside my mother in the small hours of May 29th 1979. Having asked Buckingham Palace to send a telegram for my parents' 60th wedding anniversary, I notified them of my father's death and on 6th June received a kind letter from Her Majesty the Queen expressing her sympathy. My father was a much-missed person in our family circle and had left his mark in the medical world of his time, but to this day I am sorry I was not able to have been closer to him and he to me.

BUCKINGHAM PALACE

6th June 1979

Dear Miss Vlasto,

I am writing to say that The Queen is very sorry to hear of the death of your Father only a few weeks before the sixtieth anniversary of his Wedding Day, and I am commanded by Her Majesty to express to your Mother and to yourself her deep sympathy.

Yours sincerely,

Robert Fellowes.

Miss N. Vlasto

My mother was keen that we should buy a wooden bench in his memory to be placed outside the council offices in Oxted at the corner of our road. This we did and it is still there to this day. As someone who had difficulty walking and with the need to sit down frequently she was particularly glad that this would be of help to many people living or visiting in Oxted.

Chapter Twelve

In January 1980 we had a visit to Lindon Bennett School from the newsreader and broadcaster Angela Rippon. She came to present the school with a television which was a donation from Shrewsbury House, a prep school for boys in Surbiton. We were delighted to have it and took it in turns during the week to have it in our classroom. For the occasion, my classroom was turned into a makeshift refectory with tables laid out along the sides with white clothed trestle tables laden with cakes, biscuits, cups and saucers and tea and coffee. She chatted freely with everybody before taking her leave. And so it was back to work and the children all trying to draw their idea of a television. This they thoroughly enjoyed.

Hounslow was a very innovative borough and around this time organised workshops, one of which was for parents of children with Down's Syndrome. In June I gave a talk on *Your Child at School*; seven others of varying disciplines also gave talks weekly over two months. In addition, I was invited to the opening of a 'Hounslow Toy Library for Handicapped Children', in what was the International Year of the Disabled Child, in new premises at Smallbury Green Centre in London Road, Isleworth. I was on the Toy Library committee for some time but had to resign due to other commitments.

During school time I attended a Professional Tutors' course *Society, School and the Community* and one day gave a talk on *Special Schools and the Wider Community – the Present and the*

Future. This course lasted a month and at the end of it I took my mother back to Oxted. On January 29th I gave a talk at the Keith Grove Centre in London to the Invalid Children's Aid Association. I returned to Surbiton where I examined members of Malden Emergency First Aid Society (MEFAS) in *Home Nursing*.

In February I sang in the chorus with the Oxted and Limpsfield Choral Society, with full orchestra, Monteverdi's *Beatus Vir*, the Beethoven *Choral Fantasia* and Brahms' *Requiem*, a lovely programme which was a joy to take part in. I always received such a warm welcome from the conductor Wilfred White and all the choir members.

1981 was a most difficult year which began with the death of my beloved Pandy who was put to sleep following abdominal problems – losing your dog is like losing a member of the family. My friend, Jo Leach, knowing how upset I was, gave me one of her puppies, Karen, as a replacement. Karen was also red and equally sweet-natured and not long after, produced her own puppies.

My mother, being on her own now in the Oxted house, was lonely and I took to bringing her over to my flat for trial periods to see how we would manage and I loved having her with me. Although I was aware that she was used to being in her own environment I couldn't see how she could manage the house and garden on her own. By this time she was physically disabled with arthritis and her mental capacity was not as good as it had been. I had in my mind that possibly she could join me for the rest of her days. However, having observed her over several days when I had to go to school early every morning, I was concerned that she might have an accident while I was out and felt that it would not be in her best interest to live permanently with me at this time.

On April 2nd we took off on a visit to my sister in Karachi. I collected my mother from Oxted and with suitcases and Mum's wheelchair went to the airport. We were hysterical with laughter when the airline staff had to put us, plus wheelchair, into the food lift to get us into the plane! We arrived in Karachi on what Christians call Good Friday and were met by a bevy of family at the exit gate. I do not know what negotiations had gone on before our arrival; I only know that we did not have to go through customs.

We did many things in Pakistan, one of which was to visit

Clifton Beach and Hawks Bay and the market which buzzed with activity. On the 11th April my niece Mariam, my mother and I flew to Lahore to spend five days in the house they had there, where we joined her husband who was there on business. An interesting and memorable event took place during this time. Mariam asked me to keep an eye on her chickens. She told me birds might fly down and go off with them. Unfortunately, I looked the wrong way momentarily and heard squawking noises and turned around to find the bird had flown away with a chicken in its beak disappearing into the distance.

We also visited the beautiful gardens of Shalimar and were able to push my mother everywhere we went in her wheelchair. However, I had a severe stomach upset and spent some time on my bed with diarrhoea and vomiting. Luckily it just cleared up before we were due to fly back to Karachi on the 16th, spending a night at the Midway Hotel before flying home early on the 17th.

We arrived back at Heathrow, collected 'Sootie' (Mum's dog) and I drove my mother back to Oxted, then I returned to Surbiton and back to school the following day.

From now on my visits to Oxted became more frequent and I was finding it quite tiring while keeping my work at school a priority. My friend Joyce kindly spent several weeks sleeping at Mum's house so she would not be alone. I brought my mother over to stay with me ever more frequently. It was easier for me having her here; she spent much of her day watching television and playing with the dog. She became progressively forgetful and restricted in her ability to walk. She would come into my room at 2 or 3am with her nightie, coat and hat on, letting me know she was ready to go to the shops. Having put her back in her bed she would repeat the process about half and hour later and it became increasingly difficult.

At that time there were few clubs or day centres for the elderly in the vicinity. The only one possible day centre sent transport around to pick up clients, but I would have to go to work and my mother would not be able to get herself dressed properly or be aware of the time they would call for her. One day she was seen by one of my neighbours walking along the pavement trying the door handles of each of the cars. When she went out to talk to her, she said she was looking for me as she was going to the hairdressers. The door of my flat was left wide open. Friends and neighbours kindly came and spent time with her but I could not expect them to go on doing this indefinitely.

At the weekends I took her home to Oxted. It seemed at this time that *life* was crowding in on me. I am sure my sisters would have liked me to leave Surbiton and my school job and go to Oxted to live with Mum, although they never said so. I asked Helen if Aidan, her husband, could recommend anyone to live-in with her or if there was a residential home nearby in Oxted. She told me he didn't know of any. I realised then that they didn't want to be involved and it was down to me to decide what to do and I discussed the matter with Mum's solicitor who was looking after her affairs.

With great sadness and with my mother present, my sister Helen and I spent hours clearing up and sharing out the furniture at our mother's house as she sat by watching. It was deeply distressing but at least Mum was able to choose which pieces of furniture she took with her. These came by removal van to dress her bedroom at Russell Court and those left over were housed in my garage until we moved to a house where they would furnish her room.

On his death, my father had left us children a sum of money which would enable me to move to a house of my own – something I had long wished to do. I began driving around the area looking at houses for sale with two to three bedrooms, where my mother could live with me. I saw one very near the tennis courts, a charming little place with a small garden round it. I made an offer but several months later they decided to take it off the market, which meant that my mother was unable to make full use of the furniture she chose to bring with her, which remained in the garage.

My mother's health had been cared for by my own GP (the late Dr Archie MacArthur) who was very good to her. Having seen the deterioration in her mental condition and the predicament I was in, he asked Social Services to see her. In February 1981 we visited a nearby residential home run by the council, but it did not seem to be the right place for her. Since the house by the tennis club had come off the market, my mother was less and less physically able and I realised I could not give her the care she needed even if I were to give up my work.

Another house, the one I live in now in Surbiton, was

advertised and I went to see it, still with the vain hope that my mother would be able to live there too. It was exactly what I wanted but despite being a bungalow there were three steep steps up to the front and back doors and, by now, I could not risk her being on her own with a gas cooker to manage and no one to help her as we were in a completely new environment. She had become very unsteady on her feet and was unable to work a wheelchair, either by hand or an electric one. I knew I would not be happy leaving her at home alone and when eventually I moved in, I knew I would have to try and find her somewhere where she would receive daily care and attention.

I asked Helen to come over and see the house, which she did. She agreed that it was a fair price and we discussed the need for an extension. It was obvious she wasn't happy about our mother going into a residential home any more than I was.

17 Russell Court sold. I had made an offer for the bungalow which was accepted, and I was to call it Gresham Cottage. I brought this name over from our house in Oxted with the agreement of my sisters. This was purely a sentimental matter to keep the memory alive of my parents and of their lovely home in Oxted. Roger Cowdrey, a friend and professional architect, came to the house to discuss and measure up an extension for the kitchen and sitting room. Another friend, now the late Alfred Barrett, spent a day putting up shelves in my kitchen and sitting room which are there and in full use to this day.

I moved in on 11th April 1981 and threw a party a few days later to which many of my friends came, helping in the house and bringing flowers and cards; I was so grateful for their support. It really was a wonderful welcome. I brought my mother along to join us.

The Matron of The Home of Compassion, Thames Ditton, whom I knew, had kindly taken my mother into the Home while we made the move and having done so told me that she had a vacancy in the Home if my mother would like to take it. I feared she would not want this, but said I would talk to her about it. I just wished I had my family with me to support me but unfortunately I had to do this all on my own and I was deeply distressed. The worst part was that I was told not to visit for fourteen days in order to give her time to settle. This was a terrible time. Not only did I miss her but I didn't want her to think I had forgotten her, rather, I wanted to share my love with her. But I had none of the family with whom I could discuss what to do. I was choked and was in tears at times. I had never felt so miserable.

She did eventually settle more and I visited her daily with Sootie but I knew she was not entirely happy there. So I took her out in her wheelchair for walks and to Gresham Cottage as often as I could until she became too ill to go out. She loved the cottage and called it 'our palace'. We used to go down to the river and then walk along the riverside to have a snack at the Harts Boatyard restaurant and then go back to Gresham Cottage to sit in the garden. My school work continued and whenever we put on any shows I took my mother there; she really enjoyed these outings.

In July 1981 the St Andrew's Church Choir of Surbiton kindly visited to the Home of Compassion and we gave a recital in its beautiful chapel, which was much appreciated and was attended by local people as well as those who lived in the Home.

In September I was invited to and attended the alumni party at Norland Place School. I drove up to London and was horrified to find how impossible parking had become. I was amazed since I hadn't been to London for a long time. I managed to squeeze in somewhere but did not stay long as I was scared of getting a parking ticket! Sadly I was not to see one person I recognised either amongst the past students or (not surprisingly) the staff but I was pleased to see the school again.

I went with Lindon Bennett for a trip to Bournemouth and stayed at the Eastcliff Court Hotel which was most successful and the staff were very tolerant and helpful. From there we paid a visit to Longleat, the wild animal park, in our mini-bus, which we all enjoyed. I think that we, adults, were more nervous than the children when the animals, particularly the monkeys, came all around and on top of our bus and pulled at the windscreen wipers. After we had returned to school and handed over the children to their parents I went straight to see my mother and then to collect my dog from Jo Leach.

For some months I had enjoyed attending an evening and a day class for art students in an adult education centre near my home. Annabel Bloxham and Bob Meecham were my two tutors, both superb artists in their own right. Both were equally encouraging and helpful. I felt I would never become an artist but I much enjoyed trying to be one. At the end of a summer term we arranged to meet for a picnic in the grounds of Hampton Court Palace with a bottle of wine or two and some nibbles. A rug was put down and we all settled down with Sootie sitting amongst us. We were the only ones in sight and began to feel that we probably weren't allowed to do this but decided we'd have to chance our luck. *Of course* along came a uniformed security man, who had his hands clasped behind his back. Annabel did her best to let him know how innocent we were and that we would be very quiet and not there for long. He was very kind and said we could stay and finish our picnic as long as we cleared up afterwards. We thanked him and gave him our assurance as he strolled away. We much enjoyed our party!

Later, with great sadness and with the advice of my vet, I had to have Sootie put to sleep. Mum was very sad when I broke the news to her in the Home of Compassion but accepted it when I told her of the trouble Sootie was having with her back. Sadly this is a frequent cause of problems in the dachshund breed but one lives in hope that they will have many years of happy life before it manifests itself. I have lost three with similar problems, though my first one lived for thirteen years.

On November 28th I brought my mother to Gresham Cottage for a birthday tea where two of my friends and one of my nephews, Richard, and his first wife Amanda, joined us.

December 25th my mother had been rather poorly but she had joined me for Christmas and to go to church in the morning. Unannounced on this day our GP called to visit us to wish us a happy Christmas. He had become a good friend and joined us in a drink. It was lovely.

The extensions to my house were being completed and on January 1st 1982 my mother and I sat happily in the new sitting room. Unfortunately, dry rot and wet rot was found across the front of the house with mould forming on the walls of one of the bedrooms, which may have given me the severe chest infection which I developed, resulting in hospitalisation.

Back at work, the headteacher told me he was applying for early retirement as he had not been very fit for some time. I was sad about this and it was unsettling for the school.

On April 17th I had a party at my home to celebrate one year since I moved in. As I write I am aware that, of the thirteen people who came to it, only five are still alive – a sobering thought! My mother, particularly, enjoyed the party.

This month I was asked to give a talk to the Toy Library at Hounslow. It was to be called *When is a toy not a toy?* This gave me food for thought and stimulated much discussion among the parents present.

I continued driving the minibus, taking the children riding at the Kingston Riding Centre every week. They really enjoyed this and benefited enormously both physically and mentally from the stimulation it brought them. So many volunteers for RDA made this possible, who at that time were ably led by Wendy Bott.

Driving past Tolworth Station I saw some sheds being sold outside a shop and thought that one of these would be the right thing to buy to put in the corner of my garden where I could store my tools. However, once purchased and put in place, I put my fork, spade and mower in one corner and realised I had the rest of the shed not being used. What should I do with it? It occurred to me that I could turn it into a little classroom.

So, in August 1982 I started giving reading, writing, spelling and grammar lessons for young children in 'The Little Den'. These were given individually for one hour between the hours of 4-7pm after school, which meant that I was able to help up to fifteen children a week. The numbers varied considerably for a multitude of reasons.

For some time I also taught piano and singing in the house. I was delighted when the first pupil appeared, having seen my advertisement in the paper, and seemed to enjoy coming. It was my first experience of making *others* learn their scales and arpeggios! And it was fun getting the new piano pieces they had to learn for the various grades they were taking. I did not very much enjoy putting children through their piano exam grades although, thankfully, they all seemed to do quite well. I had to keep swapping chairs in my house to suit the individual heights of the children!

Sadly, in November, news came that my sister Kish's husband Abbas had died in Karachi. At these times distance is such a barrier and one can do so little to help.

In my free time I became a member of the 'Parish Visitors' for St Andrew and St Mark's Church of Surbiton which I found very rewarding.

In February 1983 my mother had a fall in the Home of Compassion and in March she developed a cough and became much weaker and now remained in bed. I continued to visit her daily. In the early hours of the morning of March 29th, the Matron rang to tell me mother had died during the night. I had been with her during the day but had I known she would not last the night I would have stayed with her. She died peacefully in her sleep. I went straight to the Home, phoned Lindon Bennet School to say I would not be in that day, and rang my family to tell them the news. The Matron had already phoned Helen. Thankfully she and her family had been over to see her the day before.

Although Mum's end was obviously approaching, I was very distressed when the time came. My world fell apart as she was, truly, my best friend and a wonderful mother. Although one of my nephews did call in, generally I was without close family support. With the support and help of my church family, I somehow got through the days before the funeral, organising it all on my own. The funeral was held on March 31st at the Kingston Crematorium to which only family and one or two from my church came. In my distress I neglected to put her death in the *Telegraph*, so cousins were not sure where to go for the service; I felt bad about this. Nevertheless, my immediate family came to my house so I could lead the way to the crematorium.

Afterwards church and personal friends came to help with the food and doing the washing up and stayed to console me. I will never forget their kindness and hope that they will read this.

Following the death of my mother I hadn't yet managed to face up to life without her being around. I went back to school the day after and threw myself into work but I found that very hard. Particularly difficult for me was the first Easter Sunday. I needed to get away from Surbiton and have a brief complete change. I contacted my cousin in Marseille (like my sister, also a Helen Vlasto) and asked if I might pay her a short visit. I flew there and spent a few days with her in her beautiful flat. She kindly took me around the town and did most of the necessary talking in French. I understand it better than I speak it! I found Marseille, like London, to be a very frantic and bustling town but nevertheless exciting to visit. I had been there before to visit my aunt Netta, her mother, when she was alive.

On my return the first thing I did was to collect my dog from

Jo and to settle myself back at home. With the Easter holidays over, it was back to school. But the travel bug was in my blood and in the new year I was to visit my mother's cousin in America, following a visit from my sister Christian here.

I was delighted to be asked by my friend and neighbour, Louise Howlett, to help her with a piano exam she was to take. I felt very honoured to be asked since she herself was, and is, an excellent musician.

In December I sang in the Surbiton Music Festival and took part in the winners' performance. As nervous as ever I spent a considerable amount of time visiting the loo at the back of the St Andrew's Hall. I think it is sometimes easier to sing in front of strangers than it is in front of friends and family.

I was taking lodgers in to help me with my income. Students were at college most of the day and often studying at the weekends which worked quite well for me. They had a front door key and came and went as they wished. Later I took to having people who had daytime jobs and that too worked out very well.

As I had two spare rooms in my bungalow I began taking in more students. Most of the time this worked very smoothly but one autumn term I took in two girls and a young man. I noticed that at the top of the rent book I had written 'two months of purgatory'. This was because they virtually took over my house. They used to sit in the kitchen into the small hours of the morning with their feet up on the table and talking in loud voices despite my pleas for them to stop doing it. The man particularly became quite aggressive and I asked him to leave. The two girls tried to get off without paying their final week's rent but I caught them just as they were boarding a taxi at the gate. Later I discovered several items missing from my house but, of course, I had no evidence and needless to say they gave me no forwarding address.

I bought a table tennis table and put it up in my garage. I had a few games with a friend who was a very good player but she moved away and I did not manage to find anyone else interested. A few years later, I gave it to the Surbiton High Boys' Prep School.

I continued coaching children. At first I took pre-school children between three and five years old and held pre-reading and writing activities with them. This was to change to teaching

204

five year olds and upwards as I found the limited space in my garden 'Den' too restrictive for the needs of very young children.

As the winter holidays approached, I flew to Los Angeles to meet and visit with my American family, Linda, Doug and Bill Mitchell, who lived in Modesto, California. On Christmas Eve I was invited to sing in the choir of the Roman Catholic Church, where my cousin sang professionally. Of course I said yes and was delighted when I found we were to sing excerpts from Handel's *Messiah*. When the time came to take communion the choir all disappeared from the raised choir stalls at the back of the church to join the congregation below. I was left behind since as an Anglican I was not allowed to take communion in the Catholic Church. I was very distressed, and all the more so because it was Christmas Eve. I began to wish I had not agreed to help them out but there was nothing I could do except to show disapproval.

As always the Mitchells thoroughly spoilt me and, being as generous as ever, took me to the Rose Parade in Pasadena. I was sad to see all the vehicles covered in petals torn from beautiful flowers – what a waste! I then went to see the Yosemite National Park – beautiful and well worth a visit.

We had thirty family members together for a birthday party. On New Year's Eve Bill and Doris, his wife, took me to Disneyland along with Carol, their daughter, and we went on all the available rides. Among other visits they took me to the Hershey factory where chocolates were made. I was fascinated to see how the process moved from liquid chocolate to the solid bars and boxes of individual chocolates we buy in our shops. Needless to say we all bought boxes to take with us. I do not remember if mine ever stayed sealed until I reached home. I doubt it! On January 2nd I left for Modesto to visit more cousins.

Three days later, at the airport before heading towards London, there was a bomb scare, though it did not disrupt my flight which landed the next day and I was glad to have a rest from my speedy whistle-stop tour.

My 58th birthday was nothing spectacular – I just found myself a year older! However I drove to visit two old nursing friends, Janet Reeve and 'Sheppie' Tuite-Dalton, of whom I wrote earlier. I did quite a bit of getting about this month as I also drove down to my brother's and sister-in-law's farm in Devon and then to Dawlish on the Devon coast to spend a night with my friend

Eileen Conway, from Maria Gray College days. I love the way the trains run alongside the top of the Dawlish beach almost above the sun worshippers lying on the beach below.

I attended a reception by the Esher Conservative Party, in the Milk Marketing Board at Thames Ditton. My invitation stated that the chief guest was to be Sir Keith Joseph, Education Secretary at the time. Unfortunately, as usual, I never *have* recognised people, and when he came up to shake my hand I asked him who he was; I wanted the floor to swallow me up when he told me. He was very gracious about my faux-pas and in conversation it transpired he had gone to the same school as my brother! A few days later I wrote an apology to him for not recognising him and sent news and photos of my brother before his death in 1971. I also made some suggestions regarding records of achievement given to school children every year. Up to this time I believe only positive results were recorded but, from my experience as a teacher, negative ones should also be recorded as both are necessary as a base for learning upon which parents and children can build.

BGD 3M7

DEPARTMENT OF EDUCATION AND SCIENCE
ELIZABETH HOUSE YORK ROAD LONDON SE1 7PH
TELEPHONE 01-928 9222

FROM THE SECRETARY OF STATE

Miss Nancy Vlasto
Gresham Cottage
9 Avenue South
SURBITON
Surrey   8 August 1984

Dear Miss Vlasto,

I am sorry not to have replied earlier
to your letter of July 16. I was interested
to hear from you - after our brief meeting
at Thames Ditton - and to see the photographs
which I return herewith. Though your brother
and I were at school together, we did
not know each other very well as I don't
think that we were exact contemporaries.
As you realise, age groups count for much
at that time of life.

Thank you also for your comments on the
case for including shortcomings as well
as achievements in the records of achievement
which we hope to introduce.

Thank you again for writing.

Yours. Keith Joseph

Memories of my mother's death in March a year ago came flooding back. I think it takes a long time to overcome the loss of a parent; I certainly found it so. April also heralded three years since my living at Gresham Cottage and I held a drinks party to celebrate it.

At this time I had developed a fearsome cough and chest infection which meant I had to take to my bed and finally be admitted to Surbiton Hospital where no doctor, not even the

Queen's physician who attended me, could make out what was causing me to be so ill. I was encased in a steam tent and put on antibiotics but it took some time to settle. On seeing my GP a few weeks later he said all the trouble had cleared up and asked me what, if anything, different had happened in my life. I told him that severe damp had manifested itself along the front walls of my house and great areas of mould were growing along it. Since then the plaster has been taken right back to the brick and the wood and bricked areas treated for wet and dry rot and it had all been replastered and painted. '*That* was it!' said my doctor. 'I never thought to ask if you had damp.' Now I feel very knowledgeable about the danger of damp walls and the disastrous effect it can have on one's health, and in particular in the homes of those unable to pay for adequate heating.

In April and June, the St Andrew's Church choir held parties in my house, the latter was held in honour of Arthur Baxter, who had sung with the choir for over sixty years and was now retiring. My piano came in useful for parties and we didn't need encouragement to sing away the evening.

In June St Andrew's Choir went to sing at Tewkesbury Abbey which was a wonderful experience; a beautiful church overlooking the surrounding area.

On July 1st 1984 I went with a friend to see a production of *Son et Lumière* at Hampton Court Palace. It was extremely well produced and, as no visible actors take part in these productions, full use was made of the sound effects of boats arriving by water at the jetty below and the crunching of feet as they seemingly crossed the forecourt. Inside, silhouettes in the windows, the recorded voices of the people and clanking of glasses in the fully lit front room was most realistic. As darkness fell, the atmosphere became even more eerie as we were taken back into the times of Henry VIII.

In August Helen went to Karachi to attend the wedding of our great niece Neolofer. It was good that one of us was able to go. Tragically, however, Neolofer was to die from cancer when still a young woman and leaving a young family behind.

In November a major project was discussed at Lindon Bennet School. We needed a hydrotherapy pool for our children and an initial donation towards it had been made by the late Dr Bennet. It was decided to go ahead and raise the money needed. By April

Mr Spicket had retired and the new headteacher, Mrs Griffiths, was appointed and settled into the school. We had formed a sub-committee to raise the money for the hydrotherapy pool and had many meetings. The estimate was £152,000. Would we be able to find it?

In May 1985 I really 'went to town' to raise the money we needed for the hydrotherapy pool. I bought the *Directory of Grant Making Trust* book and it became my Bible for many months. I found it to be a most interesting and informative book and I learnt a lot about how to approach people for help when needing finance for an educational project. I began to understand how the wheels of the distribution of money went round and made endless phone calls and wrote even more endless 'begging' letters and was so grateful for the courteous and rewarding responses. We were certainly glad to know who to approach for help, which saved wasting a lot of time. Many meetings were held and the pool sub-committee met with the architects. The figure needed was eventually raised to £246,000.

The meetings were frequently held at my house to discuss raising money for the pool and I went on writing and phoning schools and firms, many of whom responded with great generosity. Occasionally I was given time away from my class to give talks in local schools. Other schools in the area, such as Denmead Boys' Prep School in Hampton, had kindly collected for our pool and I would go round to collect these. In October I was invited to take a collecting tin to a show jumping event at Hounslow Heath. Particularly generous were the German School in Richmond, Ibstock Place and Hampton Grammar. Their support was invaluable. It is not possible to name all the donors but we were so grateful for their help.

On the 11th a friend, Kay Newman, and I attended an 'at home' at Kingston Guildhall on behalf of the Surbiton and Tolworth Care Scheme. It was always a pleasure to attend these events and meet the mayor and councillors in their beautiful robes, and to look at the walls along the corridors where original paintings of past dignitaries of the borough were hung. Also enjoyable was the spread of food and drinks provided!

I became the press officer for the Care Scheme which was something I could do from home and, at this time, I saw an advertisement in which the Kingston Council was recruiting for their 'Stay a While Scheme'. This was when the elderly, frail or persons with special needs would be cared for to allow their families to have a break or holiday. This seemed a very worthwhile thing to do and I applied and was interviewed. After this, several people, mainly elderly, came to stay with me as well as one or two with special needs. In good weather they were able to sit in the garden and they loved to give and receive the attention of my dachshund who happily sat on their laps to be stroked. This was a great success as far as I was concerned. The visitor was brought to me and I cared for them during the holidays (24 hours a day if needs be) while their family had some time to themselves. In many cases this was very much needed. The ages and abilities largely controlled what activities I could do with them. Nearby play areas were very useful for the younger ones, but the adults fitted into my daily routine, coming with me wherever I went and sometimes ended up with an occasional night drink at the pub!

My sister Christian came over from Pakistan with her son Taimur. While he was here we visited Chessington Zoo which, at this time, really *was* a zoo and we revelled in getting close to so many wild animals. I never cease to be fascinated by the antics of the monkeys and the waddle of the penguins. In time it became more like a funfair.

Around this time I became interested in the Royal National Lifeboat Association and attended my first AGM of the Surbiton branch in the local library. One can't help noticing that it is mainly the over-forties who become involved in volunteering activities but perhaps it is natural that younger people want to be out and about and not attending the necessary meetings involved.

By now I was getting considerably more pain from my back as well as other parts of my body and decided that I should retire early, and visited my GP who agreed with me. It became evident to me that I would be unable to continue in full time teaching as I was now not able, physically, to help the children as I needed to and I decided to warn the Education Department and the school of my intentions. A visit to the borough doctor and a letter from him confirmed this as being a sensible thing to do.

X-rays now showed that I had developed osteoarthritis of my knees and hips. I think I could have told them this as my activities had been much curtailed as a result. I continued as Vice Chairman of the Care Scheme but was getting perilously close to having to cease these activities. A press article in the Surrey Comet brought us some more volunteers which was a great relief.

On March 3rd 1986 I deputised for my headteacher at a probationary teachers' meeting at Busch House School in Hounslow where nine other heads and deputy headteachers were giving talks and responding to questions from the floor. I was learning all the time what went on outside the school environment in the 'name of education'.

The day of my retirement loomed ever closer and I tried to think myself into days without a school routine. The school staff, governors and representatives from the Education Department gave me a very nice retirement party, and with considerable regret I drove away from Lindon Bennett School on March 27th. I sensed a mixture of sadness and at the same time of expectation for the future. I was sad to part from the children, the staff and my job of teaching which I so enjoyed. My sister Christian was over from Karachi and this made it easier for me to deal with the day. After she had gone back home I took in a delightful 'Stay a While' lady who was to stay for two weeks.

Having received a very kind and complimentary letter from the clerk of the Governors accepting my resignation I felt I could begin to consider what I could do to occupy my time that would not be so physically demanding. I was to go through a series of visits to my GP and Kingston Hospital.

Applying to the Kingston Adult Education Department for a part-time teaching role, I was appointed in May 1986. I much enjoyed teaching adult literacy, firstly in Kingston College and then we were moved to St Peter's Centre in Kingston. Later, my class moved to a room behind Surbiton Library, where several additional students joined us from Normansfield, a residential home between Ham and Twickenham.

I arranged with a well-known breeder of dachshunds for Karen to be mated with one of her dogs. She would be expecting puppies in June. She accompanied me in the car to Malden Manor Infants' School where I had been the school nurse and where they were celebrating their twenty-first year of being a school. Fortunately, Karen hung on long enough for me to drive home and during the night, between 4.30 and 6am, she produced four beautiful puppies in the playpen in my sitting room. I was sitting in there with her and found the arrival of perfect little puppies as amazing as the arrival of babies I delivered as a midwife. They brought me great joy and I loved looking after them until they all found good homes.

An invitation came for the opening of the 'Barbara Priestman House' inside the grounds of Ibstock Place School in Roehampton, which was described as the 'Demonstration School of the Froebel Institute'. The school still flourishes to this day but is now less closely linked with Froebel although it has its sports area within the grounds of the college.

In July I took in three junior tennis players from South Africa who were taking part in the Surrey Junior Championships at the Surbiton Lawn Tennis Club. One of them, Wayne Ferrera, was to become a well known player, also performing at Wimbledon. They were delightful lads and I enjoyed helping them, including washing their tennis clothes! Later I took in older people who were looking for bed and breakfast. I found this was less difficult than the students I had.

I continued with my role as honorary secretary for the Lindon Bennett School Pool Appeal and had particularly pleasant dealings with the Metropolitan Hospital Fund and a Mr Lynch in particular. He was one of the few who, on being approached, actually took the trouble to pay the school a visit. Following this we received two generous donations which were to help us greatly as we struggled to raise the money.

When our costs began to soar, we contacted one of the TV programmes which came to film us, both at a Riding for the Disabled session and our children having to use a paddling pool in the classroom. This highlighted the difficulties the teachers had in filling and emptying the pool, and physically supporting the children whilst kneeling on the hard floor.

At home I resigned from the Care Scheme committee but continued to move the 'case' from one Duty Officer's house to the next one, not a very onerous job but none the less necessary. It contained all the names, addresses and phone numbers of the volunteers, amongst other information. It is quite amazing how much voluntary work goes on, quietly, in the background all over the country.

I attended my first registry office wedding, which was held in

Wandsworth. It was the daughter of my best friend Betty, and who was also my God-daughter, Alison O'Neal. She was to marry Robert Coulson-Smith.

A stone's throw from my cottage, in Alexandra Drive, a beautiful new croquet club had opened and my friend, Joyce, and I decided to try out the game as the club was so near and we needed to take some exercise. Having thought it out we, independently, had both decided the game was too aggressive for us both physically and psychologically and did not follow it up.

The pool was still taking up much of my time. However I managed to do some private nursing for the British Nursing Association in Kingston, which was an interesting time. Most of the patients I nursed lived in beautiful homes in Esher; they were not heavy cases.

On the school front more money came from the C&A Modes of Hounslow keep-fit groups, the Cranford Community School, a Brentford and Fulham Football Club match and also Scouts and Guides groups. It was amazing that so many had heard of our pool needs and taken the trouble to help us. It is impossible to mention all by name here. I hope others who helped will forgive me for not mentioning them.

I continued taking in bed and breakfast visitors and particularly enjoyed the ones who came from abroad, often showing them the sights and driving them around. I once took a party of Americans, two adults and two children, down to Salisbury Plain to see Stonehenge at six o'clock in the morning returning in the afternoon; it was quite exhausting.

1987 was a bitterly cold winter. There was snow and it was freezing with -16°C temperatures. My elderly lodger at that time, Fred Bates, and I retired to our own beds for three days with hot water bottles as icicles hung down from doors and windows! I don't know whether it was the weather that made me look to the Windward Isles where I would find some warmth and sunshine but I planned a very exciting trip.

I decided to combine visiting my niece and her husband near Toronto and my ex-vet in St Lucia and, on looking at the map, also to drop in at Jamaica on the way to visit my nephew in Montego Bay. What a wonderful trip!

It was on 28th January 1987 that I flew to Toronto to stay with

Rosemary and Jonathan at their home in Pickering, Ontario. Two suitcases were packed, one for heat and one for cold. There had been quite a lot of snow and everywhere looked very picturesque. My niece was an occupational therapist and she took me to visit a special needs school, the R Lawson School, which I found very interesting. It was wonderful being taken around by car and wheelchair (I couldn't walk very far) so I could see a lot in a short time. On 1st February we celebrated mine, my great nephew's and my niece's birthday, looking out at the snowy scene as we sat secure and warm inside. In the afternoon we went to the ski slopes where my family performed in front of me while I sat by a log fire in the warm restaurant overlooking the slopes. I must admit to being a tiny bit envious of all the people, adults and little children, so happily enjoying skiing down the slope.

We paid a visit to see the Canadian National Tower and many families, mine among them, skated on the ice surrounding it. I found the Canadians to be friendly, fun-loving, out-of-doors people with a very positive outlook and willing to try anything.

On February 5th I flew to Montego Bay in Jamaica where Christian, who was visiting her son Kamran, were there to greet me at the airport. My nephew had a bungalow there, where we stayed, and I was fascinated at the way the large glamorous cruise ships sailed past my bedroom window. It was such a beautiful island but I was terrified and had my heart in my mouth as we drove up the pot-holed narrow roads with sheer drops down the sides into the gullies below. This alone would put me off going back there again! We joined in with a beach party where Caribbean music was being played and drinks served as the sea lapped on the sandy beach. The clear blue water of the sea was mesmerising!

I next flew to Barbados via Kingston, having to spend a night there to catch the plane to St Lucia where my friends had invited me to stay. I stayed one night at the Fairholme Hotel in Maxwell, Christchurch, at the recommendation of my travel agent. I seemed to be the only guest and breakfast was served outside on a little patio. It was all quite charming. The sandy beach, which was one minute's walk around the corner, reminded me of clotted cream and I would give anything to revisit this gorgeous part of the world. My nephew had arranged for a lawyer friend of his to show me round Barbados. Then they drove me to the little airport at 9.50pm where a plane flew me to St Lucia via Puerto Rico and Antigua, the tropical seaward islands.

We were faced with a very unpleasant incident in the plane. As we waited at the airport I had noticed a rather 'loud' and forceful woman nearby and hoped she wasn't getting on my plane; of course she was! And throughout the short trip she proceeded to swear at, and refuse to listen to, the calming attempts of the very charming air hostess. Concerned, I turned around and suggested she sat down and stopped being so noisy. She turned on me and told me to 'Shut your f----ing face!' Eventually, after much patience on the part of the air hostess, she disembarked when we called in at the island of Antigua and we breathed a sigh of relief. So well had the hostess handled the situation that I decided to recommend her tolerant behaviour to her employers on my return home to England. This I did and was pleased to have a very nice letter of thanks back from them.

At St Lucia the plane arrived at 10.29 (I have kept the tickets!) where I was met by John and Jo Rickards. They had a house up in the hills surrounded by banana plantations, forests and the Pitons (two mountains overlooking the sea) and the small town of Soufriere. My friends ran a tourist bus, showing visitors around, so I was very lucky to have an instructive tour of the area. The next day they drove me into the forests where parrots fly from tree to tree and to the hot-water pools where the sickening stench of sulphur fills the air. We went to Vieux Fort and had a meal at sunset in a restaurant overlooking the sea – quite stunning. We also paid a visit to the wonderful Agricultural Research Institute in Castries. I was fascinated seeing all the trucks pulling up in a long line alongside the dock area, laden with green bananas. They seemed to queue up there for ages before unloading their cargo into the waiting boats.

They also had a smallholding and, in their jeep, delivered produce to the many local restaurants and hotels; they took me with them, calling in at the back entrances, which was most interesting. Returning to their home, we sat drinking rum and I did my best to draw and paint an orchid by candlelight. There was no electricity and so no light or phone or hot water.

On February 18th my friends drove me to the airport and from there I flew back to Gatwick. Home again, I collected my dog from Jo and settled back into the English way of life. I have lived off the memories of this trip over the past 24 years.

In March 1987 a very good friend, Denis Hobkirk, died in New Malden, having been predeceased by his wife Cicely. It brought to an end close ties with that part of the Borough of Kingston and I was to miss them both greatly. I was amazed, in the months ahead, to hear he had generously left me a legacy in his will with which I bought a beautiful carpet from their house.

A presentation was held on 19th April for Gordon Reynolds at the Chapel Royal, Hampton Court. He was presented with a very special banner, to which we had all contributed, for his 20th anniversary as Organist and Master of Choristers. He was delighted with it, as was his wife.

St Andrew and St Mark's Churches both put up cricket teams to play in aid of repairing the roof of St Andrew's Church. It was hilarious. During the game, my runner (as I couldn't run myself), the choirboy Edward, unfortunately delayed his 'take-off', resulting in my very excellent partner, Valerie Baxter, being run out! Despite these hiccups we managed to raise a credible amount for the roof repairs.

I was invited to the AGM of The Kingston Riding for the Disabled Association. Their helpers kindly asked me to give out the prizes at the end of the summer term at the Kingston Riding Centre, which I much appreciated. The children looked so cute on their little ponies and were so excited to receive their progress prizes.

Further donations towards the building of the hydrotherapy pool were still arriving daily, each one requiring a letter of thanks. My dining room table was covered with papers relating to the pool. I held an informal evening at Gresham Cottage to raise money for the fund asking £5 from each person who came, which included drinks and snacks and the viewing of a film of the children riding their ponies at the Riding Centre showing the emotional and physical benefits they got from it.

On September 23rd 1987 I was appointed to supply teach juniors in dance and craft at Surbiton High School. This continued until October 23rd. I thoroughly enjoyed this month and had great fun with the most delightful girls. Among songs I taught them was one I had written for Lindon Bennett School 'The Lifeboat Tango'. Some of the girls came up to ask me to score a part for their particular instruments. Having done this, others joined them and in the end we had almost a full orchestra. The song was performed at one of the assemblies, the rest of the class and school forming the choir. The money I earned during this month paid for my new gas cooker; I only replaced it in 2010!

Cover of RNLI leaflet for *Lifeboat Tango*.

In November I was asked by the headteacher of the Surbiton High Boys' Prep School if I would cover as 'supply' for a class teacher who was on leave. I enjoyed this brief spell very much, in particular joining them playing football in the playground in the lunch break! I also taught piano which I did for many happy months.

This was also the time I was appointed to be a governor of Froebel College, which I found interesting. The functioning and future of the college was and still is of importance to me and I enjoyed the company and interaction with my fellow governors, from whom I learnt a great deal.

216

Continuing my efforts to raise money for the hydrotherapy pool I wrote to the Variety Club of Great Britain for financial assistance and crossed my fingers in the hope they might help us. They did, most generously; a cheque arrived for £15,000 which gave us a terrific boost to our funds. By 31st January 1989 the total had been reached with the support of the local authority, and the Bennett Pool was officially opened by Sir Geoffrey Dalton KCB and was immediately put to good use.

Following my retirement I linked up with my friend Joyce again to visit Holland. We saw an advertisement for a 4-day-all-in-package holiday with Saga to Amsterdam. We would leave from Victoria Station and go via Sittingbourne to Sheerness to board our ferry to Vlissingen, arriving at 7pm eight hours later. There we transferred to a coach to take us to Amsterdam, depositing us on the quay right beside our beautiful 'hotel' boat, the *Princess Juliana*, which was to be our home for the next four days. It was midnight when we arrived but the staff on board were all there with a most welcome hot dinner.

This boat was originally a Dutch barge and had been most beautifully converted with cabins down below and a dining room and sitting room at either end on the top deck. It was moored right beside the flower market and the train station and we could watch all the activities going on there as we sat and ate our meals; it was quite fascinating. We were free to explore Amsterdam and return for meals on board if we wished. Coach trips were laid on and we visited the exquisite Keukenhof Gardens where the carpet of tulips was in full bloom in outstanding vivid colours. We also went on a coach trip to Delft and The Hague. I still have the 'intact' blue and white candles on my mantelpiece!

It also seemed wrong not to see the 'night life' for which Amsterdam is so famous. So, one evening after supper, we walked the streets under the watchful and protective eyes of policemen standing at most corners of the roads. It was amazing to see many of the windows lit up with gorgeous ladies wearing precious little clothing or almost without any, posing inside, for all to see. Quite fascinating if not a little bizarre. We had a party on the last evening after sailing down the Amsterdam-Rhine Canal and visiting Schoonhoven. After breakfast on 14th April we disembarked and transferred by coach to Vlissingen again for our return, and rather rough, sea journey to Sheerness. I think

217

k

this was one of the most unusual and interesting trips I have made.

A *Dance and the Child International Conference* was held at Froebel College in July 1988 to which I was invited and I helped the committee. It was a real treat to see children dance with such energy and artistry. It was very successful, especially on the last day which culminated with a dance performance on the lawn outside.

Our family went to Edinburgh for the wedding of my cousin Kirsty's daughter, Alison Brewer, to Hector Forsyth. A very happy event followed by a true Scottish party with dancing, her father playing the violin.

I became aware that Froebel was offering courses for a Master's degree for mature students and started my course in the evenings in October 1988 finding it very stimulating. During this course I wrote an essay entitled *The Quality of Pupils' Learning Experience* and my sister Helen kindly agreed to type it for me on her computer. Early in January the next year I drove over to Brasted to take it to her. Obviously there was much reading to be done and many seminars to attend, which I much enjoyed. After submitting an essay to my tutor, Peter Jackson, I remember being so relieved!

Regretfully, the commitments of my life outside the college were such that I found I couldn't cope with the pressures and amount of reading required and reluctantly resigned part way through the course. Probably I should never have started it! I was sorry to have let my tutor down as he had tried so hard to help me.

In March the choir at St Andrew and St Mark's sang at a service for the induction of the Rev. David Gerrard as Archdeacon of Wandsworth at Southwark Cathedral. Not only did we sing beautiful music but I always revel in singing in historic churches such as this.

At home I had fun reshaping my garden and had large square stones laid as a path bordering the lawn in the middle. My garden seemed to be a haven for five pigeons which strutted up and down the lawn finding things to eat. Squirrels too dangled from the branches of a lilac tree outside my sitting room window. Hanging from the branches by their tails they would swing themselves down to the bird feeders to get to the seeds, nuts and crusts of bread put out for them. A very miserable and painfully thin fox had been trotting around the garden, obviously hungry, and I saw it eating the flower heads off my agapanthus! It left as quickly and as silently as it came so there was no chance to involve the help of any animal rescuers.

In July, while Christian was visiting me, I held an exhibition of some of her paintings in my garage. A coat of paint on the walls, a carpet on the floor, a few chairs for those who needed to sit down (like me!) and the paintings, hung from hooks in the walls, made for an attractive gallery. A table with white cloth and flowers in a vase on it complemented the somewhat unique venue. I had advertised the event in the local paper and was amazed to see hoards of people descending upon us up the garden path. A glass of sherry or wine and time to peruse the exhibition enabled her to make over £1000, which more than delighted us! My friend Johnny (now deceased) sat at a table at the entrance acting as our treasurer, which was a great help, and left my sister and myself free to welcome and talk to the visitors.

I decided to retire from teaching the piano at Surbiton Boys' Prep School and gave my last lesson there on July 10th. I knew I would miss teaching there but I was having increasing difficulty getting about and decided it would be better to 'pull my horns in' and continue with my teaching at home.

Friends from Nanaimo, Eleanor Hendy and her daughter Ann, came to stay with me and I took them to see the beautiful garden at Wisley, which we all enjoyed.

Chapter Thirteen

'Blossom' arrives. 'Who on earth is Blossom?' you may well ask. When I retired early, on medical grounds, I decided I would like to do something to entertain children at their parties. As you have read, I have always been fond of horses so I decided to have a pantomime horse's costume made, but who to approach? An actress friend in Surbiton, Sue Wall, suggested I looked in *The Stage* magazine. That I did and found a firm called *Annies*, who were costumiers in Bognor Regis. I rang them up and asked if they could make one for me. The gentleman said they only made them in two halves with back and front legs. I said that was of no use to me. I needed to have an all-in-one horse as I wished to be able to perform on my own. He said they would see what they could do. I was sent a form to fill in with measurements of my arms, legs, waist and every other part of me.

I waited impatiently for Blossom to arrive and then one day she *did!* It was brought in a parcel by a man and there was an incredulous look on his face when I said, 'At last you've brought me my horse!' He obviously thought I was mad so I gave him a brief explanation which seemed to satisfy him.

I was thrilled to bits and kept trying her on and taking her off and putting her head on and looking in the mirror to see how like a *real* horse I was. It looked pretty good to me and early on a Monday morning in September 1989 I rang the Victim Support Office and said, 'I've just bought a horse, what shall I call her?' 'You've done what?' 'I've bought a horse outfit and I want a

220

name for her.' 'Nancy's bought a horse and needs a name for her!' she called out! In the background I heard much laughter and chatter and I heard one voice call out, 'Tell her to call it Blossom.' As soon as I heard that I said, 'That's fine, a perfect name for her. We'll call her Blossom!' and that was how Blossom was born.

She was a skewbald (brown and white) and had a black tail. The only problem was that the inside of her nostrils were pink and I was to discover, some time later, that cows have pink inside their nostrils but horses are darker. For a long time I was asked, 'How is the cow?' or 'Does your cow run races?' I had a job to persuade them that she was a horse. I started putting gymkhana rosettes on her bridle but they still persisted in calling her a cow even though I pointed out that cows don't jump. So I coloured the inside of her nostrils with a black pen and that improved matters considerably. After the first few outings she made I used to wash her in the washing machine. Unfortunately the pressure exerted on the material, as she rotated, made her stretch somewhat, so over time she has had various surgical 'tuck' procedures to tighten her skin up so she still fits me!

I advertised in the local paper to perform at parties but only got two requests: one from one of my church friends and another from my family! I set up rows of little jumps about two inches off the floor and stood little green trees, like the ones used on Christmas cakes, at the sides of each one. The children were seated in a long row down both sides of the hall and were encouraged to cheer Blossom on in her race over the jumps. Unfortunately, I was having increasing difficulty moving about. I got over the first one, but then found it was too painful to do so. I decided to turn it into a fun event by tripping over one jump then creeping round the next; this got the children howling with laughter, it was a great success! At tea time I sat and had tea with them after giving a couple of 'rides' on my back which I found I also couldn't do again.

So, regretfully, I had to give up this idea and think how else she could usefully be employed. *Then* an idea came to me. We could go out in the street collecting for charity. In 1990 Blossom became a charity collector. I used to wear her head over mine but I found that it was too frightening for young children and I wasn't able to talk to people. That is when I decided to put her head into the front basket of my scooter while I still wore the rest of her!

A chat with the local Constabulary and the Mayor's secretary put me in the business of charity collecting. For those who did not have their own, I got tins and seals and labels to put on them from a local firm. I carried out my first collection which was for Victim Support. For many years Blossom was to collect money for various charities which I was in the fortunate position of being able to name. Then she increasingly went out to collect money in the wake of severe disasters.

School children whom I continued to tutor in my Den at home had lessons which consisted of reading, writing and spelling; any words for which they did not know the meaning were written on strips of paper with the meaning on the back. In order to ensure they understood them I used to ask them to write sentences incorporating the word. You may imagine how I had to contain my laughter when one little boy, who had been given the word 'erect', described as meaning to put up; such as a tent or building, wrote: 'I had to *erect* with my supply teacher today.'

I joined the Kingston Support Counselling Team of Disaster Planning and attended regular meetings held in the Kingston Guildhall. Recent indiscriminate attacks by terrorists in the centre of London and elsewhere were particularly concerning and it was essential to prepare for any eventuality. The original working group was formed from council officers, social services, representatives from the police, voluntary organisations and the health authority, all of whom could be involved were they needed.

For some years I had been a member of the Malden Emergency First Aid team (MEFAS), attending meetings and taking part in practical workshops, some of which took place in the open country simulating accidents which were acted out by members and were very realistic! I remember hiding in some bushes with a 'broken leg' and having to be found as soon as possible. On being located they had to make a stretcher and manoeuvre me down a rather steep slope after giving me first aid. I was then placed in our old out-of-use ambulance (used to carry our carol singers around the area to raise money at Christmas) and driven to the nearest first aid post. It was difficult to keep a straight face, particularly as I was far from being a minimum flyweight and they nearly dropped me off the stretcher!

Sadly, in January I lost my beloved dachshund Muffin. I had to put her to sleep as she was now nearly deaf and blind and not the happy dog she used to be. She had been such a good friend to me, even helping my students with their reading! Sometimes I would sit her on my lap as I listened to the child reading aloud and I would say to the child, 'Muffin thinks one of those words wasn't quite right, do you know which one it might have been?' Muffin would then be helped to put her paw under the offending word. After we had discussed it I would put Muffin's ear to my mouth and ask if she had put it right and the child would look at her and I would say, 'She says it's right now, well done.' I sometimes wondered if the children deliberately misread a word so that this little play could be re-enacted! I think children learn much better when having fun; I know I did.

In June 1991 I received a disabled badge for my car allowing me to park where others could not – what a blessing that was to be!

There were a great many celebrations this year: ten years of happiness living at Gresham Cottage, a UCH reunion of my Set 86 and the centenary celebrations at Froebel College, with all past staff and students invited both by letter and by an advertisement in the *Telegraph* newspaper. At the latter event, many hundreds came and balloons were released at the back of Grove House. It was a great event and raised much-needed money for our cause to build a new academic building.

Throughout 1990 I gave talks on *Teaching Adults with Learning Difficulties* to various groups of students studying social science subjects at Hillcroft College in Surbiton. They appeared to be interested in my role as a teacher and several came to help with my special needs class and gain experience in this area of work. I received delightful letters from them following their visits. It was good for my students to experience talking to and receiving help from someone other than myself and my two wonderful volunteer 'helpers' Lorna Brindley and Carey Grosse.

These students needed help in many areas, such as reading, writing, spelling and handling money as well as social behaviour and other activities. To this end, we used to mark birthdays and special events by a visit to a local pub. Here they had to pay for their drinks with money we gave them and count the change and be generally sociable to the people around them. Some of them found this difficult but people were very helpful. We generally had about six to ten students at any one time which was good when it came to playing football or cricket in our nearby Fishponds park. We made sure we used a tennis ball and not a cricket ball as theirs and our sense of direction was not always very accurate! This was an excellent activity to aid hand/eye coordination and using numbers to score runs.

The last lesson I taught was held in my garden at Gresham Cottage. All the students staggered in through the back gate, assisted by Lorna and Carey, carrying a beautiful model of a fox, as a leaving gift. To this day, despite losing his beautiful brown colour, he sits at the top end of my garden, now an 'Arctic' fox as his surface has turned white, gazing across the lawn at my house, a reminder of the happy time I had with them all.

I was still singing with the newly named Kingston Choral Society and we sang Mozart's Mass in Kingston Parish Church in November. I must admit I missed the atmosphere of the excellent Surbiton Oratorio Society (SOS) as it had been called and the expert conducting of our former conductor John Wilkinson. I found the changes difficult to take and did not sing with Kingston Choral for very long, although they, too, were a good choir.

My friend Louise Howlett and I sang a duet in the Kingston Festival and were amazed to be awarded the 1990 Gerald Bentall Cup for our performance. We were both delighted and decided to share the cup for six months each so we could enjoy having it around.

At this time I joined volunteers working with the Macmillan Community Care Team of Kingston and Esher Health Authority, being allocated patients to visit and offer help, by the Kingston Hospital Team. One could not always do much for them but a listening ear and a gentle touch, or doing some shopping, was always welcome. Most of the Care Team's meetings were held in the post-graduate medical school of Kingston Hospital.

In 1991 I was invited to be a representative of our parish churches to meet the candidates for the post of Team Vicar Designate. This was a 'first' for me and not only was I pleased to have been asked to do this but I saw another side of a church activity about which I knew very little. I felt great empathy for those involved. It reminded me of the procedure for appointing Head and Deputy Heads for a school and how I had to sit facing seven professionals throwing questions at me one after the other – nerve-wracking!

I was somewhat shocked to receive a letter from the National Blood Transfusion Service telling me that, 'It was not considered to be medically advisable for anyone over the age of 60 to give blood for the first time or to recommence as a donor if there had been an interval of several years since their previous donation. We greatly appreciate your wish to help this service and I am very sorry to have to disappoint you.' I *was* disappointed as I thought I had plenty of blood left in me to be of use despite their having taken several pints in the past!

Once a week I played the piano for the Surbiton Hill Nursery School, a few minutes up the road from where I live. Jo Gregory, the headteacher, had told me that they would be glad of someone to do this and I very much enjoyed watching their little faces and the effort they put into it when singing the words. Christmas time, with carols, was quite a favourite too. In 1992 I joined the governing body and was pleased to take on this role and remained as governor until 1997. During this time I attended a helpful course in the training of school governors organised by the council. Times were changing fast and we had to take into consideration the needs of working mothers and the integration of some special needs children with the others in the main part of the nursery, at times thought to be mutually beneficial to all.

Another involvement with my church, apart from singing in the choir, was to be elected to the Parochial Church Council on 1st of April 1992.

In October, I joined the Victim Support Scheme for Kingston and commenced training as a volunteer. It was being coordinated by Heather Benians and Cynthia Felstead. This was a very rewarding activity and I got a lot of pleasure from helping people who had been traumatised, for whatever reason, and hopefully relieving some of their distress. The aim of the scheme was to give empathetic and practical help to victims of crime. We all worked hard but also had fun together at meetings and when raising money for the scheme. Blossom went, whenever possible, to draw attention to our cause.

After some years I began training for *Working with Families of Murder Victims* in seven two-hour sessions led by police, involving the inner London Probation Service and a coroner, at Shepherds Bush Police Station. The well-known coroner Sir Montagu Levine gave talks on the role of the coroner. Following this course, I visited many families of murder victims and found this to be the most difficult and challenging area of volunteering, but equally rewarding. Several years later it was decided that volunteers working with families of murder victims should themselves receive counselling which was to prove extremely helpful.

Among the experiences I had were several visits with victims to the Old Bailey and the high security prison Belmarsh where we attended an identification parade. I was acutely aware of the extremely high level of security that met us as we turned every corner. On one occasion, as we left the Old Bailey by police car, with the victim, a witness to a shooting, we were told by the police driver to, 'Get down on the floor. I think we're being followed. Hold on tight. I'm going to go very fast. I'm going down back roads to throw them off.' Perhaps it was then that I realised how much victims (and volunteers!) needed support.

This year I bought a Peugeot 205 GRD, a second-hand car, with the help of Graham Hill, the son of footballer Jimmy, who has a car salesroom in Wimbledon. I was delighted with it and it rarely let me down. However, it died on me eighteen years later! It was the last car I was to own and without it my activities were greatly limited.

My parish church was taking part in an audit and I was asked to help in this programme. This involved knocking on the doors of complete strangers, showing them a letter of authority from the church, telling them about our church, inviting them to ask any questions they wanted, finding out what people felt our churches should be offering and asking for suggestions. There had been an article in the local press to warn people, but not everyone takes in or reads the local papers, so many were taken unawares; nevertheless we had many pleasant receptions. In one of the houses I came across a poor young lady lying flat on the floor. 'I've done my back in and this is the only way I can get comfortable.' I fully understood and we had quite a long chat about back pain. I think she was glad to find a fellow sufferer!

I was making occasional visits to Holly Lodge, Richmond Park, as a volunteer. It was a Learning Centre for those wishing to know more about the park and the flora and fauna within it. Run by Dr J. Pat Eley, it was particularly aimed at groups of people, visits from schools and for those with special needs. In the centre of two busy, bustling towns, Kingston upon Thames and Richmond, the peace and tranquillity of the park was a welcome relief. A pond had been dug for people to go pond-dipping. The day I joined them doing this several cows hung their heads over the surrounding rails to see what was going on. I really felt I was in the country. After several years my days became so full that I had to retire as a volunteer.

A visit from my sister and family from Karachi was a pleasant surprise. I must have had more stamina than I realised, for I drove them all in my car to Oakford in Devon and back again in one day, approximately 500 miles, which, for me, was quite an undertaking!

There were occasions when, hearing about disasters on the 7am news, I would get dressed in Blossom and set off for the Kingston streets to collect money for the Red Cross Disaster Fund. Blossom was to be used more and more to collect money in the wake of severe disasters of all kinds, although I still collected for other charities. My records tell me Blossom went out collecting on 92 occasions and collected for 32 different charities and in the aftermath of disasters, several of the former were annual events. At that time, in all she had collected around £125,000.

During a recent tsunami disaster, Blossom collected £600 in six hours. One hundred pounds an hour was a great deal of money, most generously given, with all three of her tins full to the brim. And more recently she collected for the bomb and flood victims.

We rode through the streets with her head in the basket of an electric scooter, firstly loaned to me by Kingston's Shopmobility, but more recently on my own red scooter. I was able to talk to anyone willing to listen and, for my part, I was able to listen to many ladies, gentlemen and children who came up to tell me their troubles or just pat Blossom or pass the time of day chatting to us.

Major changes I noticed over the time I was doing this were the pace and apparent urgency of the rushing feet of many of the shoppers. Speed seemed to be vital for whatever reason and I wondered how many had got high blood pressure! Another very marked change was the sound of voices – *endless voices*! I was driven mad when someone would be talking behind or beside me, thinking they were saying something to me and saying, 'Sorry, were you talking to me?' before I realised they were on their mobile phone! One day I looked around and counted eighteen people on their mobile phones! What did we do before they were invented?

Of course, Blossom was vulnerable to the weather but a horse with an umbrella up overhead, I was told, looked quite a funny sight and I could see people in the far distance pointing and laughing at her. I suppose this was really what I wanted, not only did it mean more money in my tins but I realised I had the power to make people happy and even laugh, which must surely have been a good thing.

I used to take sandwiches with me, as I spent from 8 or 9 o'clock in the morning to 2 o'clock in the afternoon away from home and would get quite peckish! At one time I used to take my dachshund pup with me in a basket at my feet and she certainly drew people to me, but as she grew up it was not safe to have her there so I had to make other arrangements at home for her and the ones that followed.

Shopping for a bottle of cherry brandy one day I was given a tiny complimentary sample bottle to go with it. In the icy winter days I used to fill this up from the big bottle and take it with me. As I sat having a 'swig' from it, I used to hear hoots of laughter from the people around. I guess it must have looked quite incongruous, a horse drinking from a bottle!

Blossom was always quite busy out collecting for various charities. I had started a routine, which was to last for many years, of taking her out daily for the three weeks leading up to and including Christmas Eve. People used to come up with their offerings and tell me, 'Now I know that Christmas is nearly here.' With this routine we were able to collect quite large sums of money which allowed me to help two or three charities.

Unfortunately I had a nasty habit of getting into the driving seat of my car and shutting the door with her tail trapped in it! Over time it grew shorter and shorter until eventually it disappeared! I tried everywhere to find a replacement tail but without success. I even wrote to Elf Toys, who sold rocking horses, but they said they were very sorry but the horses arrived ready-made at their stores. A Nigerian friend of mine, Ada, was cutting off some of her long hair, so I attached some strands of that but it was too fine to last and just pulled out of the band holding it together. So eventually Blossom was tail-less and nobody seemed to mind, except me; I was sitting on it most of the time anyway.

I am told now that many miss seeing Blossom at Christmas, but I guess that even horses need to have a rest sometimes. I am including some photos in the hope this will help the reader to appreciate what a character she is. Presently she is lying on the bed, resting, and giving me the 'glad eye' every time I go near her. I think she is getting restless again!

February 1992 was very traumatic for me and I had to have my beloved dog, Karen, put to sleep. She was deaf, nearly blind and very unhappy. It was hard to watch her although I knew that it was the kindest thing to do. I wish I didn't get so close to and fond of my dogs. It is such a wrench to lose them.

However, there were lighter moments which provided necessary relief such as when priceless alterations to my name appeared on some advertising letters: *Mrs Blapton*, *Mrs Gresham Cottage*, *Miss Vlastoto* among others! Also, I was watching television one day and saw a film of a horse seated on top of another horse and galloping along in the distance. It was one of the funniest things I have ever seen and I decided to try this out with Blossom. I asked the Kingston Riding Centre if they would like to help. They kindly provided me, dressed as Blossom, with a beautiful horse and a young lady groom brought him to me in Canbury Gardens by the River Thames in Kingston. She led him alongside the tow path where the public were, and returned him to the riding school. It was very generous of them and hopefully the Riding Centre T-shirt she was wearing would have been an advertisement for them. It would be the last time I was able to get up on a horse's back. It was extremely painful.

Also, one day I was sitting in the outpatient department of Kingston Hospital. There were about forty or so people sitting around the sides of the room when a lady burst in carrying her shopping bags. Looking around, her eyes alighted on me and she shrieked out, 'Mrs Blossom!' and said to the assembled audience, 'You know Mrs Blossom, who collects for charity, the horse?' One or two people muttered, 'So it is,' and 'I thought I recognised her,' but I just burst into laughter. I had been re-christened and married off as well!

As August was the month when police held their horse shows at Imber Court Police Sports Ground, I would ask permission to collect money on behalf of Victim Support. With some colleagues we released a large number of balloons into the air which was a lot of fun and hopefully made a number of people aware of the work of Victim Support. One of them reached France! Once, Graham Cole from the television programme *The Bill* visited our stall to thank us for the work we were doing. On another occasion I took Blossom there where we collected over £100 for Victim Support. Blossom was invited to bring up the rear of the procession of hundreds of mounted police in front of the top brass of the Metropolitan Police in the viewing stand. It must have looked quite funny with Blossom, head in air, following the marching policemen, the crowd seemed to think so anyway!

In September I was elected Chairperson of the Michaelis Guild of Froebel College Alumni. I felt very honoured to be elected to this role and over the next few years made sure I did my best to carry it forward in the way others before me had done.

In October, to my great surprise, I was nominated by a colleague, Jill Raine, for a 'Brighten Up London Award' under the category 'Community Service'. The award was sponsored by LBC and London Electricity and I was one of the finalists. The prize was that *she* would have her electricity paid for and I would get a certificate! We were invited to dinner at the Corte Crest Hotel, Regent's Park, with Olympic athletes sitting among us at each of our tables. As well as a meal, presentations of all the nominees were shown on an enormous screen with details of everyone's activities. The lady who won it certainly deserved to win; she had collected thousands for cancer sufferers. I much enjoyed the whole experience and still have the certificate hung up on my sitting room wall to remind me of the occasion.

It seems that the saying, 'When one door closes another one opens' is true. I gave my last talk at Hillcroft College on 11th November but the very next day was elected coordinator of the Froebel College Centenary Appeal (the predecessor having recently left). This kept me busy for some months, which eventually culminated in a new building for the Education Department. I carried out my voluntary work in the Froebel office and spent most weekdays up in a turret room on the phone or writing letters appealing for financial help.

In November my poor sister lost her daughter, Neelofer, to cancer having brought her from Karachi to England in the hope that she could be treated. But sadly it was not to be and she returned to Karachi for her burial.

This also was the month of the catastrophic fire at Windsor Castle. I wept when pictures were shown on television of the Queen standing forlornly by watching parts of her home going up in flames as the smoke poured out of the building. It was devastating.

In January 1993 The Bolshoi Ballet performed in the Royal Albert Hall in aid of Victim Support, and the Princess Royal and her husband attended. I went up with some other volunteers and we were treated to a wonderful Royal Gala performance.

A Sotheby's valuation day was held at Froebel in February, in aid of our Education Building appeal. It raised over £3,000! It was held in the beautiful portrait room overlooking the banks of rhododendrons in the garden outside.

Also MEFAS held a Silver Jubilee party to which the Mayor of Kingston came. I noticed how many of us were on the 'elderly' side and wished more young people would join. I think it is so important that we all know, at least, basic first aid.

Lindon Bennett School celebrated twenty-five years and the retired headteacher Royce Spickett and I attended. It feels so different going back to a school and seeing some of the original staff, even the same cook! I remember so well the occasion when I poured her beautiful gravy over my pudding thinking it was chocolate sauce!

At the Chapel Royal in April we celebrated the 25th anniversary of the Organist and Master of the Choristers, Gordon Reynolds. Former choristers, scholars and gentlemen who had served under him in the chapel were invited and a small party was held in the Great Hall of the Palace, which I will long remember. History is all around you in the Palace, with echoing halls and enormous portraits on the walls.

Fred Bates, who had sung in my church choir over many years, was still lodging at my home. He stayed with me for several years and was a pleasure to have. Eventually he was to be offered a flat of his own where he happily ended his days.

It was about this time that I decided to retire from the Chair of the Michaelis Guild. I felt I had done my 'stint' and needed more time to do other things. I had so enjoyed my association with past members, many of whom were now in their 80s and 90s, that I was quite sad to have to give it up.

For many years the headteachers of Shrewsbury House School in Surbiton had each in turn kindly invited me to their lunch and Speech Day under an enormous tent in the school playing fields. I so much appreciated this and had enjoyed dropping in to watch their cricket, football and rugby matches throughout the year. I finally brought this to an end, as I was no longer able to walk without great difficulty. What a happy time it had been.

Now it was Surbiton Hill School's turn to celebrate twenty-one years, this time with a delicious international supper with everyone contributing their national dishes. It was interesting to see how many different nationalities were represented.

Another reunion lunch of my Set 86 of University College Hospital was held at a most unusual venue, the Grafton Hotel on Tottenham Court Road, London. This was the last time I was to meet some of my past colleagues. Later a few of us used to be invited to lunch by one of our set, Jean Smart (née Hughes) in her beautiful house in the country. Sadly she has now died.

My friend Joyce and I went down to Brighton where we saw a sign saying *Hinge and Bracket – Last Performance*! We were dismayed that they were retiring and decided there and then to stay the night and booked in at a hotel, and drove to the Dome. When we arrived we discovered that it wasn't that they were retiring but only that it was the 'last night' of the Brighton Proms! We learnt our lesson! Dr Evadene Hinge and Dame Hilda Bracket were as good as ever and we were very glad we had gone.

In January 1994 I stopped teaching piano and singing because I found it too difficult now to walk up and down the garden to be ready for the next English lesson in the Den.

A new vicar had been appointed to St Andrew's Church, Rev. Geoffrey Owen, who was to have joint ministry with Canon David Jackson at St Mark's Church. Geoffrey Owen was very interested in art and drama and put on excellent Christmas pantomimes involving the parishioners. I much enjoyed being cast as 'Fairy Nan' in *Cinderella*. In an article in the church magazine John Perry amusingly wrote: *Whilst wandering round Kingston one lunchtime in the Christmas rush, I was intrigued to see, in an electric Shopmobility wheelchair, a horse with a stick,*

232

*bombing around the town centre, with arm outstretched and a tin, collecting for Victim Support. A few days later, I telephoned St Mark's Vicarage on some matter of import (as Churchwardens have to do) to be told that **the same horse** was in the lounge, being fitted for a tutu by the Vicar's wife. Is it me or is it all the others?*

Later in the year, Victim Support took up a lot of my time following a shooting incident which had been witnessed by someone who was driving her car between the actual cars involved. She was sandwiched in the middle. A bullet shot past her car window intended for and aimed at the car behind her. She was deeply shocked and I attended court with her on several occasions when she was called as a witness.

In December I was invited to a party at my friends', Sue and Tony Wall's, home and was asked to wear fancy dress related to either the film or theatre world. The only person I could think of to impersonate was Dawn French's character of the *Vicar of Dibley*, which I also used several years later in one of the church pantomimes. Donning my black choir cassock, white surplice and a make-shift stole, I approached my vicar to see if he would kindly lend me his 'dog collar' and biretta. Much amused he agreed to this. I really quite looked the part after I bought a black wig from Kingston's *Bits and Bobs* and cut the hair to make a fringe. Arriving at the house on the night of the party, Tony came to the door and obviously did not recognise me (or presumably was unsure that Dawn French had been invited)! He looked beseechingly up the stairs, where Sue was standing, desperate for a clue as to who this person really was! A loud call from Sue to me, 'Nance!' gave him the answer he needed and we all burst into laughter. Later they were kind enough to award me the prize for the best fancy dress. I still laugh when I think about this.

January 1995 brought us the news of the devastating severe earthquake in Kobe, Japan. The last figure I noted was that 5,300 died, with thousands injured and missing. These were the occasions when I felt grateful to be free and able to go out with Blossom and collect money for the Red Cross for help which would be needed so badly. I was out in the streets of Kingston with Blossom two hours after hearing the news on the radio and was almost besieged by people grateful to be able to put money into my hastily labelled tins. On these occasions, and knowing the police don't need me to contact them, I ring or send a message to the Mayor's office to let him or her know what I am doing. I think they turn a blind eye to me now!

In February, following pain in my knee after a fall, I entered Queen Mary's Hospital in Roehampton to have a knee replacement by the surgeon Peter Hutton. A week and a half later I was allowed home and I was able to make a radio broadcast on behalf of Victim Support with my colleague Cynthia in a studio in Kingston.

I made many visits to Ferring in Sussex where friends of mine, Dr Lionel and Mrs Mac Wright, had a large permanent caravan on a site. It was wonderful for me and my friends to be able to come and go as we pleased – just locking up behind us. The inside was as good as any flat with a kitchen, shower and toilet, sitting room with television and two separate bedrooms. It really was delightful and only a short drive to the sea front. From there I kept my eyes open for a beach hut I could hire, but it wasn't until I looked along the huts at Littlehampton that I found exactly what I wanted. *There*, right beside the car park was a hut, in close proximity to a public toilet, an area laid out for croquet, clock golf, tennis court and a small café. It was perfect for my needs and I took many of my friends for visits down there. It was ideal for dogs, who loved sitting beside us in the hut or romping on the beach. After seven years I had to part with it when the rental costs went up and I did not feel I could make sufficient use of it to justify the cost, but to this day I miss it!

In April Canon Jackson asked if I would go with Blossom to one of his children's services in St Mark's. I was quite embarrassed that he used me as an example of 'helping others' but as it was for children I did not mind so much and they enjoyed seeing Blossom!

At this time, once a week, I was teaching a young disabled student at her hostel basic reading and writing as well as continuing with all my other activities.

I drove a colleague to the Victim Support Midland Regional Conference at Nene College, Northampton on *Young People Victims of Crime*. I never liked driving long distances on my own and was glad to have her company. The college was in an enormous campus out in the country and appeared to be quite modern.

I went to see a production of *The Diary of Anne Frank* in the

234

Market House in Kingston and found myself sitting next to the well-known singer Constance Shacklock. I had heard her sing many times in the past and was delighted to talk to her. The *Anne Frank* play was an excellent and realistic production.

In May I attended a one-day course at Kingston General Hospital on *Post Traumatic Stress* led by Kingston Bereavement and Critical Incident Stress Debriefing Group.

The sad news of the death of Gordon Reynolds LVO was announced and I attended his funeral service at the Chapel Royal on Sunday 15th July 1995.

In October I gave a talk on Victim Support to the Mothers' Union of St Andrew and St Mark's churches. Their interest was evident by the number of questions they asked.

My sister, Helen Long, came to Surbiton to promote and talk about her book *Safe Houses are Dangerous*, published by Kimber, which retells the story of the escape of some British and allied airmen during WWII down the line through France to Marseille, where my father's sister, Fanny, and her nephew, Georges (Boysie), undertook to return them to England via Spain. The talk went very well and she sold all the copies she brought with her. Much help was given to her by my friend Sheila Hyson.

Helen had become a journalist which allowed her to investigate, in depth, her many and varied interests, particularly in the arts. And among the many articles that she wrote was one for *The Lady,* 9 April 1987, in which she wrote about the Ionides family within the London Greek community. Our Aunt Caliope Ionides lived just a few doors down from us in Porchester Terrace and almost opposite to the flat of my grandmother (her sister).

In October 1995 the whole town of Surbiton was involved in a festival celebrating fifty years from the end of WWII. A festival of flowers, given the title *Aspects of Peace* was held in St Andrew's Church. For this reason I chose to make an arrangement of orange flowers depicting the flames of the bombing of London and overhung these with white flowers to represent the sprays of water to extinguish them. It was also the 150th anniversary celebration of our parish of St Mark's, which was the first church in Surbiton and was badly bombed in the war.

I continued doing occasional intercessions in the Sunday services at my church. I was particularly pleased to be asked to intercede on one Remembrance Sunday, which brought back memories of so many thousands of people lost in past wars.

Following training in Adult Literacy I gave lessons to my first adult pupil wanting to improve her English and found this to be quite an interesting new experience. I stepped up the number of private students I had, teaching from 4-7pm workdays and 9-1pm on Saturdays. My volunteering with Victim Support continued and at this time I was giving two weekly one-hour talks to groups of prisoners in Latchmere Prison in Kingston.

In February something else I was to do for the first time was to invigilate for Surbiton High School for some of the girls' art exams. I was surprised and somewhat incredulous that they were horrified that they weren't allowed to listen to their music on their headphones!

Old friends of mine, Bruce and Mary Watt, from Russell Court days, invited me to join them for their son, Craig's, 16th birthday in 1996. We had a gorgeous Indian meal at The Rose restaurant on Brighton Road in Surbiton. The new theatre, opened in Kingston in 2007, took the same name – a trifle confusing!

May was a very special month for me. My friend Joyce and I decided to pay a visit to my much loved seaside town of Frinton. We planned our route taking in places we wished to see and any churches and cathedrals we noted which were in the vicinity. This time we went via Chelmsford, meeting Simon the organist of St Andrew's Church for a meal in a local pub, and afterwards we stayed for one night at the Snows Oaklands Hotel before driving on to Frinton. I had booked rooms at the very pleasant Maplin Hotel at Frinton-on-Sea where we spent three nights. The front overlooked the greensward with the sea in the distance. We were fortunate in the weather and visited many of my old haunts such as the tennis club and the beach (where we had filled the wartime sand bags in 1939). Then we paid a visit to the garden made by the townspeople near the railway crossing and the museum. I gave the museum my brother's silver cup which he and I had won when playing in the junior tennis tournament in the summer of 1935. We sat in the beautiful little garden sipping cups of coffee as the public came and went; a veritable little haven. They had recently erected the 'Vlasto Arch' which I donated in memory of my wonderful grandmother and our family, and which had been made by someone locally. I was so happy to see it there. I took

Muffy with us who behaved impeccably and was even invited into the hotel against the rules!

Before we left we reserved a room in a delightful B&B in the village of Boxted at Round Hill House owned by Colonel and Mrs Jenny Carter, where we received a most warm welcome and where we spent a very enjoyable two nights in a room overlooking the garden and fields of sheep before returning home.

On our return to Surbiton Joyce offered to take me to a Kneller Hall concert which is put on annually and open to the public. I very much enjoyed this as we sat out in the gardens with the light slowly fading and the band lit up and playing very sensitively. We also went to Wimbledon in the summer with tickets given to me by an old family friend, Doris Howard, who, herself, had played at Wimbledon in years gone by. Our tickets entitled us to use the members' enclosure; we felt very posh and made full use of the strawberries and cream offered to us!

At Surbiton Hill Nursery School I continued as a governor and joined the sub-committee responsible for 'safety' in all areas. We looked thoroughly around the building and garden to check for any potential areas of danger.

I held a 'bring and buy' garden party in aid of St Andrew's Church. My friends, the O'Neal family, played as a quartet at the top of the garden. The sun shone and it was a delightful afternoon.

A 'Contact the Elderly' tea party was held in my garden. Fortunately the weather held and all had a good time. I had twelve helpers for twenty-four guests and it was organised by Michael Pierson; such a worthwhile volunteer group and much appreciated by all. Any older person could join and would be invited to the outings, local and mostly once a week, with lifts in cars provided when necessary. Past Mayors of Kingston upon Thames have told me that they had their eyes opened to the incredible amount of voluntary work that went on throughout the year when taking up their posts.

I was now helping out with the pram service, Praise and Play, held in our church and played the piano for the songs and hymns sung by the mothers as they cuddled and cared for their babies and children. It was a veritable oasis of peace and quiet only punctuated by the occasional cries of a baby or the prayers spoken by Celia O'Neill, a church member.

237

A teacher, Saba Shafi, came from my niece's school in Karachi to attend a course for teachers being held at Froebel. She returned to Karachi in December 1996.

In September a colleague, Su, and I attended a Victim Support meeting on *Traumatic Stress* being held in St Pancras Hospital in London, which was interesting and invaluable for the work we were doing. Also this was the year I became a member of the Victim Support Management Committee and a trustee.

The St Andrew's choir, along with others, sang in Lincoln Cathedral and stayed with the Reverend Richard Crossland (who was being ordained) and his wife at their lovely house in the minster yard. It was a very beautiful service.

I started reading for the *Talking Newspaper for the Blind* and those with visual problems. It was nice to be back behind a microphone again and I thought this was a very worthwhile voluntary activity which I continue doing to the present day.

With a friend, Bobbie Ellis, we went to see *Evita* at the Richmond Theatre. This is a theatre of which I am very fond but that evening the sound was absolutely deafening and we sat with our hands over our ears!

I gave a talk on Victim Support to the boys at Richard Challoner School in New Malden. Their behaviour in the first half was appalling, talking and giggling throughout. They were distracting me so much that I decided to face them and asked why they thought the content of my talk was so funny. At that, the master sitting quietly at the side of the room got up and sent the four ring leaders out of the room. It was quite a relief! They were sent to apologise at the end, which gave me a good impression of the school.

On February 10th and 11th 1997 performances of *Cinderella* were given in St Andrew's Hall by members of St Andrew and St Mark's Churches. I much enjoyed performing as the Vicar of Dibley and 'Blossom' was given a part too! Of course, this required me to wear her head and it was rather difficult to know where I was on the stage. I nearly fell off the edge at one point. This was the first time I used a large sized handkerchief as a prop which caused some amusement.

Again in June I was involved with the Surbiton Tennis Week.

On June 30th the terrible news of the death of Princess Diana in a car crash in Paris shook not only this country but the whole world and I watched her funeral on television with sadness – what a waste of a life. Few seemed to talk about Dodi, although his death was equally tragic.

I was beginning to wind down some of my activities as I was feeling rather overloaded. I resigned as governor from both Surbiton Hill Nursery School and from Froebel Guild, having served my five years in this capacity.

Accompanying victims to the Kingston Crown Court and giving talks to the inmates at Latchmere Prison continued. This was an 'open prison' where prisoners could be allowed out to work in the community if thought suitable.

Lynn Devivo, formerly the organiser of Shopmobility in Kingston, lead a trip to France on 26th September for members of Shopmobility and their partners or friends. It was a wonderful idea and gave many of us an opportunity to go abroad who might not otherwise have been able to do so. We made a visit to Le Touquet, travelling by coach and crossing the Channel by Le Shuttle to Calais; the coach being carried by the train under the Channel. Surfacing in Calais we went to an *enormous* hypermarket where many of us bought bottles of drink, perfumes and other items at much cheaper rates than at home. Personally I was a bit bored as we seemed to spend a long time going round and round the shop and I was having difficulty walking. I did not want much in the way of shopping but others collected quite large quantities of food and drink. From there we went to Le Touquet and drove along the sea front. Unfortunately, by then it was raining and we were not really able to see very much of the town. We returned back home via Le Shuttle and I was very grateful for having had this opportunity.

Surbiton held its Festival again and I was asked to be secretary of the committee. It ran from September 27th to October 3rd and the theme this year was to be *The World of the Movies*. I thought perhaps our church would like to be involved in this. After putting the idea to the Festival Committee I approached the vicar who was very interested, and I asked the organist if he would like to be involved himself, with our choir, putting on a concert in the afternoon, to which he agreed.

A final rehearsal took place on the afternoon of the concert, Sunday the 28th, but before it had started I stepped backward, falling down the vestry steps at the back of the church and, unknown to me then, fractured a bone in my foot. I was in a lot of pain and, assuming the verger, who saw me fall, would tell the choir, went straight home, driving my car with great difficulty. On arriving I rang my friend Joyce and asked her to take me to Kingston Hospital A&E, which she did. When the X-ray showed a fracture, my foot was put into plaster and I was sent home, too late of course to join the final rehearsal and no one would be at home to receive a phone call. I had taken with me the music we were to sing, including a duet piece, scheduled in the event, to assure myself that I would be note perfect. To my great disappointment the duet piece was cancelled because of my absence from rehearsal.

I got a lift down to the church in time for the concert, where we were all wearing long skirts so no one was apparently aware of what had happened. The concert was a great success and a virtual sell-out, so no one was any the wiser of the events of the day, apparently including the choir. Shortly afterwards, following an altercation with the organist, who was also the choir master, I left the choir with great regret, bringing an end to over 60 years of singing in church choirs.

The day after my term of office at Froebel College came to an end, the refurbished and enlarged Education Building, 'Cedar', was opened by the Dean of Education of the University of Surrey. It was wonderful to see all the hours of work put into action and I was pleased to have been a small part of it. This month I had recorded the oral history of a former Froebel College student and member of the Michaelis Guild at the request of the governing body; it was suggested that other members of the Guild be approached and records kept in the archives.

In November I joined with colleagues from Victim Support to 'man' a marquee in the Queen's Stand at Epsom Racecourse where the police were operating a 'Bumble Bee' Crime Prevention Roadshow. Thousands of suspected stolen items were displayed which were found following burglaries of all kinds and we were amazed, as we walked past dozens and dozens of ceiling-high display cases, to see all the items beautifully presented, from guns to jewellery. Several people came to our base to tell us of their distress at being burgled.

December found me talking to a multi-disciplinary team of health workers called 'Community Action Team' at Hook clinic who met regularly over lunch and had talks from various representatives of other disciplines. Mine was on the work of Victim Support volunteers. So ended 1997.

In January 1998, knowing I had lived through the war, I was offered a wartime stirrup pump by a family I had visited in my role within Victim Support, which I gladly accepted. It brought back memories of the war and I kept it in my broom cupboard. However, one day on walking round our lovely little Kingston Museum I noticed they did not have one on show and offered it 'to join' other memorabilia of the time. It was gratefully received.

In February I gave a talk to the Round Table in Kingston on the work of Victim Support and on February 12th I sat in the first General Council meeting on *Racial Violence and Harassment* at Welcare House in Kingston.

In this month I also sadly attended the funeral of my much loved singing teacher Fabian Smith in Croydon.

Several cousins of the Mitchell family came to visit from America, staying at the YMCA in Surbiton and joining me for the odd meal. I really enjoyed this contact with my mother's relatives.

In May I was interviewed on the radio at studios in Thames High Street, Hampton Wick, on the work of Victim Support.

June found me helping on the staff at the Powder Byrne Trophy championships at Surbiton Tennis Club, now called the Surbiton Racket and Fitness Club. I always enjoyed being involved there.

In July, my friend Joyce and I went to the magnificent Hampton Court Palace Flower Show. I was in a wheelchair and she, poor thing, had to push me around slithering on and off the duckboards that made pathways over the grass! The whole experience was a joy; the layout of the grounds with flowers and marquees everywhere, it was as if we were soaked in colour and scent wherever we went. This has now become one of the most popular events of the year in the south of England. Incidentally, I had one of the cooks from the show stay with me during the events and each evening on his return he would bring with him a very different scent to flowers!

In August, I hosted another 'Contact the Elderly' garden tea on my lawn and again the sun shone and about thirty elderly people seemed to enjoy themselves. However I was now having

l

difficulty putting up the table and chairs in the garden and always had the dread of what I would do if it was raining. My ability to walk and lift was declining and I decided that this would be my last effort.

With Joyce, I went on a lovely bed-and-breakfast trip to Wales. In Aberystwyth we stayed in a hotel overlooking the sea. A worrying incident happened when I locked my car key inside the car and lost the spare key. We were absolutely stuck until we found a policeman who took off his cap and produced a lethal looking piece of equipment which opened the door without any trouble. I could have hugged him! During that trip we visited St Brides Super Ely where we spent two nights. We also spent two nights in the Mumbles visiting the many beautiful beaches and one night in Findon Village, sleeping in a room of a pub, over the kitchen, permeated by the overpowering smell of fatty food, before finally returning home.

Everywhere we went my dachshund came with us and every place where we stayed had allowed us to have her up in our room. This was always a condition of our going there. I used to sleep on top of the bed inside a double sleeping bag with my dog beside me so she never touched the bedding. En route we passed through Llandaff and visited the cathedral which was built around 1220 and was very beautiful. I was horrified to hear that it cost £4000 *weekly* to maintain it!

An old friend, Emily Mayhew, came from Penticton in British Columbia to stay with me and we visited the museum at the Wimbledon Tennis Club, a very interesting place to see, with memorabilia, film and photos of past players. There is also a small café which helps to make it a very attractive place to visit.

I also visited Imber Court Police Sports Centre in Esher with Blossom for their horse show. I was allowed to collect for Victim Support but the police horses used to react when they saw me and started prancing about, so this privilege came to a rather sad end and I did not return there.

Coordinators of Victim Support had come and gone and in October a new coordinator, Maria Jarvis, arrived to take over. We were to remain friends to the present day.

Also in October the St Martin Singers and Rev W.D. Kennedy Bell invited me to his birthday party on the 25th at his son's house in Chiswick. Surprisingly we were able to sit in the garden and he

242

patted the chair next to him saying, 'Come on Nancy, sit next to me.' I have always been grateful for this show of affection as it was the last time I was to see this wonderful man and I still miss him being around.

On 25th November, Ryhohei Yamanaka came back from Tokyo to visit; he had been a young student of mine referred to me by the headteacher of Shrewsbury House School many years before.

In December Blossom set out, as usual, collecting daily for three weeks to raise money for Kingston Hospital Chest Unit, Kingston Action on Homelessness and Victim Support and, as always, enjoyed every minute being out on the local streets. I was particularly aware not only of the increase in number of people shopping but also how many came from outside the area, with a large number from overseas.

As already mentioned, in the light of various terrorist action it had been decided that an emergency planning group would be formed in anticipation of any trouble in the locality. Meetings were held in the council chamber of the Guildhall of Kingston and were attended by many volunteers from a variety of associations as well as representatives from the council and the emergency services. These meetings continue to this day due to the need for awareness of inherent dangers of terrorism. It became apparent that we would be required to go to a designated area anywhere in the borough (or even outside the borough), night or day, and would be expected to cope with anything asked of us. Obviously this would require a level of physical fitness for the many roles that would be needed. Sadly I had to withdraw from this group as I felt I was becoming more of a liability as time passed due to my increasing disability.

And so another year passes and January 1999 brought me the sad news that my dear friend Eleanor Hendy of Nanaimo days had died in Victoria, Canada. Now both she and the Rev Albert Hendy had both passed away I needed to keep in touch with their daughters Ann and Grace so that the link I had with that family would not be broken.

In February we held a Victim Support week in Kingston to which the MP Edward Davey came. By the end of the year, I was told, to my surprise, that I had contacted several hundreds of

243

victims in the time I had worked with Victim Support. In September they moved their office to Siddeley House, Canbury Park Road, Kingston where many other volunteer groups also had their base. We were asked to talk to the police about the work of VS and particularly how we approached the confidentiality of our cases and how we could help each other and ultimately, the victims. It was my turn this month, which I enjoyed particularly as they were very attentive and asked questions at the end.

For twenty years Maria Windmill, Italian by birth, had cleaned and generally helped look after me but was now not well and sadly, for both of us, she had to stop work. I still visit her at her home and we talk of her days at Russell Court and at Gresham Cottage.

I was invited to give a talk to the Malden Green Ladies Club in St John's Hall, Worcester Park, about my life. I wonder if this was what stimulated me to get on with writing these memoirs! I also gave talks to several clubs for the elderly on *Personal Safety*. I enjoyed these but fear that many of them were keen to shut their eyes and be left in peace as they sat in their self-allotted chairs around the room.

Joyce and I made another trip two months later, this time up to John O'Groats and then down to Lands End. You could say this was going from the sublime to the ridiculous but it was a very interesting journey and we went from one B&B to another and had some great experiences! We booked rooms in York, Coldingham Bay, Aberdeen, Canisbay, John O'Groats, Deeside Hotel, Ballater, Kendal, Chester and Ripon visiting cathedrals wherever we could; Chester was one of our favourites. Canisbay was another of our favourites where our room overlooked fields of sheep and the North Sea. The family who ran the guest house were 'into' show jumping and kindly gave me one of their rosettes for Blossom, who wears it to this day!

As we came back into England we passed Blenheim Palace, birthplace of Churchill and home of the 11th Duke of Marlborough, which was open to the public. I love visiting places of historical interest. This was a wonderful trip. One time we were driving down through a lane coming down from Scotland and decided we both needed to stop and spend a penny. Just as she had her turn a herd of cows and a dog came down the path towards us. Joyce got out of the way just in time!

In October the History channel on television ran a competition called *Photos for the Future*. I sent them the photo of the cover picture of this book and got a runner-up certificate and award! I received a Boots voucher for processing films which was very welcome. Later this photo was accepted by the Imperial War Museum for the archives.

I also received an award this month at a ceremony for *Women in the Community*. Soroptimist International honour those who help the aged or who are old themselves helping the community.

This year I seemed to go from meeting to meeting, among them KREC (Kingston Racial Equality Council) for a talk on racial harassment and to the Kingston Debating Society for a one-off meeting.

I was sad to hear of the death of my much-loved teacher of Crofton Grange days, Beatrice Martin Smith.

My church asked me to write an article about *A Day in the Life of...* As I wrote it I couldn't believe how much I managed to pack into my day!

Christmas parties abounded: the Friends at the delightful museum in Kingston, the Soroptimist Dinner at Richmond Hotel and an event at St Mark's Church to celebrate the millennium with food, drink and dancing. This use of the church was perhaps to herald the flexibility of the way we would use our church buildings for the benefit of the wider community in the future.

Chapter Fourteen

One of the difficulties in writing your autobiography is knowing when to stop! You have to make a decision which will be the last year otherwise you can go on writing 'What's Next' until the day you die! I had decided to stop at the beginning of the millennium, when I was in my 70s, but certain interesting things have happened to me in recent years which, I feel, I cannot leave out as I am still, at the age of 85, full of the zest of life (as well as my share of arthritis!). So I will mention these briefly.

The Millennium arrived! As already mentioned, I 'saw the 2000 New Year in' at St Mark's Church along with many other parishioners of St Andrew and St Mark's Churches. There was an amazing transformation of the church, pews were moved aside and a large dance space appeared in the middle. Tables and chairs were arranged along the aisles and decorations festooned the pillars. There was food and plenty of wine on the table and the atmosphere was one of happiness and expectation as the night was danced away and, with the singing of *Auld Lang Syne*, we celebrated the arrival of the year 2000.

It was in this January that I reluctantly gave up my beach hut in Littlehampton. As mentioned previously, it had been a wonderful asset but I began to feel guilty that I was not using it enough to make it worthwhile to keep paying the rent which had just gone up that year.

On February 21st, I gave a talk to the Rotary Club at the Fountain Public House in New Malden on the work of Victim

Support. I always enjoy giving a talk, not only because, sometimes, I get a very nice meal but because the audience seem to be so interested and ask intelligent questions at the end. Because of the nature of our activities, confidentiality was essential and we never talked directly about our clients.

My particular branch of Victim Support (Kingston) gave me the very great honour of representing them at a meeting with the Queen and Princess Anne at the old London County Council building on the South Thames Embankment in London. Tables were placed at the end of each of the rows of books in the large, long library, upon which were laid cups and saucers and plates of cakes and biscuits. Her Majesty walked down one side of the room and Princess Anne the other and then they crossed over at the end and came down the other side shaking hands and having words with everyone. It was a very special moment and I felt privileged and grateful to have been selected to go.

A somewhat amusing moment for me occurred while we were there. Having arthritis of my knees and hips, I had great difficulty climbing in and out of a taxi. One had been thoughtfully sent to take me to and from my home in Surbiton. The taxi which turned up to take us home had a very high step-up to get in and I got stuck trying desperately to push up from my less severely affected leg. I'm not exactly the smallest of people and it must have been quite a sight to behold as I tried to push up on my two sticks and literally fell inside! I prayed that the cameras, that had been filming the royal party, had already gone away or I could imagine what fun they might have had filming my antics!

In March, the Mayor of Kingston, Councillor Jane Smith, awarded me a delightful memento for the voluntary work I had done in the borough. I found this somewhat embarrassing as I knew so many people, including my colleagues, were doing similar sorts of volunteering.

My association with Froebel College led to my being invited to the Service of Dedication on the Inauguration of the University of Surrey Roehampton in the presence of the Duke of Kent at Westminster Abbey. I was given a front seat on the aisle and the Duke of Kent came to stand right in front of me while he read the lesson. Unfortunately I had a coughing fit just as he came. I was choking and didn't know where to put myself! I fear that, if it was recorded, my guttural sounds will have drowned out part of what

247

he had to say. My apologies! After the service we all withdrew to eat and drink in the Westminster School hall, a wonderful occasion which I was so very happy to witness.

In April the newly built Millennium Dome (now called the O2) was opened to the public; I went up with a friend to see it. We found the car park, once we had wound our way through a maze of streets in South London, which was absolutely enormous and almost empty. With my disabled access card we were able to park right up near the entrance – there were several of them – where my friend was able to collect a wheelchair and push me into the building.

Much had been said about the building: critical, uncomplimentary and extremely negative; I did not agree with their findings. I saw a vast space of such enormous proportions that my mind ran riot thinking of the different ways it could be used. At this time the displays and activities were few and far between, access to many parts of the building was by steps and queues leading to the restaurants were long and wearisome. But apart from that, the central area contained hundreds of seats around the display area and there were timed performances of the most amazing acrobatics I have ever seen. They were performed by volunteers who had been invited to attend for training and I thought it was superb. I understand the building is now expected to be incorporated into the programme for the Olympic 2012; I am delighted! I am sure it will be successfully used for many years to come.

Having taken part in the only performance since the war of Coleridge's *Hiawatha* in the Albert Hall, I could imagine what a wonderful place it would be to put on that and similar shows. I could also see it being used for sporting events and even show jumping. The area was enormous and the seating well placed for excellent viewing. My friend pushed me around the entire circumference of the building and I was quite fascinated by it; she must have been exhausted! I wonder how many of the 'powers that be', who were mocking its future use, had actually visited in person: I met one MP who had not!

At the end of this month I attended a wonderful open-air Millennium Christmas Celebration in the market place in Kingston. A stage had been erected at one end and rows of seats placed across the area beside the market stalls. I was pleased and surprised by the number of elderly and particularly young people who turned up to join in. Hymns were sung and there were readings and prayers and the silence in the usually bustling marketplace was almost eerie. The pigeons flew around and landed, hopefully, near the tables, but must have been disappointed at the lack of crumbs which they usually found there.

This year saw the Mayor of Kingston attending endless events (such an important year it was) and I admired her stamina and seemingly endless good nature. She presided over a multi-cultural Kingston University Fashion Show at McCluskys, beside the River Thames, to which I went. The noise of the music was so deafening in the small room where it was held that I made an earlier exit than I had intended! In May she came and sat at our table (Joyce Griffin was there also) on the occasion of the Surbiton High School's generous party for the elderly in the locality.

During this time I continued taking in visitors for bed and breakfast and I attended a course called *Welcome Host* organised by Kingston Leisure which I found interesting, but I think I was already carrying out the ideas that were suggested. Among my guests were two Russians who stayed for two nights. As I have only ever taken B&B visitors in small numbers when it suited me, I was not really 'geared' to go advertising in a big way, including on the internet. So shortly after this and because I was having some physical problems, I decided not to continue taking in paying guests.

Some time later I was carted off to hospital by ambulance. One of my knee replacements had become infected and had to be replaced. I went to theatre twice in order that the infection could be cleaned out and I could have a new one put in its place. I don't recommend knee replacements, the operations are extremely painful. However, the eventual release from pain must be worth it. I was quite poorly at the time, but recovered and returned home two and a half months later in October.

In January 2001, on returning from several weeks in hospital, I retired from Victim Support mainly due to my inability to move without a considerable amount of pain. I had completed fifteen years as a volunteer.

I joined the Kingston upon Thames Museum's Oral History

Project and was interviewed regarding my time spent in the borough. I was glad to do this.

In February I gave a talk to the Surbiton Rotary Club at Glenmore House in Surbiton on the work of Victim Support.

March saw a truly epic event! The installation of my new Sky digital satellite! My neighbour's young son was duly impressed and told his parents, 'She is really with it for her age!' Another surprise was the arrival of snow this month which rather shook everybody.

By contrast in May, in the sunshine, I helped on the tournament staff at the Surbiton Racket and Fitness Club for The Open Tennis Powder Byrne Trophy. It went on till the evening when we enjoyed light music, buffet and wine. Several past Surrey grass-court and Wimbledon champions were among the invited guests.

I also took a friend to a dinner given by the Leprosy Mission in Cobham which was given as a 'thank you' to people who had helped to raise money.

Later in July, I saw an advertisement in the *Surrey Comet* for volunteers to 'man' the front desk at the New Malden Police Station – that sounded more stationary. On applying and following an interview and police check, I joined others on the rota of duties. Although I found it interesting and I learnt some of the roles carried out by the police (everything in triplicate!), I did not get the same satisfaction as working for victims of crime. Also I found myself unable to stand for long at the front desk. Even though there was a stool to sit on, one was continually having to get up and down and move around the office. When frequent trainings required us to climb steep steps in this old Victorian building to the lecture room, I realised that I had to call it a day. There was a visitation by the Chief of Police, Sir John Stevens, to thank the volunteers for their work. A party was held in a tent put up in the car park and during his speech we were informed that we had had 1,300 contacts since we first started working there. Amazing!

My sister Helen died on July 5th and later a celebration of her life was held in the Brasted Parish Church to which I went. Losing a close member of one's family is like having a tooth drawn and leaves a raw pain in the pit of one's stomach.

On September 11th I sat, mesmerised, by what I was seeing on the television as planes flew into the Twin Towers in New York. Was there ever such a heinous crime? Like everyone else I was mortified by what was happening – in cold blood – in front of our very eyes.

The next week my beloved dachshund, Muffy, had to be put to sleep and my best friend, Betty Lewis, died. It was a very low time for me. Fortunately I live alone and no one was there to see my tears.

Our new theatre, to be named 'The Rose' was being built in the centre of Kingston close to the market and a stone's throw from the River Thames. The building had reached a level of safety which would allow visitors to see certain areas of the interior and I joined a group to do just that. It was most exciting and although far from complete, it was possible to visualise what a wonderful asset it would be to the town once it had been opened to the public and was in full use. During the next few years, and as a founding member, I was to be an avid fan of the theatre and all that went on there, and spent many hours raising money and distributing leaflets for it.

By January 2002 I think my friend Joyce and I were ready to get away for a break and to find some warmth and sunshine. We went to Cooks travel agents in Kingston and telling them what we wanted, suggested that the Mediterranean was a nice place to go? They laughed and said that it may be even colder than here. The suggestion was that we went west and someone said, 'What about the West Indies? I would go to Cuba if I were you. I was there last year.' He gave us the name of the hotel – Club Santa Lucia (I think) – and strongly recommended it to us. We took away some literature, thought about it overnight and returned to book a two-week holiday leaving on the 31st. Payment for the holiday included return flights to Cuba, landing at Santiago de Cuba, and full board. We took my wheelchair.

When we arrived they saw our problem with the wheelchair and we were allotted a lovely little ground floor flatlet all to ourselves with its own sitting area and front door. We could not believe our luck. Full board meant there was a never-ending supply of 'help yourself' delicious food and drinks in the dining room; the choice was limitless.

The sea was at the end of the most beautiful, well-cared for and colourful gardens, and a river, complete with flamingos, ran right through the complex. There were also two large swimming pools which we made full use of. It felt as though we had arrived in paradise!

251

We took a horse-drawn carriage drive around the area, largely because we felt sorry for the poor little man and his equally miserable looking horse sheltering from the heat under the trees near our hotel.

We also took three other much longer trips. One was to Holguin, where we swam with the dolphins in a large sea water pool near the beach. A wonderful experience! They went very fast and were exceptionally strong animals. Donning a life-jacket, I was pulled along between two dolphins holding on (for dear life!) to their hard and wet flippers. I had left my glasses on and as we rushed through the water at great speed, there was a wall of water coming at me pushing the glasses into my face. I should have been told to take them off before starting out. The dolphins are highly trained and even at the end they posed, smiling, for a photo with me. They loved to be treated with affection and responded pleasurably to my hands stroking them.

On another visit, after a long coach ride through the countryside, we arrived in the capital Havana. It was like going into another world. Poverty was evident everywhere, but along all the streets and parked several deep in the main square, in the shopping areas, were literally hundreds of gorgeous old vintage cars, all makes and sizes, an incongruous mix with the many old crumbling buildings lining the pavement. Salsa drums and music seemed to flow from every area and particularly the cafés. It was wonderful and very relaxing.

We had been driven to the centre of the town and instructed to return to the coach by a certain time so we could get back home. We said goodbye to our fellow travellers and set off to enjoy the sights as true tourists do.

It was evident that years of neglect had allowed what must have been beautiful palaces and houses to deteriorate but in the new part of the town, overlooking the sea, we saw buildings which were being renovated and painted in the most delicate pastel shades. There was evidence of Fidel Castro, Ernest Hemingway and Che Ghevara everywhere, with their pictures and names throughout the city.

We managed to get lost. No one spoke English and we began to panic as the hours went by and the time approached when we should have been back at the coach. So we went from street to street trying to recognise our destination. Eventually, on going into a travel agent where we found an English-speaking person, we were able to be directed to where the coach and passengers were impatiently waiting. After our profuse apologies we set off, sad to leave behind this fascinating history-laden town.

The roads were covered in holes, even craters, and pedestrians walked anywhere on them. There were queues at the bus stops and many thumbed lifts on the back of lorries. Coloured number plates indicated which vehicles *had* to stop, by law, to offer lifts. Banderos (cowboys) riding horses and wearing cowboy hats and spurs on their boots rode in and out of the traffic. It was fascinating to see. I think it is true to say we were quite relieved to arrive safely back at our hotel.

During our visit we went to see a school. The children were on holiday but a small group had huddled around a television which had just been given to them. They were really excited. The school room was bare of books and writing materials. Fortunately, we had been told that donations of pencils and paper would be gratefully accepted and we had taken some with us.

We returned from our holiday relaxed and pleased that we had decided to go to Cuba. It had been an interesting and good experience.

Back home, a notice was put on the internet inviting past students to join with some other old Croftonians and pay a visit to our old boarding school in Hertfordshire. This was an opportunity which I could not miss. A friend of mine, Phil, drove me all the way there and back which made it possible. Crofton Grange looked exactly the same on the outside but it now housed a business called Hamels Mansion, owned by Hubert C. Leach Ltd, a construction company.

We visited all our old dormitories and found them inhabited by typists at their computer desks. Our beautiful library area was also filled with desks and computers, a far cry from the chairs put out for our assemblies or cleared for our Saturday night dances! We were booked in for a lovely lunch at The Town House, in Barley near Royston, a charming place deep in the countryside. What a memorable day that was to be. I was just sorry that no others of my era were there. I was saddened to find that the younger ex-pupils had not been as happy as I had been in my day. I do not remember the bullying and unpleasantness that some of them were recounting to me as happening in their time at the school.

Elizabeth the Queen Mother died on March 30th which was a sadness for the royal family and also for the country.

Despite their loss, the Queen and the Duke of Edinburgh came to Kingston for a brief visit on June 25th and dedicated a stone commemorating the 1100 anniversary of the coronation of King Edward the Elder. I was invited as a guest to have a seat in the parish church where the Queen passed right beside us. The sun shone throughout the day and it was a happy event for the many people who thronged to Kingston.

In July I gave a eulogy at the memorial service for my school music teacher, Margaret Channon. It was a very sad occasion but I felt proud to have been the person to value and recount her many virtues as she was laid to rest. I probably knew her better than the other pupils at school and was aware of her bravery during the war driving ambulances through the streets of London during the bombing.

Another sad event this year was the final winding up of the Michaelis Guild of Froebel College as it had not been possible to find enough members to serve on the committee. I found this all very traumatic and after many years of keeping in touch with past and, particularly, older past students, I feared we may have betrayed their trust in us to keep them in touch with their peers.

On a more cheerful note, weeks earlier I was notified that I was to receive an honour from the University of Surrey; a great and quite unexpected surprise. And so, on the 26th July I was honoured to receive the award of Honorary Master of the University Honoris Causa by Douglas Robertson CBE, DL, FRICS, Pro-Chancellor of the University of Surrey, at Guildford Cathedral. I was presented by Dr Peter Weston, then the Principal of Froebel College and Pro-Rector (Academics) at University of Surrey Roehampton. Afterwards I had to make a five minute speech to the many hundreds of graduates and their families and friends. The whole event was nerve-wracking but profoundly moving.

Another happy moment was when I attended *A Double Celebration* concert by the St Martin Singers at St Martin-in-the-Fields. It was a celebration of Kennedy Bell's life and work, who was one of its founding members and the original conductor, and to mark the Diamond Jubilee of the St Martin Singers. I sat with one of the other founder members, Marjorie Stewart, whose husband, Gordon, was still singing in the choir. I felt quite emotional that evening.

In April 2003 I paid another visit to Canada. This time I flew from Heathrow to Vancouver staying one night in a hotel at the airport. The next day I flew direct to Penticton where I stayed with my old friend, Emily Mayhew, for two nights. I had arranged to stay two nights only at each of the places I was to visit, as I had so many people to catch up with. So from there I was driven to Kelowna by my cousin Barbara Croil who came to fetch me. We visited Uncle Tom in Summerland briefly and then I flew to Vancouver to see Uncle George, Aunt Ailsa and family.

My other 'two-nightly' stays were spent with my cousins Heather Croil and Ailsa Milligan on Bowen Island. From Bowen Island I took a ferry to Victoria to stay with my cousin Tom Croil. On the 23rd I went up the island to Ladysmith where I stayed with Gill and Don Godkin who had been bed and breakfast visitors at my house. From there I went to Lantzville to stay with Mabel and Jim Hurford who, along with their daughters, had much influence in my life when I lived in Nanaimo. I then went to Gabriola Island where I spent two nights with Anne Hendy-King, John and Henry, their dog. Back in Nanaimo I stayed with Grace (now deceased) and Evan Mitchell and their dogs Gaby and Tzar. I also stayed two nights with Mary Holmes. To my surprise I had found that there was now an airport at Nanaimo from where I flew back to Vancouver. I spent one night at the airport hotel before flying to Toronto where I stayed with my niece Rosemary for three nights before leaving for Heathrow on May 4th. And so, back to London to be reunited with my dachshund.

On July 3rd I had a total hip replacement in Kingston Hospital with no complications and returned home on the 9th and it was very hot. In fact, in August the hottest temperature of 38°C was recorded. Apparently there were a thousand deaths in Great Britain due to the heat.

In 2004 I attended the Soroptimist International of Kingston and District Diamond Jubilee Dinner, a good event which I much enjoyed.

On February 11th I flew to Karachi on an eight day visit to see my family. As always, the time flew by and I just spent time with them, visiting their schools and the fascinating shopping markets. This time I flew both ways.

255

In 2005 I received the Year of the Volunteer Award which took place in the refectory building beside Guildford Cathedral. Of course I appreciated the recognition of my efforts to help others in need; however, I must put it on record that at no time did I feel that I needed or wanted the attention of having my efforts rewarded!

I have enjoyed every moment of the hours spent collecting for many and various causes and have had particular pleasure meeting and talking with a great variety of people. I have become aware of the many courteous and generous people who daily walk the streets of our towns. I am also grateful for the fact that, because I am single with no ties of a husband or children to consider, I have had the freedom to turn out at a moment's notice, and with the use of my mobility scooter, dressed as Blossom, take to the streets.

Once again, I joined the borough's celebration of *Diversity and Culture* for the day-long festival. It was the third time they had run it and I enjoyed very much being part of the happy and relaxed Caribbean atmosphere.

My interest with Froebel College continued and in September I attended the retirement party for the Deputy Vice-Chancellor, Dr Peter Weston. Also in November I was invited by Vice-Chancellor, Professor Paul O'Prey, to a ceremony to mark the installation of John Simpson as the first Chancellor of Roehampton University. Having seen him on television many times, I felt this was a very suitable appointment and have been delighted to meet him on frequent occasions at Froebel and Roehampton functions.

As usual Blossom went out at Christmas to collect for charity. In past years I had been followed around the town by a dear little old man carrying a bag of pennies and this year was no exception. He used to hand these to me quite quietly saying, 'Would you put these in your tin. I've been collecting them all year for you.' Blossom and I collected quite a few kisses from the public at Christmas time, which was rather nice! In recent years I had been concerned about taking Blossom out because I had found it almost impossible to do the fastenings up down the length of my back due to arthritis. And so I had the undoubted embarrassment of going up to the first suitable person I met and asking them to do up my fastenings for me. They all seemed highly amused and willing to do this.

Having been in the public gallery of the House of Commons I have always wanted to see what the House of Lords was like. In 2006 I had the opportunity to visit, through an invitation from the Baroness Perry of Southwark, at a reception celebrating Roehampton University. It was held in the Cholmondeley Room and we were allowed to take our drinks out onto the balcony overlooking the Thames. As the daylight drew to a close it was a wonderful sight to see the lights on the opposite side of the river. It was interesting to see the wording on my invitation: *Please present this card at Black Rod's Garden Entrance.* When we arrived the security was impeccable, our car was scrutinised from every angle. It was quite a relief to know we were safe to go inside as everyone invited had had the same treatment.

In 2007 I went with a friend on a wonderful boat trip up the Thames on the *Richmond Venturer* run by the charity Thames Boat Project, an experience I would recommend to anyone. The boat was a specially converted Dutch barge and was fully accessible to people with disabilities. We had lunch on board and were most impressed by the opportunities they were giving to school children, the elderly and other groups with educational input on what is to be found in and around our wonderful Thames River. A year later I was to join with one of the founders of the project to give a talk to the Berryland's Women's Club in Surbiton to raise awareness of their activities.

Perhaps the event in my life which was to be the most delightful and fulfilling was when an invitation arrived through my letterbox from the Queen inviting me to one of her Garden Parties at Buckingham Palace, on Tuesday July 10th 2007. Throughout my childhood I had passed the gates of the palace and wondered what the garden behind the walls looked like. I was to find out!

A friend, Ray, kindly took me and another friend, Valerie, into London with my scooter and we parked under the trees on the other side of the road opposite the front gates of the palace at the special garden entrance. We then crossed the road, assisted by friendly smiling police officers who appeared to enjoy the sight of me in my large hat swanning along on a large bright red scooter! As we approached the palace gates we were met by equally smiling servicemen who scrutinised our invitations and personal photo identity cards, which were issued by the Palace.

257

We then walked up past the side of the palace walls where a discreetly marked 'toilet' caught our eyes and was visited with great relief! After we had emerged we continued over the thick pebbly driveway until we came to the massive area of grass where two bands were playing (different music!). Marquees housed rows of delicious food-laden tables and the invited public were sauntering around, like ourselves, trying to take it all in. It was perfect weather, neither too hot nor too cold, and we wandered through the garden to try and find a seat. This was quite difficult as most were already taken and Valerie stood most of the time. Tea was served throughout the afternoon and we were assisted everywhere by gorgeous-looking Gentlemen at Arms with a great sense of humour!

After we had a delicious tea we went right round the garden and down by the lake. All the flowers and trees were labelled and we enjoyed every minute of our visit. I was fortunate to shake hands with the royal family twice! Neither of the princes, William or Harry, was there. It was a wonderful occasion.

ER

The Lord Chamberlain is
commanded by Her Majesty to invite

Miss Nancy Vlasto

to a Garden Party
at Buckingham Palace
on Tuesday, 10th July 2007 from 4 to 6 pm

This card does not admit

Following this, a visit to my home from the Second World War Experience Centre, in Leeds, gave me the opportunity to tell of my wartime experiences. I related to the interviewer some of my experiences but forgot to mention the event of the bomb going through my bed which I have mentioned earlier in this book. The interview was to be used by future military and academic historians, researchers, authors, broadcasters and schools, and was placed on the website (www.war-experience.org) as well as tape recordings. I felt this was a very worthwhile project with which to be involved. At our local Kingston Museum and Library I had an opportunity to share with school children some of my experiences during the war as a nurse and I went dressed in a nurse's uniform, which from their questions, seemed to have stimulated their interests. These children were from St Paul's in Kingston and Surbiton High School.

I noticed in the *Surrey Comet* in August that the Koreans in the area were holding their annual festival at Fairfield Recreation Ground in Kingston and as I was free that day I decided to go and join them with Blossom. It was a beautiful and warm day and I felt privileged to be accepted in my own right as an English person, not to mention Blossom, who drew a great deal of attention to herself! The speeches made by the dignitaries from the dais were all spoken in Korean, fortunately somebody kindly gave me a transcript which was an undoubted help. There were many tents around the sides of the ground selling delicious Korean food of which I partook!

July 26th 2008, I was invited to the official opening of the Sir William Rous Unit (cancer care) at Kingston Hospital in the presence of Princess Alexandra, to whom I was presented. It was a lovely day and we had tea in a large marquee accompanied by an orchestra.

Teachers at Surbiton High School asked if I would give talks to the girls of my wartime experiences. On two occasions I did so and was most impressed with their attentiveness. I pray that they will never have to face living through a war.

I was invited to a celebration of Roehampton University's fifth year of university status, which was chaired by John Simpson CBE, Chancellor of the university. A friend, Annabel Bloxham, kindly gave me a lift up to London and we found the British Academy, where it was held, without too much difficulty. Apart from getting stuck in a lift it was a delightful evening with interesting speeches and very tasty canapés and drinks provided. I do so love going back up through the centre of London, especially when it is all lit up at night.

Finally I feel that the time has come to bring my memoirs to an end. I hope you have enjoyed travelling with me through my eventful life as much as I have sharing it with you.

A listing of some music sung by Nancy:

Date Pieces, composer and venue

1947 *Jesu Priceless Treasure* – Bach
1948 *Sing Ye to the Lord* – sung at Downe House
1949 *My spirit was in heavenlies* – Bach, Downe House
1949 *Dream of Gerontius*, Royal Choral Society
1950 *The Kingdom* – Edward Elgar, Royal Choral Society
1951 *Largo* – Handel, Solo at Ladysmith, Vancouver Island, Nanaimo Choral Society
1951 *Belshazzar's Feast* – W. Walton, Royal Choral Society at Festival Hall in the Festival of Britain
1951 *The Apostles* – Ed Elgar, Royal Choral Society
1951 *Samson* – Handel, United Hospital Festival Choir
1952 May 31st – United Hospital Festival Choir – Royal Albert Hall
1952 Oct 25th – *The Creation*, Royal Choral Society, Royal Albert Hall
1952 Dec 13th – *The Creation*, Royal Choral Society, Central Hall
1952 *The Creation*, Royal Choral Society, Albert Hall
1953 May 29th – Brahms *Requiem*
1953 *The Music Makers* – Edward Elgar, Royal Choral Society
1954 *Pastoral* – Arthur Bliss, Downe House Summer School
1954 *Messiah*, guest singer, Free Church Choir Union in 68th Festival Concert at Westminster Central Hall
1954 *The Canterbury Pilgrims* – George Dyson, Royal Choral Society
1954 *Creation* – Haydn, RCS
1957 *Hymn to St Cecelia* – B. Britten
1959 Various – Surbiton Oratorio Society
1960 *Requiem* – Brahms, Oxted Choral Society
1960 *Requiem* – Faure, SOS
1960 *Judas Maccabeus* – Handel, SOS
1961 *Jesu Priceless Treasure* – Bach
1961 *Hear ye, Israel* – Mendelssohn, Westerham Parish Church
1961 *Recit & Aria from St Matthew's Passion* – *Although our eyes with tears* – Bach, Westerham Parish Church
1961 *Requiem* – Faure, SOS
1961 *Stabat Mater* – Rossini
1961 *Christmas Oratorio* – Bach, Royal Choral Society
1961 *O Thou the Central Orb*, Westerham Parish Church
1961 *Blessed be the God and Father*, Westerham Parish Church
1963 *Solomon* – Handel
1963 *The Seasons* – Haydn
1963 *When I laid in Earth* – Purcell, Acc. Margaret Brown, St Andrew's Hall
1964 Twickenham Festival – I won vouchers for music
1965 *Mass in D* – Dvorak, SOS
1965 *Church Cantata No. 49 Ich geh and such emit Verlanger* – JS Bach, KCMS, St Andrew's Church

1965 Soprano, *Let Us Wonder, Lost is my Quiet* – Purcell, *Shepherd on the Rock* – Schubert, Percy Road School, Hampton, KCMS

1966 *Magnificat* – Bach

1966 St Martin Singers, Maida Vales, Home Service Broadcast. Rev. J Long

1966 *Shepherd on the Rock*, Schubert, Sang soprano solo , organ: Ursula Brett, clarinet: Alan Baker, conductor: Edgar Walker.
Sógennd Leise, choir and Pat Bayliff and self, piano: Audrey White.

1966 *Before the Paling of the Stars* – B.J. Dale (copy given to me by Norman Askew)

1966 *'And Suddenly There Was with the Angels'* from *Messiah* – Handel, Chapel Royal Hampton Court,

1966 *I was Glad* – Purcell, Chapel Royal (Norman Askew)

1966 Solos, Raynes Park Methodist Church:
Recit: *Although our Eyes with Tears Overflow*
Aria: *Jesus Saviour*
An die Musik – Schubert
'Rejoice' from Handel's *Messiah*

1966 English songs solos, KCMS:
My Lovely Celia – G. Munro
Orpheus with his Lute – Vaughan Williams
Sweet Chance that Lead my Step – Michael Head
My Heart is like a Singing Bird – Parry

1966 *Silver* – Armstrong Gibbs, St Andrew's Hall

1966 Dec: Tolworth Hospital, Christmas carols

1967 Jan: Sang solos at Old People's Welfare party, Graham Spicer Hall, New Malden

1967 Annual Church Concert in St Andrews, KCMS
Trio *Sonata in C Major*, Bach
Second organ concerto, Handel
KCMS choir, conductor: Donald Perkins, sang *motets* by Palastrina, Victtoria, Morley, Weelkes, Purcell and Arthur Wills. Roy Pullen (bass) and I sang solos in Bach's Church cantata, *Ich gen und suche malverlagan*, conductor: Edward Walker

1967 Solos, excerpts from *St Matthew's Passion* – Bach, KCMS, St Andrew's Church
Solo, KCMS, St Andrew's Church:
How Calm is my Spirit – Mozart
Let Thy Merciful Ears O Lord – Thomas Weelkes
Ave Verum – Mozart
St John Passion – Chorale – J.S. Bach,

1967 *Songs of love* – Brahms, Gipsy Hill College

1967 *Jesu, Joy and Treasure* – Buxtehude, Kingston Chamber Music Society, St Andrew's Church

1967 Apr: KCMS, Sang solos from *St Matthew Passion*, Bach, with Chamber Music choir and orchestra
Aria *Jesus Saviour I am Thine*

1967 Apr: Sang *Messiah* solos, St Christopher Church, Hinchley Woods with

Joyce Taplow (alto), Richard Wilkins (tenor), and Harold Spurr (bass)

1967 Apr: Sang solo excerpts from *Messiah* for a Bible Society meeting in Surbiton, Surbiton Oratory Society.
From '*Elijah*' *If with all your heart*, Mozart
How calm is my spirit, Mozart. Choir sang motets.

1967 May: Madrigal Concert – Surbiton, Kingston Chamber Music Society
Conductor-Edgar Walker

1967 June: KCMS choir sang Monteverdi's *Beatus Vir*

1967 June: Solos to housebound at Holly Lodge

1967 Aug: *Acis & Galatea* – Handel, Gipsy Hill College
Small solo part among others

1967 Sept: I sang solos at Kingston RBK Hymns Festival, Kingston Parish Church

1967 Oct: Solo, St Christopher Church, Hinchley Wood:
A Hymn to the Virgin and Jesu Kin – Edmund Rubbra
How Long Wilt Thou Forget Me, O Lord – Sven Lekberg
Organ: Ursula Brett

1967 Nov: Four duets by Monteverdi, KCMS, St Andrew's Hall
Acc Pat Amey, conductor: John Walker

1967 Dec: Solos, Advent Music, Raynes Park Methodist Church:
Jesu, Joy and Treasure – Buxtehude
Messiah – Handel
Canticles of the Virgin Mary – Michael Hurd

1967 Dec: Advent Recital of Music – Chapel Royal

1967 Dec 25: Last Service sung – Chapel Royal (very emotional)

1968 *Jesu, Joy and Treasure* – Buxtehude, Kingston Chamber Music Society, St Andrew's Church

1968 Jacobean Singers, St Mary's Church, Hampton
I Wonder as I Wander – Michael Head
Ninth Day of Christmas

1968 Northwestern Polytechnic Singers and Players, St. Richard's Church, Hampshire
Jesu, Joy and Treasure – Buxtehude
Beatus Vir – Monteverdi

1968 *The Shepherd on the Rock* – Schubert, KCMS, St Andrew's Hall

1968 Chapel Royal Choir, St Columbus Church, Pont Street

1969 A ceremony of carols – B Britten

1969 *St Matthew Passion* – Bach, Froebel

1969 Soprano, *Silver, The Horseman, The Moth* – Walter de la Mare, *Lullaby* – Sir Walter Scott, *The King of China's Daughter* – Edith Sitwell, Nancy Cooley: piano, KCMS

1969 Solo, *In the Bleak Mid-winter* – Holst, *With Verdure Clad from Creation* – Haydn, Festival of Hymns, Kingston Association of Old People's Welfare Committees, Kingston Parish Church

1969 Soprano, *Cantata 202, Weichet nur, betrübte Schatten*, St Andrew's Hall, KCMS

1970 *Sleepers Awake* – Bach, Froebel College (I did solos)

1970 *Messiah* – Handel, solos, Kingston Hospital Choir
1970 Cantata, *Corydon* – Pepusch, Solos, Flute by Rachel Thomson, Piano by Pat Amey, KCMS
1971 Solo, Festival of Hymns, with *Verdure Clad* from *'Creation'* by Haydn, Congregational Church, New Malden
1971 St. George's Chapel, Windsor
1971 Cantate, *Corydon* – Pepusch, KCMS,
1971 Cantate, *Corydon* – Pepusch , Molesey Music Club
1971 *Jesu – Joy of Man's Desiring* – Bach, St Nicholas Church, Sevenoaks, Kent, at wedding
1972 Solos, Glyn House for Surrey County Music Association
1972 Madrigal Concert – Surbiton, Kingston Chamber Music Society
1972 Cantata: *Celladon* – Croft, Soprano, St Andrew's Hall, KCMS
1973 *Mondnacht* – Schuman
       Der Ring (from a cycle by Schuman) Piano: Nancy Cooley, St Andrew's Hall, KCMS
1973 Sven Lekberg, Westerham Parish Church at wedding
1974 4 Moravian duets – Dvorak, Nos.3,6,7,10
1974 *Childhood of Christ* – Berlioz
1974 Solos, *Le Secret, Clair de Lure, Chanson d'amour, fleur Jetée* – Fauré, Betty Lewis piano, KCMS
1974 Arias and Songs: *Pie Jesu* – Faure, *A Hymn to the Virgin, Jesukin* – Rubbra, *How beautiful are the feet* – Handel, sang solo, Organ: Bertie Stiling, St Andrew's Church, KCMS
1974 *'Mikado'*, Thames Side Opera Club
1975 *Il Trovatore* – Verdi, Court Opera group, Conductor Lesley Woolf
1975 *Schottische Lieder* (13 songs) Solo, Pat Bayliff-contralto, Michael Musgrave, (the late) Derek Pedder-bass, Margaret Venables-piano, St Andrew's Hall, KCMS
1976 SOS, Choir for Arts Festival at De Lissa Hall, Gipsy Hill College, Kingston upon Thames
1976 Quartettes: *Der gang zum liebchen*
       An die heimat
       Spatherbst
       Abendlied – Brahms
       Nancy Vlasto-Soprano, Pat Bayliff-Contralto, Tony Ellis-Tenor, Derek Pedder-Bass, Pat Amey-Piano, KCMS, St Andrew's Hall
1976 Attended and sang as a member of the St Martin Singers at the memorial service of Wendy Loveday, in the church of St Martin-in-the-Fields.
1976 Soprano solo, *O come all ye faithful*, Church of the Peace of God, Oxted Surrey
1976? Orchestral Concert – all vocalists attended the Chiswick Polytechnic Music Centre for coaching in Lieder singing. Sang soprano with Andrea Whittaker and David Knowles-bass. Trio from *Cosi fan tuite* – Mozart, Bath Road W4
1977 Mar: Soprano solo, *Vergebliches* – Brahms, *du bist die Ruh* – Schubert, Pat Amey-piano, St Andrew's Hall, KCMS

1977 Solos, *The Cloths of Heaven* – Dunhill, *Pie Jesu* – Faure, *Jesu Joy of Man's Desiring* – Bach, *Art Thou Troubled* – Handel, *How Beautiful are Thy Feet* – Handel, *Come to Bethlehem* – Warlock, *Torches* – Joubert, *The Little Road* – Michael Head, East Molesey Methodist Church

1977 Soprano, *If God be for us* (from *Messiah*) – Handel, *How long wilt Thous forget me, O Lord* – Sven Lekberg, *I will sing new songs of gladness* – Dvorak, Bertie Stilling-organ, St Andrew's Church, KCMS

1977 Maurice Durufle Requiem, SOS

1979 *Te Deum* – Bruckner, Oxted Choral Society

1981 *I waited for the Lord* – Mendelssohn, duet with Karen Middleton, St Andrew and St Mark's

1987 *Towards the Unknown Region* – R.V. Colliers

1989 Service in place of cathedral choir, on occasion of David Gerard leaving our parish to become Archdeacon of Wandsworth, Southwark Cathedral

1991 *Requiem* – Cherubini, Kingston Choral Society (ex SOS)

1993 Southwark Cathedral, sang the service

1993 Claygate Parish Church at wedding